Play, Learning and the
Early Childhood Curriculum

Liz Wood and Jane Attfield

P·C·P
Paul Chapman
Publishing Ltd

Paul Chapman Publishing Ltd
A SAGE Publications Company
6 Bonhill Street
London EC2A 4PU

British Library Cataloguing in Publication Data

Wood, Liz
Play, learning and the early childhood curriculum
1. Early childhood education 2. Play
I. Title II. Attfield, Jane
372.2'1

ISBN 1 85396 252 X

Typeset by Palimpsest Book Production Limited,
Polmont, Stirlingshire
Printed and bound by Athenaeum Press Ltd.,
Gateshead, Tyne & Wear
E F G H 3 2 1 0

For Liz and David, two master players

Contents

Preface

This book is the outcome of our joint experiences of working with young children in school and nursery settings, with novice and experienced teachers on pre- and in-service courses. It arose from our shared concerns about play, its relationship to learning and its place in the early years curriculum. In our endeavours to make sense of play we found a vast literature drawing on different disciplinary perspectives which give varying and often conflicting accounts of the value and purposes of play. There was the additional problem of the predominant focus on children under five with relatively little written about older children, from either a theoretical or practical perspective. Some of our concerns were addressed in the existing literature, but many questions remained unanswered. We were dissatisfied with the vague and often romanticized views of early childhood.

With the introduction of the National Curriculum play came under attack. In the new era of accountability play lacked credibility. Therefore new ways of thinking about play seemed timely in the face of some persistent criticisms from successive government ministers about the early childhood curriculum.

We were aware that our joint concerns and emerging areas of enquiry might be idiosyncratic. Consequently the ideas presented in this book have been explored with colleagues in schools, at Exeter University and in higher education institutions both here and in other countries. They have also been discussed at length with many groups of PGCE students and early childhood educators on modular and higher degree courses. These have included a broad spectrum of practitioners including nursery and primary teachers, nursery nurses, playgroup leaders, and classroom assistants.

One of the driving forces behind this book has been the enthusiastic response of practitioners to these ideas. They have assisted greatly in our own passages of intellectual search by opening up their thinking and articulating their approaches. We have used many examples from our own and other practitioners' experiences as we felt it important to maintain a balance between theoretical ideals and practical realities.

On the thorny issue of educational theory we have found that educators welcomed the opportunities to explore different theoretical viewpoints in order to clarify their own thinking and establish a sound rationale for their practice.

The decision to include a substantial chapter on Vygotskyian ideas was in direct response to teachers' requests to explore these further. In their view, these ideas helped them to make sense of their practice and enabled them to think critically about teaching and learning, particularly their interactions with children in play activities. This valuable dialogue gave us the confidence to take risks in presenting ideas and arguments. We have also taken note of the plea from many practitioners that we should start a book on play by talking about children and not animals!

The book represents a synthesis of ideas, issues, questions, dilemmas and approaches. We have sought to make sense of play at different levels – ideological, theoretical, pedagogical and practical. In focusing on play in school and pre-school settings we realized the need to link play more clearly with pedagogy, that is with teaching and learning, and to explore its place in the early childhood curriculum. This is a direct response to the fact that play has too often been found as limiting, stereotypical, unchallenging and occupying rather than extending. The claims made for play do not seem to be realised in practice. Our intention is not to provide a definitive model. We believe that would be inappropriate given the range of settings in which early childhood educators work, the diversity of cultures and needs of children and their families. Ideals are important, but constantly striving to attain ideals in difficult circumstances can be frustrating and disempowering. Of equal importance are flexibility, responsiveness and creativity.

On this basis we recognized the need to create frameworks for thinking about practice, thus generating new ideas and insights. This is based on the notion that improvements in practice are enabled through a process of reconceptualization: that is, changing the way we think and act, considering alternative perspectives and attending to critical questions of why and how rather than just what. We hope that this will enable early childhood educators to provide a more secure foundation for play in the curriculum by challenging entrenchment, assumptions, polarized views and vague terminology.

Accordingly this is not a 'what and how' book. There are no neat prescriptions and definitive recommendations for practice. We realize that we may raise more questions than we explore, but hope that practitioners will find some answers through their own theorizing and practice.

Although we regard the term early childhood as covering the years from birth to eight this book focuses predominantly on three to eight year olds in pre-school and school settings. The intended audience includes all educators who work with this age group, including parents. We believe that teaching and learning is a central feature of adults and children whether at home or in other settings. This book examines the teaching and learning processes in the context of children's play. We hope that it will energize critical, reflective thinking by all those involved with young children who are seriously concerned with the quality of their learning and development.

Liz Wood and Jane Attfield

1

The Problems with Play

In early childhood education there exists a strong tradition which regards play as essential to learning and development. This is based substantially on the work of the early pioneers (Anning, 1991). More recently, this tradition has been related to current contexts and to the research and knowledge base, receiving further validation from academics (Bruce, 1991; Moyles, 1989, 1994), from HMI (DES, 1989) and from government reports (DES, 1990). However, in spite of continuing enthusiastic endorsements for play, its place in the curriculum is not secure. The role, purposes and value of play in the early years curriculum continue to be issues for debate for practitioners, researchers and educationists. Practitioners are still faced with many dilemmas in the way they conceptualize play, its relationship to learning and to the curriculum. These are more acute for teachers of infants, particularly in reception classes, given the demands they have faced since the implementation of the Education Reform Act (1988). The underlying belief is that play is essentially a good thing and that it promotes learning. However, we need to question whether this is an uncritical assumption, based more on ideology than on reality, particularly as there is relatively little evidence on which to base such claims. This chapter will explore some of these dilemmas in the context of current realities for educators in pre-school and school settings.

Play is undoubtedly problematic, more so in the current political and educational climate than ever before. Its status and value continue to be questioned at the level of policy by politicians; at the level of practice by parents, governor and teachers; and at the level of theory by academics and researchers. In identifying some of the reasons why play continues to be problematic, we will draw on these three perspectives. We begin by looking at current tensions for early years educators and at some of the problems which have emerged as a result of post-ERA changed realities.

What is play?

In any discussion of play, the first problem to be encountered is usually one of definition. The word 'play' covers a range of behaviours related to many different activities both for children and adults. Play can be regarded as deeply serious and purposeful or trivial and purposeless. It can be characterized by high levels of motivation, creativity and learning, or it can be relegated to little more than just messing about. Ambiguities surrounding the definition of play have done little to substantiate claims that children learn through play or to support a play-based curriculum. While the search for clarity is important, for teachers definitions can limit how play is conceptualized and how it is represented in practice.

Hutt *et al* (1989) argue that play is a jumbo category which encompasses a multiplicity of activities, some of which are conducive to learning, but many of which are not. For example, for many children in school, outdoor playtime can be dreaded where it provides opportunities for conflict, aggression, bullying and other unacceptable behaviours. For the youngest children, playtime can be traumatic, as this observation by a beginning teacher shows:

> It appeared to me that for many of the children playtime was a total mystery. They did not know what was going to happen to them and were very apprehensive. I headed for the staffroom and soon became aware that I was being followed by Luke (aged four). I explained that it was time to go out to the playground. 'I'm not doing it, I'll come with you', he said. It became apparent to me that he was afraid to lose sight of the adults into whose care his mother had entrusted him. He did not know which (if any) adult would be in the playground. Probably his entire life up to that moment had been spent in the sight of his trusted carer, and suddenly he felt he would be abandoned.

Here the notion of playtime was not a welcome interlude but an apparent threat to a young child. In school contexts, playfulness can also be seen as unacceptable, even naughty, behaviour where it disrupts work. Neill and Jamel (both aged five) did not settle immediately to a maths activity. Instead they began play-fighting sitting on their chairs, using their pencils as swords. Their play was not aggressive or malicious, but inevitably as it became more energetic they both fell off their chairs, were reprimanded and separated for the rest of the session.

In contrast, deep and serious play can be respected and encouraged by teachers. In a nursery, a group of boys were playing with Duplo and made a large layout on the floor. As the complexity of their play developed, they used other resources to create a town. The teacher realized the need to 'go with the flow' of their ideas and asked other children not to cut across their space or take away any of their equipment. The children were not made to join in with mid-session circle time as their layout continued to evolve. At review time, after two hours of effort, the group proudly explained their layout to the whole class, and were persuaded to dismantle it only after it had also been shown to parents and caregivers at home time.

Considering these three contrasting observations, there is little wonder that defining play has proved elusive. Garvey (1991) suggests that not all that young children do together can be classified as play. There is rather a continuous moving back and forth among different activities with different modes of action, interaction and communication. She regards play as an attitude or orientation that can manifest itself in numerous kinds of behaviour. What can be played expands as new areas of experience are encountered and appropriated for playful purposes. The purposes and goals of play often shift as children manipulate play and non-play situations because they understand implicitly that different types of behaviour are permitted in play, whereas others, such as mock-aggression and play-fighting, are often banned.

These play behaviours and activities are themselves not easily defined or categorized. Academics and practitioners use a variety of terms to describe different types of play such as role play, imaginative play, socio-dramatic play, heuristic play, constructive play, fantasy play, free-flow play, structured play, rough and tumble play. These may have different meanings for different people and can be represented in many ways in the curriculum. Moreover, they can be qualitatively different in terms of the learning and development they might encourage. For example, Smith (1989) maintains that fantasy play involving characters and events is considered to be a higher form of play as it encourages representational thinking.

Another problem in defining play is that it can be chaotic, making it difficult for teachers to articulate intentions or predict outcomes. Pellegrini (1991) and Saracho (1991) used Rubin, Fein and Vandenberg's criteria which define play in terms of dispositions:

- Play is personally motivated by the satisfaction embedded in the activity and not governed either by basic needs and drives or by social demands.
- Players are concerned with activities more than with goals. Goals are self-imposed, and the behaviour of the players is spontaneous.
- Play occurs with familiar objects, or following the exploration of unfamiliar objects. Children supply their own meanings to play activities and control the activities themselves.
- Play activities can be nonliteral.
- Play is free from rules imposed from the outside, and the rules that do exist can be modified by the players.
- Play requires the active engagement of the players.

The value of these criteria is that they can be used differentially to categorize children's behaviour in play situations:

> As a result, play can be categorized as 'more or less play', not dichotomously as 'play or not play'. Behaviours meeting all criteria might be categorized as 'pure play', whereas behaviours with fewer components are 'less purely play'. Simply put, acts should not be categorized as 'play' or 'not play': they should be related along a continuum from 'pure play' to 'non-play'.
>
> (Pellegrini, 1991, p. 215)

A similarly broad definition is given by Fromberg (1987, p. 36), who states that play is:

> *Symbolic*, in that it represents reality with 'as if' or 'what if' attitude;

Meaningful, in that it connects or relates experiences;

Pleasurable, even when children engage seriously in an activity;

Voluntary and intrinsically motivated, whether the motives are curiosity, mastery, affiliation or others;

Rule-governed, whether implicitly or explicitly expressed;

Episodic, characterized by emerging and shifting goals that children develop spontaneously.

As both these definitions indicate, play is infinitely varied and complex. It represents cognitive, cultural, historical, social and physical interconnections between the known and the unknown, the actual and the possible, the probable and the improbable. It is a dialogue between fantasy and reality, between past, present and future, between the logical and the absurd, and between safety and risk. Given these complexities, it is hardly surprising that play has defied neat, tidy definitions.

Saracho (1991) argues that although there is limited empirical support for characteristics to be used in identifying a play episode, the widest set of criteria available should be used to classify children's activity as play. Utilizing broad categories can also help to free teachers from some of the guilt they may feel about the work/play divide and the supposed benefits of certain types of play. For example, Bruce (1991) emphasizes the status of free-flow play and states unequivocally that 'if I had my way nothing else would be referred to as play'. However, imposing a form of political correctness about play does little to enhance its status or secure its place within the curriculum. Definitions should take into account different contexts as well as the needs, interests and preferences of children at different ages. They should frame our understanding but not limit our practice.

In the urge to explain and categorize play, we may be in danger of overlooking the fact that children define play themselves. They often establish mutual awareness of play and non-play situations. They create roles, use symbols, redefine objects, and determine the action through negotiation and shared meanings. Often their enactments of play themes and stories or their creation of play scripts reveal far more subtleties than academic definitions can capture. Moreover, play is not just about fantasy. It doesn't have a life of its own which is divorced from reality. Children continuously weave in and out of their play their knowledge, skills and understanding gleaned in other areas of their lives. Play is also rich with meanings which children create for themselves. Educators may not understand these meanings if they are unable to devote time to observing and interpreting children's play. Play doesn't just defy precise definitions, it also has a status-problem.

The status of play

Play is widely regarded as an essential part of childhood and its significance has been idealized. But there are two contrasting views about its status. Within early childhood education there are various ideological, theoretical and practical justifications for its centrality to the curriculum. Outside early childhood education play tends to be regarded differently: 'The fact is that "play" has been defined as trivial by a male-dominated society which emphasises the power of rational thought. Work is the serious, rational business of life and play is for leisure and fun.' (Anning, 1991, p. 30.)

As we have seen, play is difficult to define in terms of its characteristics, purposes and value to children. Depending on the contexts in which it occurs and the form that it takes, play is indulged, encouraged, tolerated or banned. The unpredictable nature of play also makes it difficult to plan and assess clearly specified outcomes which, in the current educational climate, undermines its status. As Hall and Abbott argue: 'Play, being something that apparently does not have to be worked at, is deemed less valuable by society than those activities which have outcomes that are susceptible to evaluation' (1991, p. 2).

Assumptions about the centrality of play to children's learning and development and its place in the curriculum have been taken for granted. However, perspectives from practice reveal a different picture of play. Meadows and Cashdan argue that play has been heavily idealized and has been portrayed as spontaneous, absorbing, refreshing, enjoyable, creative and the ideal way of learning:

> If children aren't enabled to play as they choose, it has been claimed, their development will be impaired. Enthusiasts for play suggest that human beings have evolved so that they need to play in order to learn, to work off their surplus energy, to practise skills they will need in later life. While each of these claims has some truth in it, none of them is an entirely watertight reason for elevating them into *the* way of learning.
>
> (1988, p. 47)

Tizard *et al* (1988) argue that the commonly-held view that early years teachers encouraged learning through play was more myth than reality. This was confirmed by Bennett and Kell's study of four year olds in reception classes which revealed a mismatch between aims and practice. Although teachers mentioned play in their aims, only six per cent of the observations were of play activities and they were regarded as

> ... very limited and very limiting. The teachers appeared to have low expectations of it, often acting as a time filler, and far too frequently there was no clear purpose or challenge, a lack of pupil involvement, very little monitoring or attempt at extension. In other words, play tended not to provide learning experiences of an acceptable quality.
>
> (1989, p. 79)

On the basis of these observations, they conclude that: 'The view that the education of young children is founded on play has attained the status of a commandment, but it is a commandment far more observed in the telling than in the doing.' (1989, p. 78.)

Similar perspectives from a survey of 141 reception classes were reported by Ofsted:

The quality of learning through play presented rather a dismal picture. Fewer than half of the teachers fully exploited the educational potential of play. In more than a third of schools play was only recreational; it lacked an educational purpose and was usually undertaken only after work was completed.

(DES 1993a, p. 10)

The gap between rhetoric and reality can be seen as one of the main weaknesses of play in schools. As Moyles (1989) states, most teachers say that they feel play is valuable and has a place in the classroom, yet most also by their attitudes indicate implicitly that it does not have a prime place but is rather secondary to the activities which they themselves direct and supervise. These issues raise questions about the status of play in relation to the particular contexts and constraints within which teachers work. There are many complex reasons for this gap between rhetoric and reality. How teachers conceptualize play and their role within it; how they manage their time, space and resources; the prevailing ethos within the school; class size; and the demands of the National Curriculum all impact on whether and how play is represented within the early childhood curriculum. This indicates the need for a more secure theoretical and pedagogical underpinning to enable teachers to resolve some of these tensions. The status of play can also be seen as related to the status of children. Giving children a voice and allowing them to make choices and decisions can be threatening to adults' control and may not accord with their choices or fit comfortably with their values.

Play and learning

The relationship between play and learning is also tenuous. Even in the pre-school phase, play can be seen as preparatory to 'real' learning in 'big school' and may not be taken seriously by parents. There are even misconceptions between practitioners in different phases. One reception teacher told a nursery teacher not to teach the children anything to do with reading because she liked to set them off in her own way. Another was heard to tell her newly arrived group of four year olds that they didn't need to play any more because they were in real school now. The experience of many cohorts of students tends to confirm the view that the role and status of play in schools do not match how it is represented in their reading and course work.

There is a sense in which play is also seen as having a life of its own because it belongs to the private worlds of children and childhood and is often invested with mystique. Perhaps because of this adults have sought to control and manipulate play both inside and outside the home to make it educationally worthwhile.

A further problem is that we often make value judgments about 'good' and 'bad' play and potential learning outcomes. Left to their own desires, young children frequently demand endless supplies of the latest essential collectable such as Barbie dolls, Action Men, Transformers, Ninja Turtles or Power Rangers. These are the very things that are often consigned to the home tray because teachers regard other play resources and activities as having more value. Teachers and parents understandably may resent the commercial exploitation of children, as well as the economic strain of successive fads. But such toys, as well as characters from television programmes and films, can provide rich 'springboards for fantasy' (Cohen, 1993, p. 62). The difficulty is that even in settings where play is valued, adults may provide the springboards and control the fantasies.

There are wider influences outside education which shape aims and practices and question the value of play. Elkind (1990) has argued that, in the USA, the last quarter of a century has seen the demise of play as the major occupation of children. Reasons for this include the 'earlier is better' trend towards formal schooling. In their leisure time, many children are channelled into clubs and activities which their parents may see as more worthwhile or of higher status. In Elkind's view, childhood has become a period of work and not for play:

> perhaps because domestic roles have been devalued and many adult occupations have become too technologically sophisticated to be easily dramatized, play is no longer seen as a preparation for adult life, but rather as indulgence at best and regression at worst. In contemporary parlance the best preparation for the work of adulthood is childhood work.
>
> (1990, p. 5)

There is an assumption that play becomes less relevant beyond the age of five although it may be allowed in 'choosing time' in the infants school. For junior children, play in school tends to become a distant memory except as organised games and outdoor playtime. There is relatively little research to inform practitioners how children's play develops as they get older and what provision for it might be made in schools. This is ironic given that toy and games manufacturers have perceived the inherent need for play to change and develop throughout childhood and into adulthood. Lego is a prime example of this with its carefully sequenced range from Duplo right through to the more complex LegoTechnik.

Adults need to play too. We are encouraged to use our leisure time productively in playing games to maintain health and fitness. Business and industry also use role play techniques in their training programmes as a way of enabling people to deal with difficult situations, rehearse strategies and cope with feelings. A stroll around a toy department or superstore reveals a wide range of board games for adults and increasingly sophisticated electronic games. Some of the latest virtual reality computer/video games are based on role play. In some, participants are assigned a character and then have to work out strategies and actions in response to problems.

So far from being an exclusively childish occupation, play is an inherent feature and need throughout our lives. Cohen and MacKeith (1991) show that imaginary worlds constructed in childhood can last through adolescence and into adulthood, becoming increasingly elaborate and sometimes channelled into our working lives. This is perhaps most evident in the work of writers and artists. Playfulness and creativity are inextricably linked. Increasingly in adulthood we engage in different forms of play – playing with ideas, roles, words, media, meanings and relationships between events, people, concepts, materials, and systems. For teenagers, sense of self is created by projecting certain images and adopting the requisite roles. Similarly an adult's wardrobe is often an extension of the dressing up box as we often need to project different images and roles according to different contexts. This may be seen essentially as a form of play even though it is more subliminal. For many adults, play is still a deeply enjoyable experience. Observations of families at the seaside consistently reveal the playfulness of adults, with or without children. It is often the adults who continue digging the channel to the sea long after the children have lost interest!

Sometimes it is useful to look at issues through a different lens. In elevating the status of play within early childhood, are we being patronizing to children? Whilst children undoubtedly play naturally and spontaneously, not everything they do can be categorized as play. There are many other things which they find equally enjoyable, often with an adult. Studies by Dunn (1989) and Tizard and Hughes (1984) revealed children's interests in the real world and the need to make sense of it through participating in real activities in and around the home. By organizing exclusively play-oriented environments we may be in danger of creating an unreal world for children, particularly where there is over-reliance on manufactured toys and resources. For example, by creating diminutive home corners with plastic kitchen equipment, are we failing to recognize the skills and competencies learnt in the home? When real crockery and cutlery were introduced into a nursery class, one mother expressed concern that somebody might get stabbed with a knife or fork. But the children were already using real equipment in the cooking area and understanding about safety and appropriate use was an important part of their learning. Play cannot live up to its assumed status if it is benign, unchallenging and repetitive and if it excludes the real world.

This is not an argument for less play and more adult-directed activities in early childhood settings, nor for less play and more work. Maintaining a critical perspective on play can enable practitioners to clarify the what, how and why of the curriculum rather than just proceeding on the basis of assumptions. This is even more important in the educational climate of the late twentieth century. The mismatch of perceptions about the status of play has been made worse by the dichotomy between play and work and, more recently, by the demands of the National Curriculum.

Play and work

The play/work divide is a recurrent tension for teachers, particularly as the two are conceived differently by people outside education. As we have seen, society has a general mistrust of play and the lack of a precise operational definition of play in educational contexts ensures that it is viewed as the opposite of work. Whilst industriousness and playfulness may be tolerated in the pre-school phase, the boundaries between work and play become increasingly evident in the primary school, even in reception classes. Another confusing element in the search for status is that children often work quite hard at their play in terms of effort, motivation, concentration and outcomes.

In reality, evidence suggests that teachers are clear about what constitutes work and play in classroom contexts. In a sociological study of infant schools, King (1978) observed a diversity of opinion amongst teachers about activities defined as play and those defined as work. His findings indicate that in general work was done in the morning and play in the afternoon. Work was done for the teacher and play was seen as more important for younger rather than older children. Bennett and Kell's study (1989) also found an explicit distinction between work and play. However, Cleave and Brown revealed a range of views about play, work and learning. In their study, teachers commented that 'children "need to play"; "it's the way they learn"; "a style of learning"; "I've never thought of it in terms of play versus work"; "the children enjoy what they are doing without realising they are learning. Play is their work."' (1991, p. 64.)

The distinction between work and play has done little to further the case for play beyond the pre-school phase:

> Some teachers of older children will have made rigid demarcations between work and play to the extent that play, far from being a medium of learning, is seen as something that actively interferes with learning and is relegated to the edges of the school day to be indulged in when work is completed.
>
> (Chazan *et al*, 1987, p. 54)

This polarization between work and play has evolved because of diverse definitions of play and conflicting perspectives about its relationship with learning. With more value being given to formal education, teachers are faced with increasing demands for evidence of achievement from parents who typically undervalue play as a learning process, as the following example shows. A small rural primary school with a strong commitment to play devised a model whereby play was integrated successfully across the curriculum. However articulate the teachers' justifications to parents, the use of the word play was objected to because of its trivial, anti-work connotations and a concern that the children would not be 'doing' the National Curriculum. It was decided to call play-based sessions workshops. Such a compromise might be seen by some as a betrayal of ideals and practice, but this was a pragmatic response to a difficult problem.

Children themselves evidently have their own distinctions between work and play. Cleave and Brown (1991) report that children associated work with producing something or sitting still. The following comments made by children after a morning of play activities organized by student teachers on an Early Years PGCE course, confirm this view:

- No, we haven't been working this morning because we could choose.
- Play is what you do when you choose, like Lego and things, but work is what the teacher tells you to do like reading and writing things down.
- I think we've been playing and working. It was hard work making that go-kart because it kept falling to bits.

Teachers are pragmatists as well as idealists and accommodations to changed realities have been necessary in the post-ERA phase. Teachers need to clarify and articulate their ideas about work, play and learning so that they can communicate effectively with parents and children about curriculum contexts, activities, aims and approaches.

Some of these debates in early childhood education tend to go round in ever-decreasing circles. Just as rigid definitions are unhelpful to practitioners, so too are narrow demarcations between work and play. One further point is important here. It has been suggested that we need to distinguish between play 'as such' and play in schools (Guha, 1988). Play 'as such' has been studied intensively from many different perspectives with the intention of understanding why children play, what they play, and what effects it has on their development. Play in schools must inevitably be scrutinized for its educational and developmental potential. It is within the power of teachers to value and promote children's play through creative, informed management of the learning environment, clear aims and intentions and systems for observation, assessment and evaluation. Play in schools (particularly beyond the pre-school phase) will be different because of the various situational constraints and the broader aims of schooling. Wood makes the point that

> Learning *how* to think and learn about things that are relatively *unfamiliar* are not 'natural' achievements that occur with time, but special forms of 'self-regulation' which rest on *relevant* experiences . . . any changes that occur in children's ability to learn, think and understand may, in part at least, be a *product* of schooling.
>
> (1988, p. 54)

Clearly for play to have a secure and legitimate place within the early childhood curriculum it must incorporate such learning-relevant experiences. Even in the pre-school phase, David has argued that we need to justify play as a vehicle for learning or at least prove that it is useful for something (1990, p. 79). Now, more than at any time, educators need critical, informed perspectives about play and to clarify its relationship to other activities and areas of learning in the curriculum. However, with the introduction of the National Curriculum, this has proved to be a difficult task.

Play and the National Curriculum

The Educational Reform Act (1988) was based predominantly on a political agenda and introduced an unprecedented degree of control of the curriculum for five to sixteen year olds. Predicated on coercion rather than genuine consultation and co-operation, it appeared to threaten teachers' traditional autonomy in determining what should be taught, when and how. However, in early years education traditional autonomy was synonymous with idiosyncrasy, insularity, lack of clarity in aims and approaches and of accountability. The extent and pace of change were daunting and in the early stages of transition there was a clash of ideology and counter-ideology. It was understandable that teachers felt threatened since the package of reforms could quite easily be seen as a conspiracy against the educational establishment. Initially at least this led to polarized views and entrenchment.

On first seeing the original statutory orders as they emerged as part of a rolling programme between 1988 and 1993, many early years teachers were dismayed that little status was given to play. They were concerned that they would have to teach to attainment targets which would be seen as ends in themselves (Lally, 1989). This seemed to imply more teacher direction at the expense of child-initiated activities. Content overload as well as testing and assessment procedures appeared to militate against play, and teachers were faced with the erosion of what was thought an important part of the early years curriculum. The notion that teachers needed to 'hang on to' and 'defend' play was a recurrent theme on in-service courses, at conferences and BAECE and NCB meetings.

Opinions about the impact of the National Curriculum were divided. In Anning's view, infant teachers knuckled down to making the best compromises they could between their preferred ways of designing and implementing the curriculum and the requirements of the Programmes of Study (1991, p. 104). Other commentators noted the potential for a more proactive role to enable early years teachers to contribute to the processes of change by becoming more directly involved with curriculum development. The role and status of play within the context of changed realities have been viewed pessimistically. According to Hurst, play was increasingly seen as the enemy of education and was relegated to the margins of school experience. Furthermore, the top-down pressure of the National Curriculum on pre-school education became a 'malign influence' (1994, p. 58). It became increasingly evident that teachers needed to clarify what it was they were hanging on to and defending.

The status of play was already tenuous, particularly beyond the pre-school phase. A lack of clear principles and firm theoretical base had resulted in discrepancies between aims and practice. There were disagreements about the role of the adult in children's play. The dichotomy between work and play meant that play lacked status and credibility, particularly in relation to children's learning and tangible outcomes. Its vulnerability was not caused by the National Curriculum but was undoubtedly made worse by it.

There were attempts to legitimize play within the new curriculum framework. A report which examined the implications of the National Curriculum for children under five accorded central status to play with particular emphasis on planning, structuring the learning environment and developing skilled interactions between adults and children:

> Purposeful play features strongly in good pre-school education. It is not a free or wholly unstructured activity. Through the selection of materials and equipment . . . teachers ensure that, in their play, children encounter the learning experiences that they intend . . . Play that is well planned and pleasurable helps children to think, to increase their understanding and to improve their language competence. It allows children to be creative, to explore and investigate materials, to experiment and to draw and test their conclusions.
>
> (DES, 1989, p. 8)

The report recommended the adoption of the nine areas of learning and experience outlined by HMI in 1985 as a framework for planning:

- aesthetic and creative
- human and social
- linguistic and literary
- mathematical
- moral
- physical
- scientific
- spiritual
- technological.

This model was intended to promote breadth and balance and to relate to the subject areas of the National Curriculum. Subsequently it was endorsed by the report of the Rumbold Committee (DES, 1990) as a key aspect of ensuring quality for the under-fives, including children in reception classes.

For Key Stage 1, the need to retain play within the curriculum was also upheld. The Early Years Curriculum Group devised a model using the familiar topic web as a means of integrating play within the National Curriculum framework (1989). The underlying rationale was that play was compatible with this framework and that children could demonstrate their achievements of the attainment targets through different play activities. This gave teachers some reassurance at a time of considerable uncertainty. However, in subjugating play to attainment targets, teachers were in danger of narrowing the value and purposes of play. Other areas such as social and emotional development, creativity and imagination were neglected in this model. Also, it did not address the critical issue that the original attainment targets and level descriptors did not accurately reflect the complex qualitative changes in children's understanding.

These initiatives represented a serious attempt at securing play as an integral part of the early years curriculum, paying more attention to planning, assessment, evaluation, progression and continuity. However, the impetus for change was being externally driven and teachers needed to reconceptualize their practice in their own terms. Stitching together a patchwork of different ideas and initiatives was a short-term response to change. This was perhaps inevitable given the extent of change and the impact of the National Curriculum on the nature of infant teachers' work.

Many educationists have been critical of the National Curriculum in terms of both its design and the impact that it has had on early years practice:

> It is plain to anyone who has had direct experience of early years education in the UK that the advent of the National Curriculum has had the effect of turning it on its head. The direction of its development has been reversed; the advances it has made towards establishing a new and sophisticated form of curriculum have been discounted and arrested; and those teachers in the sector who continue to adhere to the values and ideals implicit in the approaches which have been displaced are struggling against all odds to maintain those values and ideals in a context which is not only incompatible but hostile to them.
>
> (Blenkin and Kelly, 1994, p. 1)

This forthright critique reflects some of the genuine pain, struggle and sense of frustration that teachers have faced over the last few years. However, it conveys a sense of powerlessness and pessimism. While many teachers might identify with the comments, it is also true to say that, for some, the struggles have not just been defensive, they have also been creative. It is creativity which has energized good practitioners not only to make the most of a difficult job but to create new ways of thinking about teaching and learning. The National Curriculum has generated renewed focus on teaching, learning, models and approaches, content and processes. Evidence from practitioners shows that some have been moving away from defensiveness and entrenchment to consider issues which are central to the development of play in schools. These are some of the questions raised by early childhood educators in their efforts to improve the quality of play:

• How do we extend thinking and learning through play?
• How do we measure learning in play?
• How can play be used to extend subject-based learning?
• How do we recognize and develop children's individual 'schemas' through play?
• What play activities are most successful? How can we tell?
• What is good play?
• At what point does 'valuable' play end and how do we define low-level activities?
• How do we organize for different types of play in the classroom?
• How do we balance structured play with free play?
• What is the teacher's role in play and how can they extend children's learning ?
• Should we intervene, if so, when and how?
• How much time should we spend observing play and how can this feed into assessment and record keeping?
• How can we ensure creativity and exploration whilst maintaining safety?

These questions reflect the pragmatic concerns of educators who are committed to play but want to improve their practice through reflection and enquiry. The need for theoretical rather than ideological support is a recurrent request on in-service courses:

- We need a wider theory-practice view.
- We need to develop critiques on theory and practice.
- We need to see whether our own ideas accord with the theorists'.
- We want to understand more fully the theoretical background to play.
- We'd like to learn from the experience of other practitioners in organizing play in their classrooms.

In our view it is difficult, if not impossible, for teachers to organize content in relevant, meaningful ways without utilizing play. Clearly in order to facilitate this, a more rigorous examination of the relationship between play, learning and the curriculum is imperative.

The politics of play

Play is not just an educational issue, it is essentially a political issue. The ascendant philosophy of the New Right in education brought with it the language of the marketplace. Competition, accountability, performance indicators, league tables, users and providers became buzz words. The idealistic ideology which has characterized the early years in general and play in particular was made to appear outdated and irrelevant. The political agenda was not just to change the curriculum but to change the culture of primary education. This was attempted overtly through the Education Reform Act but more insidiously by a systematic denigration of the profession. Early years teachers have taken a considerable battering from successive Ministers of Education. The emphasis on play in the curriculum did little to raise their credibility in the eyes of politicians and may have contributed to the threat of raising a 'Mum's Army' to teach young children.

Clearly there was a need to clarify the status and credibility of play. However, a significant problem here is that this is intrinsically bound with the status of early years teachers and other adults who work with young children. Issues of status, gender and power have been explored by David (1990), Anning (1991) and in Kessler and Swadener (1992). A common theme emerges: asserting principles and changing practices from within is a difficult process in a female-dominated area of the teaching and the caring professions.

Early years educators tend to be passive and inwardly focused on the demands of the profession. They have a poor record in researching, documenting and articulating their professional thinking (Anning, 1994, p. 69). This view has been confirmed by Hall and Abbott: 'It is no secret among educationists that we have been singularly unsuccessful in persuading politicians, journalists and parents that play is of tremendous significance for the intellectual, social and physical growth of children' (1991, p. 2).

It was the very insularity, apparent ideological entrenchment and 'secret garden' approach of early years practitioners which attracted criticism from Alexander (1992) and which government education policies sought to erode. In order not to feel deskilled and dispirited teachers need to develop and articulate new perspectives in order to challenge rather than just accommodate changed realities. Athey has argued that

> The problem in Britain is not an absence of excellence in early or primary education. What is lacking is a professional vocabulary that can clearly articulate the nature of excellence . . . Questions on the nature of 'learning', 'knowing', 'understanding' and 'experiencing' are psychological and pedagogical rather than political and are of central concern to teachers.
>
> (1990, pp. 8, 9)

Finding a professional vocabulary involves challenging assumptions about play, teaching and learning, and creating a discourse which goes beyond the rhetoric of the New Right and the insularity of early childhood educators. The educational reforms introduced since 1988 concentrated largely on policy issues and, initially at least, ignored pedagogy, that is an understanding of the ways teachers teach and children learn. It is through pedagogy that the curriculum is mediated and educational intentions are translated into practice through activities and experiences. For play in schools to attain greater status and credibility, it needs to be linked to pedagogy. This should go beyond surface features such as relating play to attainment targets or creating a carefully structured play environment. Desforges has argued that, in the National Curriculum documents, the teacher-pupil relationship is conceived to be subtle, complex and reciprocal (1989, p. 17). The implications are that teachers need a powerful understanding of the nature of learning, and more discriminating levels of pedagogical knowledge and expertise. This applies equally to all those who work with young children and not just to teachers at Key Stage 1. We need to consider where play fits in and how its educational potential can be more fully developed.

The National Curriculum and other education reforms were not the only forces undermining play. There are wider problems within early childhood education. There is a need to establish what the critical issues are for the design of curricula in the various early childhood settings, what are appropriate contexts for developing and maximizing play, and what types of play are important for children in the different phases of their development and their schooling. Addressing such questions means that practitioners need to draw substantially on the knowledge base in early childhood education for support. However, this in itself is difficult because play has been implemented on a disparate ideological and theoretical base. As the next chapter shows this has proved to be a further source of tension in early childhood education.

2

Ideologies, Ideals and Ideas

The disparate nature of the ideological, theoretical and research bases in early childhood reveals persistent tensions regarding the purposes of play. As we have indicated, this has led to conflict between aims and practice and between rhetoric and reality. In spite of strong ideological commitments to play and confident assertions about its value, the quality of play in early years settings is variable. In this chapter, we will examine play from three perspectives – ideology, research on play, and research on play in educational settings – with the intention of understanding how and why some of these problems have arisen.

Ideologies and ambiguities

The work of the early educationists and philosophers has been regarded as the basis of the early childhood tradition (Bruce, 1987). This tradition is not easily defined since it emanates from a wide variety of philosophers, educators and developmental psychologists from different ages and cultures as well as from 'hundreds of speeches, discussions, resolutions, reports, texts and taken-for-granted assumptions' (Webb, 1974, p. 3). It includes a heady mix of ideas about the nature of childhood, the purposes of education, rights and responsibilities and the role of play. These ideas range from the rhapsodic to the pragmatic. Central to this tradition is the work of Pestalozzi, Freidrich Froebel, Rudolf Steiner, Maria Montessori, Margaret McMillan, Susan Isaacs and Anna Freud as well as the literary and philosophical writing of Rousseau, Wordsworth and other nineteenth century 'Romantics'. Useful summaries can be found in Bruce (1987), Anning (1991) and Cohen (1993). We consider that a critical appraisal of the ideological base is necessary in order to develop a professional vocabulary which can clearly articulate the nature of excellence.

First, the ideas of these and other pioneer educators were highly relevant in their own historical and cultural contexts. Until the nineteenth century, childhood was seen as an immature form of adulthood and children from all classes had little status in society. Children were frequently abused and exploited and had few legal rights or protection. For many, childhood was cut short by the need to work either in the home or in factories, often for long hours and in dangerous conditions. The concept of original sin meant that children were regarded as naturally evil and had to have moral rectitude instilled in them by whatever means adults thought acceptable, whether at home, in schools or in the workplace. Froebel and Rousseau took the opposite view that children are naturally good and that their goodness could be harnessed through nurture, care and educative processes. The early pioneers were striking out to persuade society of the need for new visions of childhood, to change entrenched attitudes towards children and to make appropriate provision for their development, care and education. Intrinsically bound with this movement were ideals about social justice and ultimately a more egalitarian society.

The pioneers of the nineteenth century sought to establish the uniqueness and importance of childhood as a stage in its own right. Part of that uniqueness lay in children's natural affinity for play. The Romantic, child-centred ideology emphasizes the importance of allowing children to indulge their naturalness and playfulness. The word 'kindergarten' represents metaphors of growth, freedom, and an idyllic balance between nature, nurture and spirituality. Kindergartens represented a safe haven away from the harsh realities of the adult world. The curricula devised by the pioneers were not just innovative but revolutionary. Froebel's new system of education was perceived as a political threat and, by the mid-nineteenth century, he was regarded as a subversive by the authorities in Germany. He was accused of being an atheist and a socialist and all of his nurseries were closed down (Cohen, 1993, p. 27).

Play was valued differently by each of the pioneers but they were all concerned to harness its educational potential in different ways. Montessori did not believe that children needed to play and did not value play as a creative force in itself. In designing special child-sized environments, she was not directly stimulating imaginative role play, but encouraging practical independence and autonomy. She had an instrumental view of play as a means to further cognitive, social, moral and emotional development. The pioneers recognized that play allows children to express their inner needs, desires and conflicts but, in terms of their curriculum models, it was not the dominant activity. The models devised by Froebel and Montessori were based substantially on the use of special materials to be used in a particular sequence and in carefully structured environments. The curricula designed by all the pioneers included sense-training, self-discipline, orderliness, cleanliness and habit formation.

These curricula were very much products of their times. They were designed with reference to particular values and for specific purposes. But times change and education is subject to fads and fashions. It is interesting to note that the Progressive Movement which developed in America at the turn of the century criticized the programmes of Froebel and Montessori as being highly structured, formal and ritualized. Montessori's emphasis on sensory training, individualism and academic learning was considered to be at odds with notions of freedom, creativity, play, fantasy and self-expression which were fundamental to the Progressives.

Although Bruce (1987) has outlined some commonalities and areas of agreement, the work of the pioneers reveals different emphases on the value of play, the role of adults, the organization of the learning environment and the content of the curriculum. They held different views about the nature of learning and development. Many of their ideas combined philosophy and psychology and provided guiding principles but not a unified theoretical, psychological or pedagogical base for early childhood education. McAuley and Jackson have argued that the pioneers present such a bewildering contrast of ideas that 'the onus is surely on those who claim to see consistency to demonstrate it' (1992, p. 20).

As conceptions of childhood changed and investment in schooling expanded, education was seen as playing a vital role in the social and economic welfare of the nation. However, there were radically different views of what form that education should take and the Romantic and Progressive movements, both in Great Britain and America, sat uneasily with the more utilitarian view which came to dominate infant schools from the late nineteenth century. Control of the curriculum became a political and economic issue and, as public investment in education increased, so too did the need for evidence of effectiveness, accountability and value for money. Curricula based on drill, rote-learning, sequenced exercises and prioritizing 'the three Rs' seemed more likely to deliver a literate, numerate workforce. As Anning (1991) argues, this resulted in two distinct theoretical and pedagogical frameworks which informed policy and practice in the twentieth century. On the one hand, there was the naturalist, developmental tradition derived from the pioneers. On the other, the instrumental, utilitarian elementary tradition derived variously from the public schools and the Protestant work ethic.

The tension, confusion and ambiguity at the level of ideology, policy and practice derived from the past have a familiar resonance in the present. What constitutes an appropriate curriculum in the early years has been subject to scrutiny throughout the twentieth century. This is appropriate because education must both respond to and determine change within societies. However, confusions in the ideological base have contributed to the vulnerability of play and some of the weaknesses inherent in early childhood education. The developmental, child-centred tradition, whether characterized as Romantic or Progressive, lacked a clear, unified theoretical, psychological and pedagogical base for early childhood education and systematic guidance for practice. It did not address issues such as how play is specifically responsible for educational and developmental effects, what purposes it serves at different ages in a child's life, and what forms of play are appropriate at different ages.

Confused practice may also have resulted from the blurred distinctions between philosophic principles and pedagogical and psychological theories. Ideology of any historical, educational or political description should not be received as dogma. It either creates entrenched practices which rest on partial understandings and outdated assumptions or creates conflict for educators and serves to widen the gap between rhetoric and reality. The ten common principles distilled from the past and redefined in a modern context by Bruce

(1987) represent a synthesis of ideals and ideas, both traditional and modern, but again these are not easily translated into practice in coherent, consistent ways. As DeVries and Kohlberg (1987) argue, philosophic principles cannot be stated as ends of education until they can be stated psychologically and tested empirically.

Do philosophic principles located in the past continue to provide a realistic theoretical, moral or ethical framework for the early years curriculum? At worst, this body of received wisdom has deteriorated to little more than mantras which are recycled for familiarity in times of stress. While we may look to the past for guidance, the direction must be located in the present and towards the future. Principles need a theoretical grounding, to be related to practice and to articulate the value system on which they are based. A philosophy of practice that does not generate a set of values by which to examine that practice may be less a philosophy, more a set of polite words on a page (Drummond, 1989, p. 5).

The influences of the early pioneers today is difficult to detect let alone demonstrate empirically. The apparent entrenchment of this ideological framework and commitment to the centrality of play has rendered early years practitioners vulnerable. We have already indicated that play is poorly represented in infant schools, and that the quality of play in nursery and other early years settings has been questioned. This is not altogether the fault of teachers. In their critique of the ideological base in early childhood education, McAuley and Jackson have argued that there is little that is firm or clarified to take from the early childhood tradition with the result that 'Teachers must fall back on classroom experience and seek to develop professional expertise without much theoretical guidance. Conspicuously absent from the common law of early childhood education is, simply, knowledge about what has been going on' (1992, p. 31).

It is not just the lack of consistent guidance which has contributed to the ambiguities surrounding play in early childhood education. As the next section will show, the theoretical base is as disparate as the ideological base.

Theoretical perspectives on play, development and learning

We do not provide an exhaustive review of the research base on play – it is simply too vast. But shifting perspectives and broad trends can be identified. It is important to note that different types of play have been investigated from a number of disciplinary perspectives; different methods of enquiry have been used and not all of this research is easily applied to educational settings. As Meadows has noted, an inspired and practical pedagogy and curriculum are not inevitable outcomes of research as the field is too heterogeneous (1993, p. 345). Early childhood education has been constrained by its reliance on psychological theory and research, particularly where there has been an emphasis on understanding child development (Kessler and Swadener, 1992). A wide range of theories has influenced decisions about what and how children should learn and the contribution of play has attracted considerable attention.

The main focus of research on play has been directed towards establishing what play is and what purposes it serves. Theories of play have changed over time. Hughes (1991, p. 15) outlines a broad overview of classic theories of play which, as Saracho argues, justify the basis for play in human activities, but constitute conflicting pairs:

> The surplus energy theory and relaxation theory conflict; one theory suggests that play consumes energy, while the other suggests that it creates new energy. Similarly, the pre-exercise theory describes play as a way to anticipate the future, while the recapitulation theory reflects the past history of civilisation, again a contradiction. Indeed, none of the classical theories provides a satisfactory justification for play in the early childhood curriculum.
>
> (1991, p. 89)

There has been a distinct change in emphasis from theories which describe play as a natural, instinctive way of promoting optimal physical development, to those which focus on the social, emotional and cultural adaptation of children. More recently, the emphasis has shifted again to theories which explain play in terms of its contribution to children's learning and development within social, historical and cultural contexts. In the current educational climate which is concerned with outcomes, measurement, testing and accountability, the need to link play with cognitive development has become more pressing for early years educators in order to justify its place in the curriculum. Thus how we conceptualize play depends on our understanding of learning and related cognitive processes and on our interpretations of what is educationally and developmentally significant to children about play.

Many researchers have distinguished between different types of play and have sought to define their characteristics or qualities. Piaget's three stages and categories of play are often used as a framework for research:

- *Practice play* – sensori-motor and exploratory play based on physical activities (six months to two years).
- *Symbolic play* – pretend, fantasy and socio-dramatic play, involving the use of mental representations. When play becomes representational, it is regarded as intellectual activity (two to six years).
- *Games with rules* – from six or seven years upwards.

These stages and categories have been challenged, refined and extended. Smilansky (1990) added a fourth category of constructive play because of the dominance of such play in early childhood. This is characterized by the manipulation of objects to build or create something. It can be based on blocks and other constructional equipment, as well as playdough or collage materials which can involve symbolic, spatial and multi-dimensional constructions to allow children to represent their own reality. There has been substantial research on the first and second categories, and on constructive play, but less on games with rules. Because of Piaget's influence on research and practice, a brief outline of his theories on play and learning is necessary.

Piaget was interested in the origins of logical, mathematical and scientific thought and wanted to establish the relationship between biological and cognitive development. He was less concerned with the role of language, communication, social interaction and teaching. Piaget's theory of cognitive development placed action and self-directed problem-solving at the heart of learning and development: 'By acting on the world the learner comes to discover how to control it. Learning how to act on the world and discovering the consequences of action form the bedrock of thinking'. (Wood, 1988, p. 5.)

Piaget saw the child as a lone scientist working actively on materials, objects, events and the environment to construct knowledge and understanding (hence the term constructivist theory). He characterized learning by the transition through age-related stages from immature to mature forms of thinking, that is from simple to complex, and from concrete to abstract. These stages are linked to the concept of readiness – critical periods when a child is ready to learn. He theorized that only when children have constructed logical operations do they develop the capacity for sustained and systematic perceptual analysis and rational thought (Wood, 1988). Interventionist teaching which ran ahead of these stages could not facilitate development or learning. Meadows challenges this theory: 'The development of performance is age-related, but being stagelike in the sense of being clearly discontinuous, cohesive, synchronous or even across tasks requires stronger evidence than is available in most areas' (1993, p. 349).

Piaget proposed that three processes are important in learning – assimilation, accommodation and equilibration. Accommodation is the child's ability to adapt to the environment, whilst assimilation is the child's ability to change the environment to suit the imagination. This involves transforming experiences within the mind, whereas accommodation involves adjusting the mind to new experiences (Sutherland, 1992, p. 26). When children encounter new experiences, concepts or knowledge, their existing internal frameworks or schemata have to adjust, causing a state of disequilibrium or cognitive conflict. This acts as a motivation to learning until a state of equilibration is reached again.

Piaget argued that children's play tended to promote assimilation rather than accommodation, and that it led to consolidation of newly learned behaviours. Therefore playing was not the same as learning but could facilitate learning as it exposes the child to new experience and new possibilities for dealing with the world (Hughes, 1991, p. 21). Thus play in itself was not seen as a leading source of learning and development. Piaget's theories were interpreted to imply that educators should create environments in which children could be active learners, free to explore, experiment, combine different materials, create and solve problems through their self-chosen and self-directed initiatives. In this framework, the role of the educator has been characterized as that of enabler and facilitator, someone who responds to children's initiatives and values their thinking processes and ongoing cognitive concerns, but who does not seek actively to impart knowledge which children ideally should construct for themselves.

Rightly or wrongly, this has been interpreted in practice as a non-interventionist stance, even though Piaget considered that interaction with other children and adults has an important part to play in children's education. So early childhood practitioners who accepted Piaget's descriptions of child development found that they could interpret his work according to their own beliefs and preferred methods. Curriculum designers have, therefore, drawn implications leading to a variety of approaches to educating young children based on their needs and characteristics as learners. A teacher on an in-service course described how she had been 'born and bred' on Piaget's theories and, as a consequence, tended to stand back from children's play. Increasingly this was causing her real conflict as she recognised many instances in play when supportive interactions would assist a child's learning. This serves to illustrate the tortuous journey from theory to practice and how theories need to be subjected to critical reflection. In Piaget's work, the links between play, cognitive processes and social adaptation were not fully explored. This may in part account for the fact that play has been allowed in the pre-school years, but has been regarded more as preparatory to real learning in schools.

Continuing the theme of play and cognitive development, the work of Smilansky has been oriented towards the significance of dramatic and socio-dramatic play as a means for developing cognitive, creative and socio-emotional abilities. She makes clear distinctions between these two types of play:

> Dramatic play consists of children taking on a role in which they pretend to be someone else. They imitate the person's actions and speech patterns, using real or imagined 'props' and drawing on their own first-hand or second-hand experience of the imitated individual in various familiar situations . . . When such activity involves the *co-operation* of at least two children and the play proceeds on the basis of interaction between the players acting out their roles, both verbally and in terms of the acts performed, the dramatic play is considered 'socio-dramatic play'.
>
> (1990, p. 19)

In Smilansky's terms, socio-dramatic play should not be confused with either symbolic or representational play because the latter stressed the mental processes involved and not the child's behaviour. Similarly role play was considered too narrow a definition as it only describes one of the elements in socio-dramatic play, that of taking a role. Both forms of play are dependent on imitation and make-believe. She links sensori-motor play with representation as, for example, when children don't just explore sand, but use it for building sandcastles. Smilansky questions Piaget's categories of play on the basis that both dramatic and socio-dramatic play develop parallel to other forms of play, beginning at around two and continuing well beyond the age of ten. She identifies six elements which characterize these types of play:

- role play by imitation
- make believe with objects
- make believe with actions and situations
- persistence in the role play
- interaction
- verbal communication.

These elements can be used as an assessment and diagnostic tool for evaluation purposes:

> The richness of play depends on the extent to which the various elements are used and developed. Thus, the evaluation of richness depends, not on the content of the child's episode or on the type of role being played, but on the degree to which each of the elements is developed and used as a play skill.
>
> (1990, p. 21)

Smilansky's work challenges some of Piaget's deficit notions of children's thinking, particularly the continuum from concrete to abstract. Children do not just play with objects and materials. They also play with meanings and ideas, and can make significant cognitive leaps and transformations. For example, Elizabeth had a collection of cotton reels which, from around eighteen months, were variously transformed into food, goods to load on a train wagon, people, items of shopping and naughty children in school, to name but a few. The ability to think in quite sophisticated abstract ways is an undervalued aspect of children's play. Imitation and make-believe are tolerated as part of children's fantasy worlds, and are not seen as cognitive processes or fully appreciated in terms of their relationship to cognitive development. As we have argued, technical and rational modes of thinking tend to be valued above creativity and imagination. However, Smilansky (1990) concludes that socio-dramatic play either uses learning-relevant capacities or contributes to their development. This relationship tends to be overlooked by educators who typically regard socio-dramatic play in terms of catharsis, relaxation or as part of the child's own private world. As Kelly-Byrne argues, this is a neglected resource:

> it is the excitement and compulsion of a personal agenda that motivates much self-initiated and self-directed play in the lives of children . . . In the privacy of a space of their choosing and among friends, the dramatic play of children is an alluring and incredibly complex kind of behaviour that is likely to encompass most, if not all, of a child's resources and integrate them into a whole. The value of tapping its momentum and power, in the child's own terms, should be obvious to those of us concerned with facilitating children's communication and their sense of their own power.
>
> (1989, p. 212)

The implications of Smilansky's work are that play activities stimulate a wide range of cognitive processes which are important for learning in a variety of contexts. She also suggests that children's cognitive competence could be enhanced through 'play tutoring', as adult involvement in play was found to increase children's fantasy play, and improve their cognitive, language and social development. However, the kinds of interactions used by the adults were both supportive of and responsive to the child's needs and potential:

> Intervention should be skill oriented and not content oriented; that is, the purpose is to provide children with tools to express and actualize their needs, to experience roles that fascinate them to their fullest, and, accordingly, to enact and develop themes with content that interests them. It seems that the basic skills that should be emphasized at early age levels are the ones that characterize well-developed play of older children: role declaration; make-believe with objects, actions and situations; co-operation; and elaboration of themes according to role. All of these should be supported with sensitivity to the child's level of play development and in congruence with the content the child is trying to express.
>
> (1990, p. 153)

The implication here is that play is not an entirely spontaneous activity in early childhood and that children need to learn how to play in different contexts and with the support of skilled peers and adults. Children have a natural tendency to be active as soon as they are born. But this activity is transformed into play through deliberate actions and interactions. Clearly the issue of how children learn needs to encompass how they learn to play and what cognitive processes are involved. There is some debate as to whether it is play that contributes to learning and development or whether the various actions and interactions within play are more influential. For example, a group of children was playing with a tray filled with autumn leaves, berries, and seeds. At first they plunged their hands in to the materials, apparently enjoying the tactile experince. They began to examine the contents more carefully, discussing and comparing their finds. This led to sorting, classifying, questioning, comparing, contrasting, sharing ideas and using descriptive language. The children then used the materials to represent trees, animals, plants and birds and created a woodland collage on a nearby table. Later they wrote poems and stories which helped to sustain the flow of ideas and experiences, making connections between areas of learning. The children were not just playing with materials, they were also playing with language and ideas which they were able to communicate and represent creatively.

Two detailed reviews of research on play by Fromberg (1987) and Johnson (1990) describe a variety of studies which indicate a relationship between play and cognitive development, particularly where play incorporates intellectual challenge as a means to perceiving new connections and relationships. Johnson (1990, p. 215) notes that play serves an important cognitive consolidating function by assisting in the child's construction of meaning from experience. Intrinsic curiosity and motivation act as a spur to cognitive processes such as developing understanding, problem solving and making sense. Therefore, understanding cognitive processes is a key to understanding more fully the role of play in children's learning. However, the difficulty for educators is that these processes tend to be specified in rather general terms. Theories about assimilation and accommodation provide a broad description but are unlikely to be of central concern to teachers as they attempt to pinpoint much more specific learning processes and possible outcomes.

Research on play reveals two problems. First, categorizing play can be useful from the perspective of researchers since they need in-depth data to test hypotheses and provide evidence. Accordingly, their research designs and methods of enquiry can neglect the overlap between different types of play. Similarly, research into children's play has tended to focus on domains of development – the cognitive, affective, socio-emotional and psycho-motor. This can result in partial snapshots and 'thin' descriptions which do not adequately capture the dynamics or complexity of play. In summarizing their review of research on play, Smith and Cowie concluded that the evidence for strong cognitive benefits, whether from theory, observation, correlational or experimental studies, is not convincing. If anything, the evidence is better for the benefits of play for social competence (1991, p. 185). Does this imply that social competence is not related to or dependent on cognitive processes? There seems to be a hierarchy or at least a distinction between what kinds of learning are most valuable to children and hence what should determine curriculum content. This neglects the fact that children need conceptual frameworks for developing social competence. They need knowledge about their social worlds, including social conventions and rituals, appropriate forms of behaviour, moral and ethical issues. Play has a particular role to play in children's social, affective and moral development, and this should not be seen as separate from their cognitive development.

The following example shows how different forms of play and domains of learning are integrated. Martin built a car with hollow blocks by himself and, for a while, was content to sit behind the steering wheel making engine noises. Other friends joined the activity and they negotiated with Martin to extend the size of the car to include extra seats, then went for a long drive, visiting different places on the way, stopping for petrol and oil. At some point Martin felt that he was losing control of his original intentions because he told the others to leave as the car was really a Grand Prix racing car and could only take one person. He removed the extra seats, returned to his solitary play and put a blanket over his head to signify a helmet and/or the cockpit, as well as to exclude other children. This sequence incorporated constructive, manipulative, symbolic and socio-dramatic play. It was also rule bound in the sense that the children negotiated the rules and had to maintain them in order to sustain the pretence. The children also displayed their real world knowledge and their understanding of social conventions. In this episode, they also deferred to Martin's ownership and control of the sequence, partly because he had made the car. This was a common pattern in the collaborative play of this group of four year old boys. Martin was popular, articulate, inventive and capable of directing imaginative play sequences. His friends usually accepted Martin's dominance simply because he was a skilled player and they enjoyed inclusion in his games, however limited that might be. Similarly Meckley (1994b) reports how children in her study accepted Jason's dictatorial style because he was 'a very good player' and his creative ideas were valued by other players.

It would be difficult to define accurately what the children were learning in this play episode in terms of outcomes, although they evidently drew upon a wide range of knowledge, skills and competencies. For educators, establishing a direct, causal relationship between play and learning remains problematic. However, if we reflect on the point made above that play acts as a spur to and rehearsal for cognitive processes, then a more accurate 'in-depth' analysis might be possible. There are two implications here. First, that educators need a clearer specification of cognitive processes, that is what is involved in learning rather than focusing exclusively on what is involved in playing. Second, educators need more detailed, 'thick' descriptions of children's play in natural contexts and over extended periods of time, rather than in controlled experiments in artificial settings.

Educators do not have to limit the way they conceptualize play to how it is defined and categorized by academics and researchers. The theory and research base in early childhood can inform our understanding about the relationship between play and cognitive development but, ultimately, educators have to derive meanings and connections through their practice. The world of research with small, experimental groups, specific designs and methods quite deliberately filters out many of the complex contextual variables which educators face in their practice. They need to appreciate and understand play in their own terms, in their own contexts and create their own frameworks for interpretation and analysis.

The research base reveals a minefield of competing and sometimes contradictory theories and hypotheses. Play encapsulates many forms and behaviours and changes according to contexts, cultures, age and gender. Where research has provided recommendations for practice, there are different perspectives on the various types of play, the role of the teacher, the content and organization of the curriculum, the balance of activities and their purposes. Questions about how children learn and develop and how that is best facilitated at home or in school are complex. There is no single theory which can explain the role of play in children's learning and development. Adopting multi-theoretical perspectives can shed light on the relationship between different types of play and different domains of learning. These need to be integrated by educators to inform their understanding of play to guide their practice.

Learning through play

Alongside the scientific, rational tradition of research into play, learning and development which has been dominated by cognitive and developmental psychology, there has emerged a critical, interpretive perspective which has attempted to understand play in terms of what it reveals about children's unique forms of learning, knowing, representing and understanding. These studies have also emphasized the complexity of the educator's role in making sense of children's play worlds, imaginary worlds and real worlds in which they integrate the knowledge, skills and understanding gleaned from a wide variety of experiences (Figure 1). They also reflect the view of Bateson (1972) that to truly understand play, one must try to assess the multiple patterns of meaning occurring simultaneously over time.

The work of Vivian Gussin Paley and Dianne Kelly-Byrne provides fascinating insights into children's play lives which capture the qualities which educators may be more familiar with in their practice. In *Wally's Stories* (1981) Paley followed a group of five year olds through their kindergarten year. She found that a wide variety of thinking emerged from the children's conversations, stories and play acting as concepts of morality, science and society shared the stage with fantasy. The children were encouraged to tell their own stories and create their own play themes and scripts. Throughout the book, the children's stories reveal many paradoxes as they weave between fantasy and reality. For example, they created stories with monsters, superheroes, good guys and bad guys, and played with concepts of danger, threat, strength, bravery, triumph and fear.

Inevitably, themes derived from well known stories and fairy tales, as well as television characters, inhabited the children's play worlds. In creating fantasies, the children were often making sense of events and concerns in their own lives in ways which went beyond emotional release. They revealed concerns with rules, power, conflict, control, coercion, jealousy, anger, punishment, justice

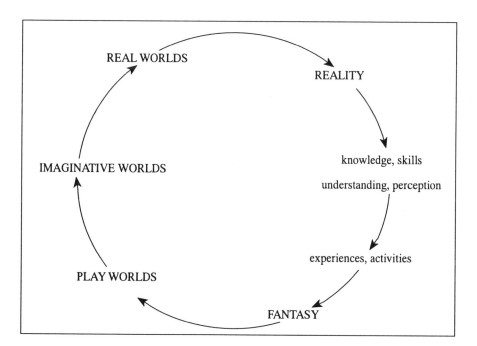

Figure 1   Integrating knowledge and experience

and self-determination. They demonstrated emerging knowledge of physics, mathematics, space and time, and made connections between actions and events in their real worlds and their play worlds. They were involved in complex actions and interactions which entailed communicating their intentions with others, negotiating, taking into account the needs and perspectives of others, adjusting the script and, in the midst of wild and wonderful fantasies, using logic, reasoning and 'real world' knowledge to sustain the fantasy. The following conversation between a group of children took place after reading the story of 'The Three Pigs'. Earlier, Wally had been on the 'time-out' chair:

> *Andy:* There's a boy Jeffrey on the other block from me. I went to his house once and he wouldn't let me in.
> *Lisa:* Why?
> *Andy:* Someone else was there.
> *Wally:* You should have gone down the chimney.
> *Lisa:* You shouldn't sneak into someone's house.
> *Eddie:* He should shape his hair in a different way and then come back and Jeffrey'll say 'Come in' and tell the other boy to go home.
> *Fred:* If he went down the chimney he might get boiled.
> *Wally:* He could come down with a gun.
> *Eddie:* Just to scare him. If he puts a boiling pot there, just jump over it.
> *Lisa:* Not a gun.
> *Eddie:* Here's a great idea. Get bullets and put it in a gun and aim it at Jeffrey.
> *Teacher:* That's a great idea?
> *Eddie:* No, I mean it's a bad idea.
> *Lisa:* Well, let him come down the chimney but not with a gun.
> *Wally:* Let's all go to Jeffrey's house and climb down his chimney and make him let Andy come in.
> *Andy:* I'll find out if he has a chimney.
> *Wally:* I'll get a time out chimney and he has to stay in there until he lets you come in.
>
> (1981, p. 19, 20)

Clearly we need to attend to the content of children's play, particularly their dialogue, as well as their behaviour in order to get a more accurate appreciation of the nature and quality of their thinking and learning. The evidence in Paley's work suggests that in their play children make creative transformations which allows them to play with ideas, roles, knowledge and concepts. Whether this kind of play is recognized and valued in the early childhood curriculum, and how it is managed (whether it is enabled or constrained), is a different matter.

Similar perspectives are revealed by Kelly-Byrne's study of the play life of six year old Helen which was a 'mass of diffuse yet intricately patterned symbols, structures and rhetoric' (1989, p. 209). Helen's home was the naturalistic setting for the fieldwork and included both solitary and peer group play. Kelly-Byrne involved herself in Helen's play, at her request and under her direction. Helen's preferred mode of play was make believe, with themes derived from myths and legends, television characters and her everyday life at home and in school. These were interwoven with immense complexity, often being further elaborated and transformed by Helen's creativity and imagination. The predominant play themes included:

> The child's origin and identity.
> The battle between good and evil.
> The testing of her powers and weaknesses.
> Her relationships with parents, peers, males and females.
> Strong women rescuing men who were weak and abandoned.
> The upgrading of her own supposedly inferior status as a girl by performing super feats.
> Understanding the polarities of smartness versus dumbness.
> Sorting out differences between good and bad mothering.
> Making sense of her own sexuality.
> Exploring the power of language to posit worlds and transform situations.
>
> (1989, p. 211)

This study demonstrates more recent theories that play has a central role in the transmission of culture through social interaction and communication. These processes contribute to children's social cognition – their understanding of roles, rules, relationships, values, beliefs, how society is organized, how it functions, and their own place in the world. Helen's preoccupation with powerfulness and powerlessness reflects her position as a child, her interpretation of her own socialization and the images of women portrayed in the media. Kelly-Byrne was struck by Helen's deep involvement, abundant energy levels and intense excitement during play sequences and argues that this challenges the 'wishy-washy' and idealized views adults often hold about children's play:

> Helen learned that play is a special kind of medium for packaging life's contradictions, for ordering confusion, and for destroying and transforming patterns and realities that are disliked; and, moreover, for doing so with a spirit of involvement, happy abandon, madness and festival. The materials she used in shaping her imaginary worlds were provided by the culture and motivated by her inner conflicts and agenda. She also had a sense of the spirit of play, one that was in keeping with the negative cultural state that play holds in our society. Therefore her play was often irrational, exuberant, combative, unbridled, and grotesque in its moments of intense passion.
>
> (1989, p. 216)

Meckley (1994a; 1994b; 1996) demonstrates how young children communicate shared knowledge through their social play and argues that it is essential to gather data on children's play over an extended period of time to fully understand its social organization. She reveals the immense complexity in children's play with repeating themes which were enacted through 'play frames' – a play sequence or action: 'in play, children actively communicate and interpret their individual and collective social realities through the play frame. This frame is a shared context that makes behaviour comprehensible and prescribes appropriate responses' (1994a, p. 295).

Meckley argues that children are amazingly competent in their construction of play frames and present themselves with tasks, problems and situations which demand complex interactions and a variety of social and communicative skills. These include inventing plots and characters, scripting the dialogue which forms the basis for directing the actions and interactions, negotiating, co-operating, representational skills and sharing knowledge. Moreover, far from being chaotic, the play of children in this study maintained stability, order, interconnectedness and consistency through an inherent rule system. Within the play events children used metacommunicative cues and techniques for communicating shared knowledge amongst all the players in the classroom and maintaining the play (1994b). In the 'Disappearing Pegs in Road' play, the children regularly construct a road layout with blocks and then pour a can of pegs into the spaces between the blocks. Some of the actions are communicated and directed non-verbally as these examples show:

- Signalling of others to join in this play is done by getting the peg can and taking it to the block area.
- Handing the peg can to a child immediately confers leadership on the peg can holder for the ensuing play.
- Changing voice by Jason, the disappearing peg play events' inventor and director, always signals a change in the play, usually that Jason is about to wreck the blocks. When other children in the area hear this voice change, they usually move away from Jason and/or exit the block area. Jason uses a specific singsong voice that always signals that destruction will follow.
- Searching for players often occurs during these play events. Disappearing Pegs in Road, once started, is a continual play event that may span thirty minutes or more. During this time, other happenings in the room attract the players away and only one may remain. When this player realizes he is alone, he searches for the others to come back to the play or he may briefly join them in their new activity.

There is substantial evidence of children learning through these peer group interactions which informs the design of further learning experiences in support-ive contexts. Meckley's interpretations of children's observable behaviour is linked to their social competence, social affiliation and social knowledge. These perspectives challenge the Piagetian viewpoints on play outlined earlier as the children were using symbolic, abstract forms of thinking and communicating these to each other in quite sophisticated ways.

Other studies have investigated internal cognitive processes in children's play which reveal patterns of learning, thinking and understanding (Athey, 1990; Gura, 1992; Nutbrown, 1994). These provide further evidence of the complex-ity of children's play and demonstrate how they reveal persistent cognitive con-cerns across a range of play activities which give educators a window on learn-ing and development. Both Athey and Nutbrown adopt a Piagetian standpoint through the exploration of children's schemas. These are defined as patterns of actions and behaviour which reveal the characteristics of children's thinking and learning. Schemas are gradually extended and co-ordinated through experience and activity and can be represented in many different ways – through action, speech, markmaking and the many different types of play. The research into children's block play (Gura, 1992) shows how children work on different schemas at different stages which indicate, amongst other things, early mathematical, scientific, linguistic and creative development. Schemas may be elaborated, integrated and co-ordinated into more complex forms of thinking and can be 'nourished' by worthwhile curriculum content, including play.

The above examples indicate two significant trends. First, research into children's play is moving out of the psychologist's laboratory and into more naturalistic settings such as the home and school. This is important as the influence of context on children's play and learning is central to the quality of their early education. Second, there is a shift away from broad-scale theories towards more detailed descriptions of the characteristics, patterns and processes of early learning and development. Meadows notes that theoretical progress is more likely to be made at a level where behaviour is clearly specified than at the level of behaviour so general and all-pervasive that it is abstract and untestable but goes on to state that 'there remains a substantial discrepancy between the practices which the developmental psychologist who has studied children's development might suggest, and the practices which an under-resourced and over-stressed school system can implement' (1993, p. 345).

We have shown that early childhood educators have been criticized for reliance on a disparate ideological tradition rather than a clear theoretical framework and have argued that they need to reconceptualize their practice. However, changing practice through conscious reflection and critical enquiry can be a painful process and, as Rodd (1994, p. 132) has argued, early childhood professionals can find themselves caught between the push for change and the pull of tradition. A further problem is that the fruits of academic research may not be made widely available to a practitioner audience. The language of research can be specialized and inaccessible so that a dialogue between theory and practice and between academics and educators can be difficult if not impossible.

If the perspectives of educators have been neglected in this dialogue, then so too have the perspectives of children. Athey (1990) has argued that we need to establish a more professional conceptualization of what children are saying and doing before teaching prescriptions are made and adopted and that teachers need a more conscious pedagogical knowledge based on greater concerns with how quality of mind in young children can be cultivated. Deepening our understanding of play is an important part of this process, but this needs to take place alongside a better understanding of children's learning. Integrating perspectives from these two fields can serve to inform and enrich practice. The following two chapters present a range of theoretical perspectives on children's learning and development. The intention is to move forward the debates about play, its place in the curriculum and its significance as a vehicle for learning.

3

Understanding Children's Learning: Multi-theoretical Perspectives

Learning and development in humans are so complex that no single theory can adequately account for all the interrelated processes involved. Instead multi-theoretical perspectives offer detailed and specific explanations. Many of these are tentative and hypothetical since our knowledge of the human brain and the development of cognition are still expanding through research. Moreover, most theories inevitably imply ideal transitions through ideal processes and into ideal states. However, as all early childhood educators know, the contexts in which they work are often far from ideal, and children are individuals who learn and develop in different ways, at different rates, but generally within broadly similar patterns. We begin by looking at the neuro-physiological development of the human brain (Meadows, 1993), as learning and development are dependent on how cognitive structures are formed, connected and coordinated.

The brain is a highly complex organ and its range of functions is not fully understood. Different parts of the brain have different functions – the left hemisphere dominates in speech and language comprehension whilst large areas at the front and back deal with thinking, storing and processing information. All areas are connected by nerve fibres which carry the messages received from external stimuli. The nature of children's early experiences determines how these networks develop and assist in the process of editing, sorting and pruning connections.

In normal patterns of development the connections and interconnections between nerve cells and between the different areas of the brain develop in response to stimulation which is actively sought and used. Hence learning and cognitive development are dependent on structures which are complex from birth. But the brain is not just a mechanical device for regulating body temperature, coordinating actions or storing and processing information. Emotion and cognition are not separate brain functions. As Meadows states, in the workings of the brain lie the subjective unity of each individual's mind and personality (1993, p. 282). It follows that the range and quality of early learning experiences are vital to forming these connections and expanding the structures as well as in the creation of self.

Many of the conditions needed for the development of the brain and for learning appear to take place during play from the earliest months of a child's life. Most theorists agree that children's natural desire to play arises spontaneously, but whether play is an evolutionary necessity is more debatable. Whilst children are active from birth, the ability to transform that activity into play is usually learnt in conjunction with adults or more experienced others from the first peek-a-boo games to fantasy play or board games. It is also stimulated by appropriate materials and learning environments. All the processes involved in play such as repeating actions, making connections, extending skills, combining materials, taking risks, provide the essential electrical impulses which help to make the connections and interconnections between neural networks, thus extending children's capabilities as learners and thinkers. Play also integrates the brain's regulatory systems and contributes to the 'unity of mind and personality' through the development of self-systems (self-esteem, self-worth, self-image and self-competence) and knowledge of cultural and gender identities.

As we have seen, recent theories of cognitive development have moved away from broad scale theories to more detailed information about cognitive processes and structures. These now acknowledge the complex interactions between the internal motivations and characteristics of the child, the learning environment and the role of peers and adults. In the following section we will examine a range of theories which seek to account for the development of different areas of learning. These will be related to play.

Information processing theory

Seifert (1993) states that the mind is viewed as having distinct parts that make distinct contributions to thinking in a distinct order. Information processing theory seeks to explain how the brain perceives, transmits, stores and retrieves information and how this is used in solving problems. It is based on cognitive psychology and computer science and focuses on the acquisition of knowledge, how the memory functions and how we learn to use and control our memory. Not everything can be remembered – that would be impossible – but control processes determine whether information is lost or transferred from one store to another (Meadows, 1993). Transfer from the sensory register to short- or long-term memory is dependent on the learner attending to the stimuli and using certain cognitive strategies to aid memorization, organization and internalization. Mnemonic (memory assisting) strategies are cognitive activities which include perceiving, attending, concentrating, imposing some structure on what is to be learnt, rehearsing, recalling and repeating. Seifert (1993) describes these cognitive processes as the 'mental architecture' for thinking, learning and processing information. Observations of children playing reveal that they do use these strategies, but probably spontaneously rather than deliberately. They often remember quite accurately how to make a dumper truck, or the details of play themes which are of current interest. However, children may have more difficulty learning to remember number bonds or spellings. There appears to be a distinction between what is remembered spontaneously and what has to be memorized deliberately.

This fairly straightforward model raises some interesting questions about whether these mnemonic strategies can be taught, and how they are learnt by children. Research has shown that young children use some strategies but these are vulnerable to mistakes because of their inexperience as learners. Wood (1988) and Meadows (1993) suggest that children can be taught these strategies which are then followed up with educational experiences in which they can be practised, applied and transferred to different contexts:

> Simply asking a child . . . to pay attention, concentrate, study, learn or remember is unlikely to bear fruit. Unless we embody the material to be learned and remembered in a task that makes sense to the child, one that involves objectives he can realize and that draws attention 'naturally' to the elements we wish him to take in, our imperatives to concentrate, memorize or learn are almost bound to fail. Young children can and will concentrate and remember but will often need the support of a more knowledgeable and intellectually skilled assistant. Such assistants act as 're-mind-ers'. At the same time, they provide living illustrations of the processes involved in memorization which eventually the child comes to 'internalize' and exploit for himself. Looked at in this way, the processes involved in deliberate memorization and contrived or formal learning situations take place first in external, observable and social terms before being internalized by the child to become personal, mental activities.
>
> (Wood, 1988, p. 61)

An example of these processes is a child learning to do an inset tray jigsaw. At first he/she may select pieces at random and 'bang' them on the tray to try to make them fit. Rotation and experimentation may follow and then more deliberate memorization through experience, repetition and success. If children are supported in this task they will develop the requisite 'mental architecture' for tackling different types of jigsaws, attending to the shape and size of each piece, using visual and tactile exploration, learning to use relevant language – back to front, upside down, wrong way round, straight/wavy edges, middle, top, bottom, fitting together, and encouraging deliberate efforts to remember the sequences and appearance of the finished product. This requires a great deal of concentration which can be aided by the support of a more knowledgeable other who is aware of the importance of such strategies. This is not simply telling a child what to do, it involves learning the tools for thinking which will eventually make learning more efficient. These can be learnt as the brain grows in size and complexity and as the connections and interconnections between areas and functions develop.

Seifert (1993) argues that children use a lot of mental energy on concentrating on new tasks. However, with practice, children attain a level of mastery which then releases energy for attending to the results and taking more control of both processes and outcomes. Howe (1992) and Meadows (1993) note that in the early years children rarely consciously use memorization strategies such as rehearsal or repetition. But their comments refer to the deliberate and conscious attempts to learn and process information. As we will show in this book, children use rehearsal and repetition extensively in their play. This can be problematic for educators who may have to make some decisions about the distinction between valuable rehearsal and stereotypical, repetitive play which leaves a child where he/she is rather than moving them forward to new challenges and possibilities. Whether rehearsal and repetition in play have any later impact on more formal learning processes has not been tested or proven, but it is possible that these valuable formative experiences might just have some lasting effects on the ways in which the brain develops and the extent and efficiency of the neural networks. As these structures develop, children gradually need to learn how to use and exert control over them.

Metamemory

An advanced form of memorization is 'metamemory' – which is defined by Meadows as 'knowledge of what memory behaviour is happening at the moment, and one's understanding of task difficulties, one's own skills, abilities and deficits, and strategies that will enable one to perform a task satisfactorily' (1993, p. 57).

Metamemory also involves transferability – the deliberate transfer of strategies and skills between tasks and problems, usually involving deliberate reflection and organization. Young children are considered to be deficient in this area because of their lack of experience as learners. But again we can see the roots of these skills in children's play since they store a tremendous wealth of information gleaned from many sources which they weave into different types of play. Often, if children are developing the structure and content of, for example, socio-dramatic play they draw upon individual and shared memories which are then interpreted and organized to provide the script and content of the play – what Garvey (1991) calls the play frame. They use recall strategies in repeated play themes, drawing on experience and imagination to remind each other of previous actions and sequences as the following example shows:

Ellie: You be the baby and I'll be the Mum.
Jen: No, I want to be the mum, I be'd the baby last time.
Ellie: No, but it's my turn to wear the dress cos Helen had it yesterday and I was the mum but I couldn't wear the dress.
Jen: O.K. then, you wear the dress but I'll be the mum as well and I'll have the baby and the pram. We'll be two mums.
Ellie: Yeah, and we'll go down the clinic for a 'jection cos my baby's got the measles. Has your baby got the measles?
Jen: No, but my baby's had medicine cos she's sick. I had medicine and I was sick.

Teaching cognitive strategies

Educators need to be aware of what develops spontaneously and what needs to be taught in order for children to become successful learners. Even where certain skills develop spontaneously, children need to become aware of the different contexts in which they can be used. Teaching children cognitive strategies is in itself insufficient. They need a wide repertoire of skills, knowledge and experiences in order to develop transfer-ability. Just as children need tools to think with, they also need something to think about. Connectionist theories of information processing seem to suggest the need for direct teaching of specific knowledge and cognitive strategies to young children. This may be a difficult concept in the context of play where early childhood educators often tend to highlight children's right to choose their own activities on the basis that this reflects their ongoing interests, needs and cognitive concerns. Seifert (1993) argues that, as we discover more about children's learning and development, early childhood educators may need to rethink their frequent, pervasive commitment to curricular self-choice. This has implications for how play is conceptualized in the curriculum. Again it does not mean more teacher direction or control, but it does raise questions about the role of the educator in designing effective learning environments. If children are to have a certain amount of curricular self-choice then the options open to them should be structured in order to maximize the educational value of play. This implies a balance between teachers' and children's intentions, reciprocity between the two and opportunities for teachers to appreciate children's meanings as they arise in play.

Information processing theory has its limitations. It provides explanations of cognitive processes and development which are based on a model of how a computer functions. But the 'unity of mind and personality' cannot be described adequately in this model. Wood (1988) has questioned whether learning can be viewed as information processing, memory as information storage and knowledge as information structures. The reality is much more complex. Children are individuals and, although they may share common experiences, how those are received and interpreted is unique to each child. Learning which is not underpinned by understanding is rarely useful or sustained even in adulthood. We can all remember instances of 'rote learning' facts, equations, scientific principles for exams. One teacher described how she learnt to 'do' logarithms without understanding their relevance or purpose. We all need to make sense and create meaning through learning and experience. Analogies with computer hardware and software provide only partial explanations of certain aspects of the brain's functioning which do not account for other influences on cognitive development.

Norman's model of learning

The process of learning involves change which is brought about through action and interaction, leading to an inter-reaction (Figure 2). It is influenced by maturation and the quality of early learning experiences. Young children develop naive or framework theories which act as working models and are subject to continuous modification and extension according

TEACHING AND LEARNING

involves

ACTION

COMMUNICATION

MEDIATION

INTERACTION

leading to

INTER-REACTION

Figure 2 Teaching and learning processes

to experience. This is reflected in a model of learning put forward by Norman (1978), which involves three interdependent processes – accretion (acquiring new knowledge), restructuring (reorganizing existing knowledge to accommodate new knowledge) and tuning (acquiring new knowledge on the basis of extended cognitive structures). With each new experience these processes are repeated, although young children may need a great deal of practice and repetition at the restructuring and tuning stages. This indicates the transition from deliberate, conscious awareness of learning something new, to a state of fluent, 'automatic' performance. In this transition, novice learners gradually spend less time concentrating on the task or skill, which liberates more time for attending to the more creative aspects of learning such as transferring, consolidating, extending, perceiving patterns and connections.

As Moyles demonstrates, this model of learning implies four different types of tasks which make different demands on the learner:

- Incremental tasks – which involve accretion and require imitation or step-by step reproduction of new procedures.
- Restructuring tasks – working with mostly familiar materials but at the same time constructing new ways of looking at problems.
- Enrichment tasks – extending the range of application of new concepts and skills rather than adding new ones.
- Practice tasks – repetitive and automatic responses with rapid application of familiar knowledge and skills to familiar problems and settings.

(1989, p. 25)

For play to be regarded as a process which promotes learning, these patterns need to be incorporated as educators plan play/learning environments for young children.

This model of learning can be related to Hutt *et al*'s (1989) model of how play progresses in young children. They argue that there are two distinct forms of play. The first is epistemic play which includes acquiring knowledge and information, problem-solving and exploration, in which children find out 'what does this object do?'. Hutt *et al* consider this to be productive play which promotes learning since children are often aware of what they are making or doing, and it leads to an end-state which is a higher level of competence (p. 224). This is distinguished from ludic play in which children find out 'what can I do with this object?'. Ludic play has symbolic/fantasy and repetitive elements, is characterized by pretence and is highly dependent on mood states. The authors conclude that it may only promote learning indirectly, or may serve some quite different function, but do not go on to speculate what this might be. Clearly the range and type of knowledge and information which children need to process goes far beyond learning to do puzzles and manipulate constructive materials. Knowledge of themselves as individuals and their place in a complex world is equally important. Learning is also about making sense and creating meaning and is determined by broader social, historical and cultural contexts, as will be shown in Chapter 4.

Structural theory

This can be seen as an extension of information processing theory since it offers some explanations of how cognitive structures within the brain become coordinated and connected through the learner's activity and experience. Case (1985) argues that children have four regulatory systems which orchestrate their cognitive activity. These are:

- a tendency to problem-solving
- a tendency to exploration
- a tendency to imitation
- a capacity for mutual regulation with other people.

In actively seeking to make sense of the world, children organize their experiences into schemas which guide the acquisition of new knowledge. As in Norman's model, learning is both recursive and incremental so that the child is able increasingly to operate at higher levels of flexibility, thus assisting the process of transferability of knowledge and skills across different domains and activities. These processes are gradual and each child will vary in terms of pace and capability. Therefore if we are to develop a more informed understanding of the relationship between play and learning, educators need to be sensitive to the learning patterns, styles, attitudes and characteristics which children reveal in their self-chosen activities. There can be no appreciation of the significance of outcomes without a detailed understanding of these processes. The problem for educators is how these can be revealed and interpreted in terms of their educational significance for children.

Schema theory

The idea of repeating patterns and actions (schemas) which lead to the coordination of cognitive structures is also explored by Athey (1990) and

Nutbrown (1994). Patterns of thinking and learning can be accessed through children's representations, language, mark-making and play. Athey (1990) identified a range of schemas from detailed observations of children at home and in pre-school settings. She describes these schemas as:

* dynamic vertical
* dynamic back and forth/side to side
* dynamic circular
* going over and under
* going round a boundary
* enveloping and containing space
* going through a boundary

She argues that schemas represent forms of thought which can be nourished by worthwhile content and will then become connected with other schemas. Nutbrown explains that:

> if a child is focusing on a particular schema related to roundness, we could say that the child is working on a circular schema. The *form* is 'roundness' and the *content* can be anything which extends this form: wheels, rotating machinery, rolling a ball, the spinning of the planets!
>
> (1994, p. 12, original emphasis)

This model reflects how the brain develops through forming connections and interconnections. Schemas are related to more complex forms of learning in later schooling. The support of adults in an educative role is critical to identifying these schemas and supporting their development through interaction, language, and the provision of relevant materials in a supportive learning environment. It is the informed diagnosis of children's schemas which informs curriculum planning and which provides for extension and differentiation. The intention here is not just to provide more of the same activities but to encourage children to make connections and to raise the child's awareness of the meaning of their activity, in particular the ways in which they use and transform materials.

For Athey and Nutbrown, the value of this approach lies in educators becoming better informed about what is involved in the processes of thinking, learning, understanding and 'coming to know'. Identifying children's schemas demands an informed understanding of what each child brings to an activity so that the educator can then finely tune subsequent interactions in the form of teaching strategies, input of new skills or knowledge, or the provision of materials. In this sense, the teacher is much more than an enabler and facilitator. He or she actively mediates in the process of coming to know and, in the process, draws on a wide range of pedagogical skills and knowledge. This implies a much more proactive but responsive role than Piaget described. If we extend Seifert's (1993) metaphor of developing a child's 'mental architecture' it follows that children need both tools for thinking and worthwhile content – something to think about and actively engage with in this essentially constructive but collaborative process. Again this implies 'hands-on' as well as 'brains-on' activity. This is equally important in the context of play. Often children are left to their own devices about choosing what they play with or what they play at. But educators may make assumptions about the value of these activities which are not borne out in practice. Hands-on activity does not automatically imply that children are learning or using learning-relevant strategies. Observations of children playing at the water tray in a nursery over a period of time revealed that they were doing things such as pouring, filling, emptying but were paying more attention to chatting about everyday things with the odd argument about not sharing the equipment which is when the adult usually stepped in.

Athey (1990) states that children's achievements need to be understood by educators at a conceptual and theoretical level, not just on the basis of what is perceived. That is, we need to understand the meaning of an activity to a child in terms of the forms of knowledge and cognitive processes which are being developed or represented. This is particularly important in the context of play. If early childhood educators make claims about the value of play to learning and development, then these must be substantiated with evidence which can be communicated to parents, caregivers, other educators and policy makers. The difficulty here is that in pre-school settings more time is usually available for play and other self-chosen activities which enables the skilled practitioner to identify schemas and patterns of learning. As children enter statutory schooling, the balance between teacher-directed and child-initiated activities, including play, tends to alter significantly, as indicated in the evidence from research outlined in Chapter 1. Where play is used merely as a time filler, then evidence of these patterns and children's persistent cognitive concerns will be lost. Therefore the educational significance of play cannot be fully appreciated and play cannot be utilized effectively as a learning process.

Moving forward

Neo-Piagetian theories of learning and development reflect a shift in perspective away from children's incapability as learners to their rapidly developing competence and potential. Usually it is the lack of an extensive knowledge base and a less reliable memory which contribute to apparent inconsistencies in their thinking. Their existing knowledge may be isolated in pockets but, as we have seen, becomes more organized and interconnected with maturity and experience. Young children's thinking may appear disorganized and idiosyncratic, but rather than seeing this as a deficit, educators need to build on children's naive theories and frameworks, even if these involve misconceptions and some confusions between reality and fantasy.

These theories also place greater emphasis on the educative role of adults. It follows that teachers need to attend to how children organize new knowledge and fit this into their existing schemas or conceptual frameworks. As well as presenting children with curriculum content as prescribed in the National

Curriculum, they need to attend to the content of children's thinking and learning and how that knowledge is represented and internalized. Seifert (1993) argues that children need ample practice at recognizing specific associations in order to form connections between schemas. Therefore to be effective experience must occur in contexts where such connections normally occur. These theories also acknowledge the connectedness between the domains of development – the cognitive, psycho-motor and affective – so that children can be seen not only making cognitive connections but also making relationships between themselves and others.

It can be argued that play acts as an integrating mechanism for these processes. For example, Athey (1990) traces how children represent their own movement and things that move (cars, machines, airplanes) in their play and drawings. Early random mark-making shows repetition of simple forms (vertical lines, crosses, circles, triangles, arrows) which children see in their everyday environment. She argues that this forms the basis of early writing, supported by educators who model reading and writing in authentic contexts and support children's belief in themselves as readers and writers. Again this is not a wholly spontaneous, emergent process. It is dependent on educators connecting children with forms of knowledge which are immediately meaningful to the children and relevant to their future lives. Recent theories suggest that learning becomes more efficient if children become consciously aware of what processes are involved and how they can gain control over those processes. This is known as metacognition.

Metacognition

It must be remembered that young children are learning to learn and learning about themselves as learners. This sometimes takes place at an unconscious level through dialogue and interactions but tends to become more formalized and systematized in educational contexts. Metacognition is the self-conscious participation and intelligent self-regulation in learning and problem-solving situations. It involves knowledge and awareness of what is involved in learning. The basic skills involved in metacognition are:

- predicting the consequences of an action or event
- checking the results of one's own activity (did it work?)
- monitoring one's ongoing activity (how am I doing?)
- reality testing (does this make sense?)
- coordinating and controlling deliberate attempts to solve problems.

(Brown and DeLoache, 1983)

Wood (1988) suggests that an important role for educators is helping children to become better learners through trying to teach them how to control their own intellectual activities: 'If this is possible, we might wish to claim far more importance for teaching in development and a greater potential for learning through instruction in young children than Piagetian theory suggests' (p. 73).

The phrase 'learning through instruction' might seem to imply a didactic, transmission model of teaching and learning, but as will be shown in the next chapter, this incorporates a wide range of teaching strategies which are based on mediation and reciprocity between the teacher and learner. In our view, this can take place in the context of both teacher-directed and child-initiated activities. Ideally there should be a continuum between the two so that learning can be extended, consolidated and transferred between contexts.

Wood (1988) argues that children do not necessarily have a natural capacity to attend or concentrate. Many of the processes involved in learning need to be learnt consciously and deliberately and, as we have seen, preferably in meaningful contexts. This can be supported in a number of ways. Educators can design activities which teach such processes to young children. An example of this is Kim's game where children have to memorize and recall a number of items. Or educators can respond to what they observe in children's self-initiated activities which they consider has educational significance for the child. For example, drawing attention to how they have used a new skill, or combined different materials, or giving recognition for concentrating, persevering or solving a problem. The development of metacognitive skills demands conscious and deliberate reflection on action. Again this is not something that arises spontaneously. Teachers have both to create the conditions and time for reflection and to teach children the skills which raise their awareness of their own learning. An important part of this process is using language about learning so that children come to understand what learning is all about, are able to describe their learning and can be enabled gradually to articulate the meaning of their activities in these terms.

Of course there will always be differences between children in how easy or difficult they find such demands, particularly in school contexts, and children's success as learners is influenced strongly by their individual temperaments, attitudes and dispositions. But teachers on in-service courses who have developed metacognitive approaches with children have reported consistently that even those as young as three and four can understand language about their own learning and will use this in meaningful contexts. The following example shows how Andrew (age six) was both aware of his own knowledge and expertise and how he used it consciously to assist Nigel (age five).

Andrew chose to make a truck from the Fisher-Technik construction kit. He had recently achieved success with making models from this kit with adult help. In this observation, Andrew did not ask for help and started to collect the pieces he needed from the kit. Nigel asked to join him.

Andrew: This is good this is. I can make a lorry. I don't have to copy a plan because I can make it.
Nigel: Let's see, can I help you? What are you doing?
Andrew: You slide them in here, down the side here.
Nigel: What, do you have to do it all the way down with all these?
Andrew: Four, you get four. They go on like this … you slide them then you get these big pieces (refers to axles) down through there. We need big

ones. We need four. Get me two more. Oh (laughs) we only need two, I thought four.

Nigel:	There's four wheels we need.
Andrew:	We only need two of these (axles) cos the wheels go like this (shows Nigel).
Nigel:	Better, better.
Andrew:	We put the wheels on now . . . there . . . (demonstrates to Nigel) you do that one.
Nigel:	It's hard isn't it, to put them on?
Andrew:	Push them hard (helps Nigel). Now we have to put these on (wheel stoppers) to stop them falling off, these little ones. Put the little ones on . . . go on. This is going to be a milk lorry.
Nigel:	Got that one right haven't I Andrew?
Andrew:	That's right. Now we put the edges on (means the sides).
Nigel:	What we have to put them on?
Andrew:	Yes.
Nigel	Why?
Andrew	So that's the edges so the people can't fall out. (Andrew continued until the model was successfully completed.)

Previous observations of Andrew had revealed that he became easily frustrated, was often dependent on adult support and had a short concentration span. However, in this activity Andrew was clearly able to show initiative and maintain concentration and perseverance until his goal was achieved. He also supported another child, worked independently and collaboratively, used reasoning, answered questions and used language to reflect, explain, and direct. The development of his confidence, motivation and self-esteem was evident and Andrew subsequently explained how he taught Nigel to make the model at review time. At this point the teacher was able to offer further support by reminding Andrew of the words axle and wheelstopper which he had forgotten (Attfield, 1992).

In the next example, Vernon (age seven) and Alec (age six) were making a racing car from a Gymbo construction kit. Vernon identified a self-created problem and articulated his thinking and problem-solving strategies.

Vernon:	This is no good, if you sit on it it's gonna touch the ground.
Alec:	What shall we do? Take that bit off?
Vernon:	That isn't a good idea because all that'll happen is that your weight will push it down.
	(They try various pieces of equipment and alterations to their design.)
Vernon:	If you put that there it'll stop your weight from making it go down, then put the wheels on there. They do this. Test it, push on it . . . Alec you've got it the wrong way, how are you going to put the wheels on?
Alec:	Oh, yeah, mm.
Vernon:	You can put them on there . . . that's it . . . just adjust that . . . you can put your legs on the side there . . . that's OK now.
	(At review time, the boys explained how they made changes to their original design and how the needs of others had been taken into account.)
Vernon:	We were going to have the seat there but we had to change it because the

Alec: weight puts it down when you sit on it and it goes on the floor so we changes it so the wheels are higher than the bottom bits.

Alec: We put these on (wheel stoppers) to stop the wheels falling off and that's for big people to put their feet on there.

Vernon: Little kids can sit there. They can't reach their legs down there so they put them there so it's easier.

This activity involved coordinating and controlling deliberate attempts to solve problems and integrated the metacognitive skills outlined above – predicting, checking, monitoring and reality testing (Brown and DeLoache, 1983). These examples indicate that play incorporates both processes and outcomes. The internal cognitive processes are externalized in the discussion, behaviour and activity. The outcomes include a successfully completed model, as well as enhanced self-esteem, social competence and the satisfaction of having engaged in the play. The discourse in children's play, the nature of their activity and the outcomes are all rich in meanings and can provide educators with insights into the content of their thinking and styles of learning. As children become more experienced learners and players, they integrate their cultural knowledge and, as the following example shows, demonstrate meta-awareness of other children's needs, as well as the rules and conventions of play.

Jenny, Betty, Lee and Paul (age between six and seven) decided to make a board game after discussion initiated by the teacher that the toy shop needed some more toys. The children went to a quiet area to discuss their ideas.

Betty: Well we could have a race track.

Jenny: Or we could have the first one to get home like a frog jumping on lily pads.

Lee: In a jungle, in a jungle.

Jenny: And you've got to go in your home in a jungle.

Betty: Or you could have quite a big one and on one side have a race track. You've got to go round the race track the right way and then you get into the jungle.

Jenny: Or what we could do is a little game for young children and put like sums on lily pads and they've got to add up the sums and they've got to jump on the next lily pad.

Lee: I like Jenny's idea.

Paul: It could be just like Jenny's but . . . you could go along with a dice and a counter and you throw the dice and if you land on a square that's got writing on then you've got to do what it says.

Jenny: That sounds good, like forfeits.

Betty: I think Paul's is quite good cos it's fun.

Jenny: What happens if it's really shy children, they might begin to cry with forfeits.

Paul: We could have easy sums like 1 + 1.

Lee: Easy peasy.

Jenny: That's easy for you but not for little children.

Betty: They put two fingers up and count with them.

Lee: Why don't we have both ideas on it?

Betty & Paul: Yes.
Jenny: Why don't we have sums and forfeits? And what did you say about the jungle, Lee?

This group of children were skilled learners and communicators, using language for explaining their ideas, reasoning, reflecting, sharing information and explaining. When they presented their ideas to the teacher, she extended their thinking by helping them to reflect on further elements of the design.

Teacher: Before you start, so you've got it clear in your heads what the players can and what they can't do, there's something you need to do. How will the players know what to do?
Jenny: Rules.
Teacher: Right, you need some rules. How many people can play?

With further discussion and teacher participation the children clarified their ideas and devised a format whereby the long explanatory sentences for the rules were abbreviated. Figure 3 shows Jenny's list of rules. Here she is writing for a purpose, in a particular style, with a conscious awareness of what has to be communicated in order for the game to be successful.

The children decided to have a pond at the end of the game as 'home' and, in the next stage of the planning, hit another design problem.

Betty: We'll stick the pond on the end here.
Lee: Cut the pond about that big, turn it over and stick it here.
Jenny: Yes, but what happens is the game breaks and that bit falls off and you can't find it and it isn't very nice in the game, you can't play it any more.
Lee: Have it round here.
Betty: Wait a minute. I think we should plan it before we draw.
Lee: On this piece of paper. We don't have to put one enormous pond.
Jenny: I know, we could have four ponds a different colour.
Paul: Yes, red and blue.
Jenny: The people with the green counters have to go to the green pond.
Betty: Yes and red counters for the red pond, and yellow for the yellow pond and what's left?
Lee: The blue one.

This example shows that meaningful contexts are essential for fostering cognitive processes such as paying attention, remembering and concentrating. The 'intellectually skilled assistance' was provided by the teacher in different ways, at different times and in relation to the particular features of the activity and the needs of the children. The teacher's role in the learning process was not to transmit empty 'procedural' knowledge which Piaget regarded as meaningless to children. This type of adult involvement reflects Tamburrini's view that teachers who interact with children in their play, and adopt an 'extending' style which synchronizes with the children's own intentions, promote play as educationally profitable and, at the same time, value play in its own right (1982, p. 215).

These examples also demonstrate how Case's four regulatory systems are

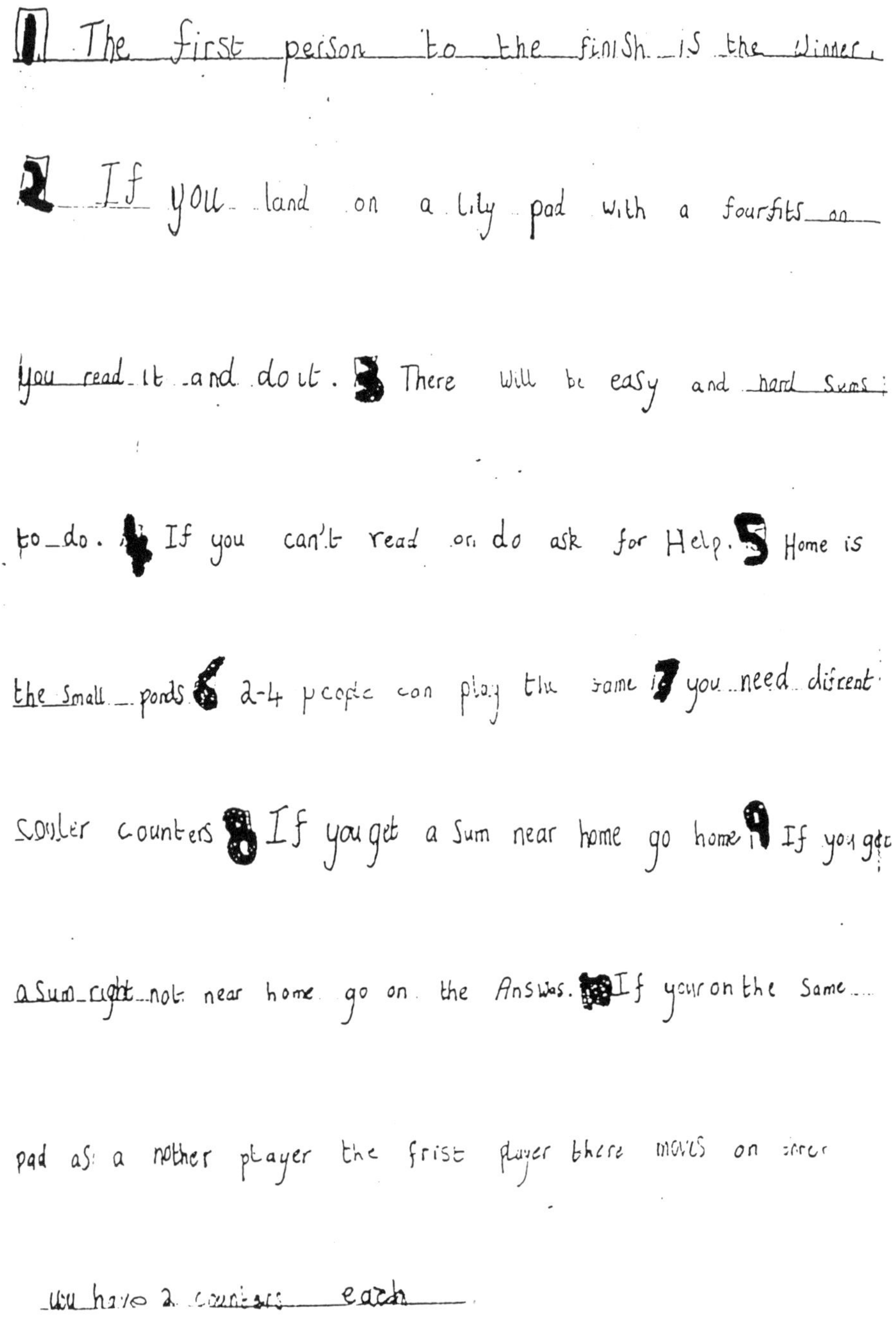

1 The first person to the finish is the winner.

2 If you land on a lily pad with a four sits on you read it and do it. 3 There will be easy and hard sums to do. 4 If you can't read on do ask for Help. 5 Home is the small ponds 6 2-4 people can play the same 7 you need dicrent couler counters 8 If you get a Sum near home go home 9 If you get a Sum right not near home go on the Answes. 10 If your on the same pad as a nother player the frist player there moves on firor

we have 2 couniers each

Figure 3 Jenny's list of rules

evident in children's play – exploration, imitation, problem-solving and mutual regulation with other people. These are not only internal, individual processes but are developed through activity and interaction. They take time to acquire, practise, consolidate and use with increasing skill and effectiveness. To some extent, they occur naturally and spontaneously and, therefore, may be used unconsciously. However, if children are taught to use these processes more consciously they can help them to orchestrate their cognitive activity and maximize their learning and development.

Language and communication

All children need language-rich experiences since this is one of the principal ways in which they make sense of what learning, being and becoming is all about. The communication between children, peers and adults externalizes their thinking and levels of cognitive competence. Often it takes the form of out-loud thinking which is an extension of self-speech. Both provide a means of regulating activity, reflecting on action, describing, articulating ideas and intentions. Etta, age four, was playing alone with a doll in the home corner:

> Now it's time to go to sleep. No, don't cry. I'm going to put you in your cot. Now shush that's naughty (angry expression and voice, points finger at doll). It's time for bed. I'll come back in a minute. (Puts baby in cot, then stands still for a few seconds. Goes back to doll.) Are you still crying? (Hands on hips, angry expression and voice. Picks up doll.) I'll have to see what's the matter. Oh dear, wet nappy. Alright, there, there, I'll change you. (Holds baby closely, gentle voice and relaxed expression.)

Here Etta was using metacommunication through dialogue and gestures to create and sustain the pretence. She shifted her emotional state in response to the baby having a legitimate reason for crying and immediately communicated this through her behaviour and attitudes. She was conveying emotion and reason through her self-speech which directed the play. It is thought that such experiences help children to make the transfer to paired or group cooperative play since they are rehearsing ways of communicating action, imagination and pretence.

Mark, age six, was trying to 'mend' a radio. He had access to some tools and a variety of old electrical equipment and was talking to another child:

> I can't think around which hole this screwdriver goes in. (Tried screwdriver in each hole.) Look, it goes in that hole there. I can't have this screwdriver. I think I'll have that big one over there. I think this one came from a robot. (Picked up hairdryer.) I wonder if we can get this working. Switch is still working. We'll have to take it apart then. I don't think this is the right screwdriver.

In both these examples, language provided a link between the child's thinking and action. Mark uses language about his own cognitive processes, a skill which was deliberately encouraged by the teacher as part of the curriculum. Play provided a context for developing transfer-ability of knowledge and skills.

He used logic, reasoning, deduction and problem-solving skills in pretending to mend the equipment. He also had to believe, for the purposes of the play, that these were repairable otherwise his actions would have been meaningless so his language conveys his suspension of reality. Both Etta and Mark used language to communicate the meaning of the activity for them.

Social cognition

The models of learning presented here should not be taken to imply an emphasis on cognitive development at the expense of the socio-affective domain. In reality, as we have seen, these are integrated and interdependent. Children need to understand, express and control emotion and, in doing so, come to regulate their behaviour. This is an integral part of making sense and meaning from learning and experience. These patterns of learning are culturally determined and are learnt from birth so that children are gradually socialized into forms of appropriate behaviour in different contexts:

> For very young children, the bridging role of adults involves assisting children in understanding how to act in new situations by provision of emotional cues regarding the nature of the situation, nonverbal models of how to behave, verbal and nonverbal interpretations of behaviour and events, and verbal labels to classify objects and events. All of these adult activities are coupled with young children's efforts (intentional or not) to pick up information about the nature of situations and their caregivers' interpretations.
>
> (Rogoff, 1993, p. 73)

Models of learning have to take into account how young children are socialized and the importance of their emotional development in this process. This is known as social cognition which is defined by Feinburg and Mindess as 'the process of thinking about emotions, feelings, and how people interact with one another. It is a developmental process that plays a critical role in the acquisition of social skills, ability to engage in interpersonal problem solving, and development of an inner locus of control' (1994, p. 238).

This is intrinsically bound with the development of self-concept, cultural and gender identities. How children come to perceive themselves is determined to a large extent by their success and competence as learners, particularly in educational contexts. The development of thinking and learning is associated not just with information processing and knowledge acquisition but also with feeling states about self and others. In coming to understand their place in the world, children need to understand and know themselves, their strengths and weaknesses, attitudes and dispositions, how to interact with others, form relationships and overcome their limitations in social and individual contexts. They also need to learn about emotions and mood states – how to identify and cope with fear, anger, jealousy, love, hatred, guilt, anxiety, betrayal and injustice. Mood states determine behaviour so that an anxious, stressed child may not play successfully because he or she may lack the motivation to engage, take risks, participate cooperatively or just enjoy an activity. Feinburg and Mindess (1994) argue that when children deny their emotions they gain expression through either inappropriate overt or covert behaviour so that unexpressed feelings will interfere with a child's ability to function, learn and interact with others.

This is often evident in play contexts as children need a wide repertoire of social skills in order to become successful players. Bruner (1991) argues that play can serve as a vehicle for socialization – teaching children about the nature of society's rules and conventions, roles and relationships. This is demonstrated vividly in the example given above of the children making a game. They revealed a range of knowledge about rules and conventions, as well as empathic understanding of the needs and feelings of younger children. They also understood the rules of interaction, turn-taking, negotiating, compromising and synthesizing ideas as well as the paradoxical nature of play. They knew that, even though this was to be a game, some children would feel distressed if they were challenged inappropriately by too many forfeits, showing an awareness of concepts of justice and fairness. As we have argued, children integrate their real world knowledge into play situations. They are not just socialized into school norms but learn a complex range of strategies, skills, cultural tools and behaviours which enable them to live successfully in society.

Teaching children to think about feelings and relationships and to make them more aware of themselves can empower children by helping them to recognize and deal with conflict, resolve disputes, take control and make decisions. The development of social skills thus contributes to their self-concept and self-efficacy. Children construct their social knowledge in social situations which are culturally determined and which involve interactions with both peers and adults as conveyors of cultural rules and norms. They learn about rules, roles, relationships, friendship skills, appropriate forms of behaviour and about the consequences of their actions, both positive and negative, for other people. Play provides an important context both for learning and testing out their social cognition. Children use play contexts to create their own rules, determine appropriate behaviours, define roles and often test their own boundaries as well as those imposed on them by adults. The success of any play situation depends on children abiding by rules and social conventions, however these are construed within the play. A child who behaves destructively or uncooperatively will eventually not be invited to play. Children may play with anti-social behaviour as a way of testing boundaries, but ultimately they cannot tolerate it for real, especially in pretend play, as it destroys the sequence and flow which are necessary for success and enjoyment. For example, in super-hero play, children play with concepts of conflict, power, aggression, dominance and control. Even where this is based on current television/cartoon characters such as Power Rangers, they will usually stop short of real physical contact because they know that this is anti-social and will not be tolerated, especially in the presence of adults but usually not by peers. This involves moral judgement and reasoning, as well as knowledge of society's conventions and appropriate forms of behaviour.

Social cognition encompasses what can be termed emotional literacy as well as self-awareness. However, these areas of learning also need to be raised to a conscious level of awareness so that their significance and meaning can be recognized. Whilst young children undoubtedly learn a great deal from observation and imitation, this may be an insufficient basis for making sense of what they are learning. Social and emotional learning need to be subject to the cognitive activity outlined in this chapter so that children learn to control and make connections between their feeling states and their behaviour. Learning in the socio-affective domain is every bit as important as discipline-based learning such as maths and science and contributes directly to the 'unity of mind and personality'. It is not enough to leave this to chance or to developmental and maturational processes. Nor is it enough to assume that children will learn and practise social skills in their play, although this undoubtedly provides valuable contexts for such purposes. We cannot just tell children to 'play nicely' without helping them to develop some of the skills which help them to become successful players.

Children often exaggerate emotions and behaviours in their play for different reasons. First, the exaggeration signals that 'this is play' and defines the boundaries and rules of what is to be accepted and tolerated. Second, children may need to exaggerate emotion, to literally play with it, to explore how it feels to be angry, frightened, abandoned, lost, powerful or powerless in a non-threatening situation. The 'what if' and 'as if' qualities of play contexts give children permission to behave differently. Their behaviours may be rooted in real life problems, dramas and ongoing concerns, or they may just want to be nonsensical, absurd, zany, even anarchic.

For example, young children are frequently observed being angry with and even violent towards dolls. They may weave into their play smacking, shaking, or threats of excessive punishments. Educators may read into this kind of behaviour all sorts of possible explanations and, in exceptional cases, this may be indicative of some problems at home. But usually children are playing out their developing understanding of the world and their place within it. They are processing a huge amount of information which has to be subjected to reasoning, sense- and meaning-making. As with other areas of learning children need the time and opportunities to develop their skills, knowledge and understanding. In order for this to happen, educators need an informed understanding of what socio-affective learning encompasses, how this is developed through play and what opportunities exist in other areas of the curriculum for further learning. This will be explored in more detail in Chapter 6 which addresses curriculum development.

Creativity and imagination

One further issue is important when discussing models of learning and development. These have tended to stress the development of rational thought and action and have rarely addressed creativity and imagination. Perhaps this reflects the concern of psychologists to isolate and study that which is easily defined or measured. Creativity and imagination are important aspects of the lives of children and adults since they embody divergent forms of thinking and can lead to the development of novel, innovative combinations of ideas and experiences. Indeed, a disciplined imagination can be seen as a form of reasoning. However, as Egan (1991, p. 11) argues, fantasy is altogether a more wayward phenomenon:

> Education is the process in which we use rationality to show and discover what is real and true, and so fantasy, which ignores the boundaries of reality, is seen as the enemy which slips out of the constructive constraints of reason and runs mentally amok in unreal and impossible worlds ... In rational activity the mind is awake, about constructive work, in accord with reality, attuned to the logics whereby things operate; in fantasy there is mind-wandering illogic, dream-like indulgence of the flittering shapes of the idle mind, disregard of hard empirical reality.

Egan argues that features of fantasy become 'constituents of a rich rationality' and represent a legitimate means for making sense and creating meaning. Fantasy and reality are intertwined in children's play. Cohen and MacKeith (1991) use the evocative phrase 'world weavers' to describe the imaginative worlds created by writers and artists. Children become world weavers in their play. For example, in order to take on a role in pretend play children have to understand the distinction between fantasy and reality, but the fantasy is informed by the reality. We have shown how children have to suspend reality in order to construct pretence. But in doing so they use logic and reasoning to create the 'as if' and 'what if' characteristics which give play its particular qualities.

In order to sustain and develop the pretence, children move between fantasy and reality because they have to signal clearly the paradoxical nature of play which is at once real and not real. In doing so, children create novel forms of thinking and meaning. Sometimes they appear to make nonsense of their real worlds in their play in order to make sense. But in their play children create their own internal logic which is based on negotiated rules and shared meanings which are often repeated, revised, and extended and elaborated. Children continuously edit their actions and interactions in this process as they play with rules, roles and ideas. Again, if we refer back to the ways in which the brain develops, the external play behaviours and internal developmental processes seem to be mirrored. So imagination and reason are not always in opposition. In order to pivot between fantasy and reality children need to develop quite complex, abstract and sophisticated ways of thinking, reasoning and behaving:

> in the construction of play and other fictitious worlds like story, the order of the everyday world is transformed and all manner of irregularities and reversals might obtain ... by adopting a nonliteral orientation to the world all manner of imaginary situations may be played into being.
>
> (Kelly-Byrne, 1989, p. 212)

Anning (1994) states that fantasy has been devalued in the current technical/rational curriculum and argues for an alternative curriculum which would aim to empower children with tools for thinking, giving them the capability to explore a whole range of ideas, experiences, feelings and relationships. Fantasy, creativity and imagination enable children to go beyond the boundaries of their knowledge and understanding, to play with ideas, concepts, reality and to become world weavers. These capabilities are not to be underestimated in subject-based and more formal learning in later schooling. For example, a well-disciplined imagination is essential in history as children have to go beyond the evidence available to imagine what life was like in another time, to understand people's motivations and aspirations, to make deductions about how they might have felt and why they acted as they did (Wood and Holden, 1995). As Egan (1991) states, it is human emotion, and human thought, that can bring to life the concrete content we want children to learn. He criticizes the trivial, and often sentimental, stories and programmed reading schemes, as well as the absence of powerful emotional, dramatic, and intellectual content of too many primary classrooms. The stories that children weave into their play go far beyond what Egan describes as 'Disney-esque sentimentality' and deal directly with powerful human emotions, painful experiences and challenging situations. Another paradox of play is that children both escape from reality but through their creativity, imagination and fantasy get closer to reality.

This may help children to learn through the processes described in the models outlined in this chapter. We have seen that cognitive structures within the brain become coordinated and connected through the learner's activity and experience. A great deal of what children as well as adults learn takes place in social situations, enabling them to glean a tremendous amount of knowledge from their experiences. Learning is both recursive and incremental so that children gradually develop flexibility and transfer-ability. Creativity, imagination and fantasy are important elements in this process as they encourage divergent ways of thinking and reasoning and help to make novel connections and interconnections between areas of the brain and different domains of learning.

We have argued that play provides a wide variety of contexts which encourages these learning processes. The value of play and its relationship to learning are therefore dependent on the quality and range of play experiences and what actually happens in play. We should remain wary of making too many assumptions that play is in itself a good thing without undertaking some critical observations of whether this is realized in practice. In an educational context, the quality of the learning environment, the role of play in the planned curriculum and the role of adults are all influential factors in developing a clearer relationship between play and pedagogy. Whilst some of this learning will be spontaneous, educators need to be able to utilize play as a window into the child's developing mind in order to understand the learning patterns, characteristics and needs of individual children. In the following chapter we will extend these theoretical perspectives to include a detailed but selective outline of the work of Vygotsky. The intention is to extend the theoretical underpinning for the relationship between play and learning and to examine how this might inform curriculum planning in school and pre-school settings.

4

Vygotskian Perspectives on Learning

We have explored some of the theories of children's learning and related these to play. However, we cannot assume that playing leads to learning or that play is the only valuable means of learning in early childhood. We know that in their practice educators face a number of dilemmas in the ways they conceptualize play and incorporate it into the curriculum. In order for some of these dilemmas to be resolved, there needs to be a more conscious exploration of play and pedagogy which goes beyond general statements about first hand experience, discovery learning, enabling and facilitating. In this chapter we present a synthesis of the work of Lev Vygotsky because it offers a supportive framework for understanding teaching and learning which can be related to play.

Any discussion of Vygotsky's work needs to be prefaced by three important caveats. First, his premature death meant that many of his ideas were still being developed and had not been fully tested. What has become known as a Vygotskian model of learning is, in fact, a synthesis of theories developed, extended and reinterpreted by both his contemporary and subsequent followers. Second, the essence of his work has been altered through the process of translation. Third, Vygotsky's ideas must be seen in their historical context. He was inevitably influenced by Marxism, because its ideology penetrated all aspects of social, political, economic, educational and cultural life in the former USSR. Vygotsky was concerned with developing innovative psychological insights into the nature of development, learning, language, thought, concept formation and play. His work reveals many contradictions and inconsistencies, because he was still formulating his ideas up to his death. It has been left to others to interpret these ideas in the light of further research and advances in our knowledge of children's learning and development and to relate them to teaching and learning in schools.

In spite of these limitations, we maintain that Vygotsky's theories deserve more accessible exploration because they have important implications for how we might think about teaching and learning in general and particularly in the context of children's play. The aspects of Vygotsky's work which we have chosen to explore are selective and should be compared and contrasted with other theories. There is no single theory of learning, and hence no single prescription for teaching, which could adequately capture the dynamics of educating young children. Hence we do not intend to be prescriptive, but to provide a framework or scaffold to enable early childhood practitioners to reconceptualize their practice and achieve an intellectually deeper understanding of teaching and learning in the context of play.

The key themes we have chosen to explore more fully are Vygotsky's ideas about learning and development, the zone of proximal development, the relationship between development and instruction and play. We illustrate some of the concepts with examples from our own and other teachers' practice and examine the implications of these ideas for developing practice.

Learning and development

Vygotsky regarded learning and development in early childhood as a complex process which could not be fully understood or defined in any of its stages solely on the basis of one characteristic. He argued that a single set of explanatory principles could not provide an adequate explanation of the complex developmental changes which occur throughout childhood. Vygotsky defined development as evolutionary and revolutionary shifts with qualitative and quantitative changes in thinking. More importantly, he argued that learning leads development, unlike Piaget who argued that development leads learning. Now neither Piaget nor Vygotsky may be wholly right or wrong. However, this is an important distinction which warrants further explanation because there are different implications for curriculum organization, and for our understanding of teaching and learning depending on the perspective adopted.

Whilst Vygotsky did not reject Piaget's research into the development of logico-mathematical operations, he placed more emphasis on development as a socio-cultural process and considered that the socio-cultural and biological aspects of development work together. This represents a challenge to Piaget's ideas about the development of cognition as internal and individualistic processes. Whereas Piaget saw the child more as a 'lone scientist' constructing knowledge through actions on objects, Vygotsky regarded social interaction between peers and adults as important in creating meaning, making sense and conveying culture within a shared context.

Vygotsky did not claim that social interaction automatically leads to learning and development of a child's abilities. It is more the means used in social interaction, particularly language, that are then taken over and internalized by the child. He defined a wide range of 'psychological tools' which assist in the learning process. These include language, various systems for counting, mnemonic (memory assisting) techniques, algebraic symbol systems, works of art, writing, schemes, diagrams, maps, technical drawings, and all sorts of conventional signs (Wertsch, 1985a, p. 74). A more familiar way of describing these psychological tools is as knowledge, skills and processes or sense-making capacities. Although Vygotsky did not distinguish these as subject matter knowledge, Newman and Holzman (1993) have argued that the subject disciplines represent important ways of thinking and learning and can therefore be seen as tools to assist in cognitive development and sense-making processes since they include concepts, ideas, beliefs, attitudes, emotions and language, all of which contribute to disciplined ways of knowing. Thus the conditions educators provide for thinking and learning determine to a large extent children's ways of coming to know and understand.

The acquisition and use of these psychological tools do not just create new capabilities but actually transform cognitive functioning. Vygotsky considered learning to be revolutionary because each successive layer of understanding transforms the meaning of previous understanding. Again this represents a challenge to some long-held assumptions about children's learning. There has been a tendency to regard children's thinking as naive and simplistic, because in Piagetian terms it has been seen as an immature form of adult thinking. In a Vygotskian model, children's ways of knowing, thinking and understanding are important in their own right as they build incrementally towards more mature forms of thought.

An important part of this process is the educative nature of relationships between children, peers and adults. Interactions with more knowledgeable others, particularly adults, enable a child to get to what Vygotsky termed 'higher ground' or the next level of cognitive functioning. Learning or 'higher cognitive functioning' takes place on two distinct but interrelated planes – the interpsychological and the intrapsychological. 'First it appears on the social plane and then on the psychological plane. First it appears between people as an interpsychological category and then within the child as an intrapsychological category' (Vygotsky, 1978, p. 57).

This process is characterized by interactions which can lean towards qualitative, internalized transformations in what a child knows, can do and understands. The means of social interaction, particularly language, are critical in this process since they provide psychological tools which help to develop a child's learning and sense-making capacities. The learning environment and the child's own internal motivations and aspirations are seen as influential.

In investigating the relationship between learning and development, Vygotsky stated that if we determine the child's level of development from observations of what she can do independently of others, then we are considering only that which has already matured. He saw this as an inadequate basis for instruction and argued that we need to consider both mature and maturing processes (Newman and Holzman, 1993). Internalization (the process by which the interpsychological becomes the intrapsychological) is not a simple transfer from external activity to preformed internal cognitive structures because it creates and develops these internal cognitive structures and is facilitated through speech, social interaction and co-operative activity. This reflects the models of learning and the development of the brain outlined in Chapter 3. Through incremental experience, children then reorganize and reconstruct these experiences, moving to higher levels of cognitive functioning on the basis of both qualitative and quantitative changes. The child is not a passive agent in this process. Active involvement and reciprocity are crucial in enabling the child to transform what is internalized through a process of guided reinvention (Tharp and Gallimore, 1991).

It is a common assumption in educational practice that children need to be motivated in order to learn. Vygotsky took a different perspective and argued that children need to learn in order to be motivated. Furthermore, he believed that the only good learning is that which is in advance of development. However, as Bruner notes, this poses an apparent contradiction – how can good learning be in advance of development if a child has not yet achieved consciousness of what is to be learned or established mastery and control? Bruner arrived at his own theory of what Vygotsky might have meant by this:

> If the child is enabled to advance by being under the tutelage of an adult or a more competent peer, then the adult or the aiding peer serves as a vicarious form of consciousness until such time as the learner is able to master his own action through his own consciousness and control. When the child achieves that conscious control over a new function or conceptual system, it is then that he is able to use it as a tool. Up to that point the tutor in effect performs the critical function of 'scaffolding' the learning task to make it possible for the child, in Vygotsky's word, to internalize external knowledge and convert it into a tool for conscious control.
>
> (Bruner, Jolly and Sylva, 1976, p. 24)

An example places this difficult concept into a meaningful context. Daniel, age five, planned to make a table from Tactic – a large construction kit. He selected the correct pieces and assembled them in the right order. However, he became frustrated and dissatisfied with the final product because it was too wobbly to stand on its own. Daniel had not correctly interlocked the tubes into the joints because he did not know how and asked an adult for help. He had created a meaningful problem but lacked the requisite problem-solving strategies. The teacher intervened sensitively to discuss the problem with Daniel and identify possible solutions. She modelled the task using the correct language to describe her actions. She showed him how to line up the lugs on the poles with the hole in the joint and twist it to lock it firmly into place. Daniel watched intently, repeating some of the words and phrases used. The teacher asked him to show her how to do it, offering further support by talking through the task again and praising his new skills. Daniel showed determination, concentration and perseverance and was more than pleased to be able to show a successfully completed table to his peers at review time. More significantly, Daniel was observed later that week demonstrating this process to another child using similar techniques to those modelled by the teacher.

This example shows how learning can lead development in the context of play. Of course, the foundations for learning were already there in terms of Daniel's interest, existing levels of competence and his confidence to approach an adult for assistance with a self-created and self-identified problem. The relationship between learning and motivation can be a two-way process. Daniel had the motivation to get so far with the task, but needed to learn new skills in order to be further motivated to complete it to his satisfaction. The scaffold provided by the teacher became an enabling framework which assisted Daniel's performance and led towards a higher level of functioning. It is debatable whether Daniel would have discovered those principles for himself without the assistance of a more knowledgeable other – although this could have been a child. He could easily have become frustrated to the point of de-motivation if he had been left to his own devices. Through appropriate interaction and assistance, learning became more efficient and provided further motivation. Whilst a certain amount of struggle is necessary and desirable, allowing children only to discover for themselves can lead to them constantly having to reinvent the wheel.

This challenges the Piagetian 'lone scientist' model and the primacy of discovery learning. It also challenges some ideas about teaching and learning. Piaget stated that each time one prematurely teaches a child something he could have discovered for himself, that child is kept from inventing it and consequently from understanding it completely (Meadows, 1993, p. 336). This implies a high level of activity on the part of the learner, and a complex range of sense-making capacities. As we have argued, children are novice learners and may need skilled assistance even in their play, particularly where the context or materials create opportunities for challenge. We cannot assume that children or even adults are always in a happy, equilibrated state which enables them to make the best of their motivation and learning capabilities. In writing this book, we could not have raised our own level of cognitive functioning without the assistance of more knowledgeable others, whether through our reading or interactions with colleagues in schools and universities.

The Vygotskian model outlined here emphasizes the social, cultural and historical factors involved in teaching, learning and development. These can be understood more fully in the context of the second of the four key themes we have chosen to explore here.

The zone of proximal development

Vygotsky's theories about the zone of proximal development (ZPD) have received some attention in books on early childhood education but again we believe that a fuller exploration of these is needed. As Smith (1989) states, Vygotsky's theories about the ZPD are inspirational but in need of some clarification. We have already established that, in a Vygotskian model, learning is embedded in social and cultural contexts and it is through activity and interaction with more knowledgeable others that children come to understand themselves and the world in which they live and in the process acquire the 'psychological tools' for thinking.

In seeking to explain this process, Vygotsky developed his ideas about ZPD and defined it as

> *the distance between the actual developmental level as determined by inde-pendent problem solving and the level of potential development as determined through problem solving under adult guidance or in collaboration with more capable peers.* The zone of proximal development defines those functions that have not yet matured but are in the process of maturation, functions that will mature tomorrow but are currently in an embryonic state. These functions could be termed the 'buds' or 'flowers' of development rather than the 'fruits' of development.

(1978, p. 86; original italics)

The ZPD can be seen as the common ground between where the child currently is and where she or he might usefully go next. This provides a foundation for productive interaction between the novice (child) and the expert (adult or more capable peer) which in turn facilitates internalization – the shift from the intrapsychological to the interpsychological. By identifying or discovering a child's ZPD a teacher can lead the child on ahead of her development. This is quite a complex task which demands a high degree of intelligent action on the part of the teacher, first in identifying a child's ZPD and second in selecting the appropriate strategies to scaffold learning. There is no set prescription for identifying or discovering a child's ZPD – Vygotsky did not specify the process. It can be both intentional and entirely accidental, but depends substantially on close observation of children and the ability to interact productively and appropriately. The teacher has to know what the child has already mastered which is relevant to the task or activity. Within the ZPD the novice and expert take different levels of responsibility. Learning takes place when the novice is enabled gradually to take over responsibility until mastery of the new role, skill or concept is achieved and internalized. In Vygotsky's view, this style of interaction (he actually called it instruction) impels or awakens a whole series of functions that are in a stage of maturation lying in the zone of proximal development.

The teacher may need to break down (but not necessarily over-simplify) the task into sub-tasks and select from a range of strategies which are relevant to the task and meaningful to the child. These may include modelling the actions or processes for the child, sharing or handing over control, correcting, refining, asking the child to perform a task or demonstrate their understanding. The assistance is intended to give the child confidence and motivation. It should allow a certain amount of struggle, but not so much that the child is frustrated and de-motivated. It should allow a certain amount of support, but not so much that the child is bored or feels that she or he has no control in the activity. Vygotsky believed that what a child can do with assistance today, she can do by herself tomorrow. The aim for the child is to achieve conscious control and a higher level of cognitive functioning, not to be continuously dependent on an adult for demonstrating or telling without that essential reciprocity between the novice and the expert. The teacher needs to recognize the child's intentions and meanings as the foundation on which to build the scaffold. Learning is accomplished with the progressive narrowing of the gap between the actual and the potential level of development. These processes and strategies are equally important in play as children often create their own problems and challenges which need the support of a more knowledgeable other.

Central to this process is language. Children are still acquiring language and consequently need language-rich environments and effective support systems. Language is, in Vygotsky's view, an essential 'psychological tool' for thinking and learning. The input of language has to be finely tuned to the child's level of development and understanding. Any new skills or concepts may need breaking down not just into sub-tasks but into sub-explanations so that the language can be matched to the child's progress and form part of the scaffold. Again this does not necessarily imply over-simplification or justify the use of baby talk. In fact the reverse is true. As Tizard and Hughes (1984) have shown, adults often expand on children's speech, giving a model of correct sentence structure, tense, grammar and word order. They also make specific inputs of knowledge, technical language or elaborated explanations in response to a child's prompt, request or defined need as the following example shows.

A group of Year 2/3 children were using Tactic for the first time. They established quickly that they wanted to make a push-along trolley for the younger children to use as a transporter for soft toys. The teacher was familiar with the equipment and, with the support of the teacher's guidebook, knew the correct technical terms for the different constructional elements. The children were able to select the correct pieces, but needed help with thinking through how to make axles, a chassis and to align the joints to build a supporting framework. As the design evolved, they had to consider strength, stability, rigidity and load-bearing capacity. The children learnt about form, function, design and quickly picked up the technical language which the teacher used throughout the interaction. This was demonstrated at review time when they were able to relate what they had done and learnt. As in the example of Daniel given earlier, the children were able to pass on their knowledge to other children, referring to the guidebook, the teacher and each other for support.

Through dialogue and reciprocal action teachers can model essential tools for learning, such as reflecting on action, posing questions, noticing cause and effects, talking through actions, requesting and offering further support or information. The adult needs to receive and to listen as much as to give and to talk. Pretending not to know can also be a powerful motivator to get a child to demonstrate a skill or articulate understanding. It also allows the teacher to monitor the child's progress through the ZPD, aids further diagnosis of the next step and thus informs curriculum planning (Figure 4).

The conscious use of these and other strategies helps to create the conditions whereby learning leads development within the ZPD. Through assisted performance the child moves towards higher levels of cognitive functioning so that the ability to think and reason is changed, as is the ability to regulate

Vygotsky's theory of the zone of proximal development

In the ZPD the novice moves from
other regulation (interpsychological)
with
skilled assistance from
more knowledgeable others (peers and adults)
in
an enabling environment
with
appropriate materials, experiences and activities
combining
social, cultural and historical influences
acquiring
tools for thinking and learning, knowledge, skills, processes, sense-making capacities
leading to
self-regulation (intrapsychological)

Figure 4 Learning in the ZPD

independent action and behaviour. Once new knowledge, skills and processes are internalized they form part of the child's individual developmental achievement. This can also lead to a growing ability in children to engage in activity willingly and with conscious awareness, thus leading to the development of metacognition.

In order to develop conscious awareness children need to learn metacognitive strategies. It is relatively easy for children to be in charge of their own actions. It is much harder for them to be in charge of their own learning without such support strategies. In our view, one of the weaknesses of classroom approaches which stress the importance of independence and autonomy is that false assumptions are often made about children's levels of conscious awareness of their activity and their ability to control and direct their own learning without metacognitive strategies or the support of a more knowledgeable other. As Smith notes (1989) self-awareness of learning is not the same as self-control of learning. We cannot put children in control of their own learning without teaching them the supporting strategies which make this more efficient or without providing challenging experiences in the classroom. Furthermore, we cannot assume that children are capable always of taking control because they may encounter novel situations in which they will benefit from supportive interactions which help them to learn.

These points are illustrated in the following examples. Joanne, age three, selected a range of jigsaws from an open shelf. The selection appeared to be deliberate, starting with easy inset trays which Joanne accomplished without difficulty. After completing each jigsaw, it was returned to the shelf and another selected. Joanne graduated to four piece tessellating jigsaws set in a frame, and again completed these successfully though not as quickly. Her next selection was a more complex twelve piece tessellating jigsaw which caused her some difficulty. She used all the correct actions, rotating the pieces, testing them against each other and against the frame. However, the level of cognitive challenge was too high and Joanne replaced the pieces randomly in a pile in the frame and put the jigsaw at the back of the cupboard. (Joanne actually checked to see if anyone was looking when she did this, perhaps because the nursery 'rules' were that jigsaws should be finished before being put away!)

This example shows how Joanne appeared to be checking through her existing competences as though she needed recognition of these to spur her on to a further challenge. She began with safe, known tasks and applied her skills to the more challenging task, showing evidence of some metacognitive awareness. Joanne had created the problem for herself by selecting the difficult jigsaw, she had recognized and tried to deal with the problem but lacked at that point a sufficiently wide repertoire of problem-solving skills to complete the task. Joanne appeared to be operating at the edge of a ZPD but could not be led through it because there was no 'knowledgeable other', either adult or child, to give the assistance she needed. This reinforces the point made earlier that children need to learn in order to be motivated. Without assistance Joanne was de-motivated.

We have concentrated on Vygotsky's theories about the ZPD in relation to the individual child. Obviously, this finely tuned approach to teaching and learning raises many problems. It demands high quality interactions, effective on-going diagnosis for ensuring accurate match between the task and the learner, reciprocity between teacher and learner, overt modelling of thinking and learning strategies and experiences which assist the transfer of learning from the interpsychological to the intrapsychological. This appears to imply a constant one-to-one relationship for it to be applied successfully. In a parent-child context this might be achievable, but for educators in school or pre-school settings the everyday constraints of time, number of children, routines, space and facilities can all militate against such an approach. In the context of play it is even more difficult to give the children the attention they may need, particularly in school contexts where other demands impinge upon how teachers spend their time.

The ZPD is a complex concept because it does not just relate to problem-solving skills but also to performance in other domains or areas of competence – social, physical, affective, cognitive. Furthermore, there is no single zone for each individual and a ZPD can be created for any skill in any of these domains. There are cultural zones as well as individual zones, because there are cultural variations in the competences which a child must acquire through social inter-action in a particular society (Tharp and Gallimore, 1991, p. 46). However, the concept of the ZPD need not be taken exclusively as an individualized process. Newman and Holzman (1993) have interpreted Vygotsky's theories to argue that the classroom or school environment should itself be a zone for proximal development. Creating a zone for proximal development means structuring and organizing the environment in such a way as to facilitate high quality interactions between adults and peers, providing resources which stimulate problem-creating as well as problem-solving, liberating time for conversation and interaction, and adopting a particular range of teaching strategies and ways of understanding children's learning. Therefore, the planned curriculum must actually promote rather than deny these approaches.

Creating zones for proximal development is not an alien or difficult concept, it is what good practitioners do anyway. It also means that children can be educated effectively and creatively within different sizes of groups and as individuals. Furthermore play creates zones of proximal development for individual or groups of children through their self-initiated activities. Here they are expressing their interests, motivation, ongoing cognitive concerns and their will. All these learning-relevant features combine to create the conditions where children can learn through play.

For Vygotsky, learning is predominantly, though not exclusively, a transactional process involving many different types of interactions and teaching styles, including play. This leads us into the third of Vygotsky's theories which we believe to be important in developing our understanding of teaching and learning, namely the role of instruction in development.

The relationship between instruction and development

Vygotsky used the word instruction rather than teaching and regarded this as central to learning and development. Lest this sounds too instrumental and didactic, we must emphasize that it refers to a wide range of strategies and does not imply a simple transmission model whereby the teacher instructs and the child learns. Understanding Vygotsky's ideas about teaching can support educators who want to improve their skills and develop the quality of their interactions with children, particularly in play. However, it must be remembered that the social relationship which Vygotsky referred to as teaching is a one-to-one relationship between adult and child. It has been left to others to interpret the implications of his theories for educational settings: 'Teaching consists in assisting performance through the ZPD. Teaching can be said to occur when assistance is offered at points in the ZPD at which performance requires assistance' (Tharp and Gallimore, 1991, p. 45).

Central to our understanding of Vygotsky's theories about the unity between teaching and learning is the concept of assisted performance. This is defined as what a child can do using internal motivations and capabilities, but with help from more knowledgeable others and support from the learning environment. Assisted performance is joint performance and relies on the active participation of the child (hands-on and brains-on). The teacher needs to draw on a complex range of strategies to maintain the interest and involvement of the child. The deliberate use of these strategies models the process of assisted performance itself and can help children to learn how to use them in their own peer group where they recognize themselves as the more knowledgeable other. Assisted performance involves learning to learn and learning about learning. Tharp and Gallimore (1991) devised a four stage model which describes different levels of assisted performance and the requisite supportive strategies.

Stage 1: Performance is assisted by more capable others
Children rely on adults or more capable peers for regulation and may have only limited understanding of the situation, task or goal to be achieved. The more knowledgeable other may offer explicit directions and/or use overt modelling strategies as the child's response is acquiescent or imitative. An example of this is the game of peek-a-boo. Usually an adult initiates the game, teaches the child the rules through modelling, actions, exaggerated facial expressions and language. Gradually the child learns the meaning of the activity and takes over the actions, initiates the game, takes turns, and may then play it with another child, adult or even with a toy.

At a higher level of cognitive performance, language plays an increasingly important part in assisting performance. The adult may model self-speech or 'out-loud thinking' as a means of regulating activity and introducing metacognitive skills. Questions, prompts, reflecting on action, directing attention, using recall strategies and praise all assist performance. It is not just the hands-on aspect of the activity that is the focus for assistance but also the level of cognitive engagement (brains-on activity) which is significant. Through this process, the adult models expertise in knowledge and action. Acquiring this expertise is fundamental to learning how to learn, to think and communicate (Wood, 1988, p. 13) and is central to Bruner's concept of scaffolding.

Assisted performance does not necessarily involve simplifying the task. The task difficulty is held constant but the child's role is simplified by means of 'graduated assistance' from the adult as the following example shows. Laura, age three, wanted to help her Dad make a new shed for the garden. She insisted on using the real hammer and nails and would not be fobbed off with child-sized, safer alternatives. Her Dad demonstrated how to use the hammer correctly by knocking in the nails part of the way and allowing Laura to finish them off. He also realized that Laura's interest and skills could be developed further by having access to wood and tools. Over-simplification of tasks and materials can be patronizing to children and can result in unchallenging learning environments.

Intentionality is an important aspect of assisted performance. As the interaction develops, the intentions of the activity may change. This may be initiated by the child in response to an adult's help or to the changing nature of the activity, as is frequently demonstrated in children's play. It may also be prompted by the teacher, who may see the ideal opportunity for the input of knowledge, skills or understanding which is necessary to the activity. This does not imply a takeover by the teacher as the essence of the interaction remains responsive. As the child's involvement and expertise develop, he or she can help the teacher to assist by requesting specific support. This maintains reciprocity between the child's and teacher's intentions. The process is gradual and takes into account that learning often occurs in bursts rather than in a logical, ordered sequence. Practice and repetition are essential *en route* to mastery and expertise. Stage 1 is accomplished when a new level of expertise has been reached where the child has begun to internalize the rules, processes, skills and concepts necessary to independent performance.

Stage 2: Self-assisted performance

Here the child's performance is not yet fully developed but they have internalized some of the strategies which are essential to self-directed and self-regulated action. One of these strategies is self-speech which the child may use to guide behaviour and actions. This can be observed as a frequent aspect of young children's play as they structure and act out roles. Self-speech can serve many purposes, as a mnemonic (memory-assisting) device, practising retrieval, as a self-regulation system, and as a conscious way of gaining control over one's unconscious thought processes. In later life it is an effective way of revising and rehearsing information which needs to be memorized (Howe, 1992). As Tharp and Gallimore have noted, it is more than instrumental in skill acquisition: it is an important aspect of cognitive development which forms the basis of communication and writing (1991, p. 53).

Stage 3: Performance is developed, automized and 'fossilized'

Here the child has internalized the rules, processes, skills and concepts necessary to independent performance. The child has emerged from the ZPD into 'self-sustained take-off' and may be able to act as a more knowledgeable other in collaboration with another child. Transition through the first two stages has led to qualitative and quantitative changes in a child's level of competence in one or more of the cognitive, affective and psycho-motor domains.

This sequence of learning through assisted performance can be observed not just in young children but throughout our lives, for example learning to drive a car, master a word-processor, or learning to teach. With practice and experience, we attain a level of 'unconscious competence', but can then use previously learned strategies in novel situations.

Stage 4: De-automization of performance leads to recursion back through the ZPD

Vygotsky considered learning as a life-long process with no final rung in the ladder of cognitive competence. The idea of learning being a recursive and accretive cycle indicates how learners of all ages can draw upon these strategies. Bruner (1966) characterizes this process as a learning spiral to indicate how learners achieve qualitative and quantitative changes in their cognitive competence. This is not an ever onward and upward progression. Young children frequently have bursts of energy, interest and motivation where they are willing to learn. At times they can appear to regress as though a plateau has been reached and they cannot cope with any further advances for a while, perhaps even forgetting things if there has been some upheaval or stress in their lives. These stages can be used to revise, maintain or enhance performance with the different strategies being adapted accordingly. There can be qualitative and quantitative changes in assisted performance, the ground rule being that it is responsive to the child's capabilities, intentions and needs. In adopting such strategies, the teacher is able to begin where the learner is, to use Froebel's maxim, but also knows where each child or group of children should go next. This implies conscious pedagogical decisions and actions on the part of the teacher so that learning is not left to emerge by chance nor is it so formalized as to deny children's interests and motivations.

Implications for practice

As young children gain expertise as learners they know how to deploy a range of strategies to assist their own performance, including specifying what kinds of support they need from more knowledgeable others. They then move between self-regulated, other-regulated and automized performance. Howe (1992) and Wood (1988) argue that children need to learn effective learning strategies so that this recursive, accretive cycle is made more effective and efficient. As we have shown in the previous chapter, this involves metacognitive activity – conscious awareness and control of learning:

> Ultimately this 'scaffolding' technique of teaching has been so well internalized by the learners that they can provide it for themselves in new learning situations; the learning child internalizes the teacher's actions and reflections, transforming them into his or her own way of solving that particular problem or doing that particular task, but also internalizing and developing more general tools – how to observe, how to imitate, how to analyse, how to scaffold one's own cognitive activity or another person's. These powerful 'metacognitive' activities contribute to making the learner into a 'self-running problem-solver'.
>
> (Meadows, 1993, p. 344)

Children need to talk about what they are doing and thinking and about what and how they are learning. The conscious development of metacognitive skills and strategies should form an integral part of the curriculum so that children do not just learn, they become aware of themselves as thinkers and learners. This links both cognitive and affective processes since children's success in school can determine to a large extent their self-image and self-esteem. More importantly, this is where real independence and autonomy lie. Giving children choices and allowing them to make decisions is one thing, but becoming a self-running problem-solver and a successful learner promotes authentic autonomy, whilst maintaining the child's ability to ask for assistance and specify what kind of assistance is needed.

Vygotsky's ideas about the importance of teaching to learning were explored by Leont'ev and Luria:

If all the development of a child's mental life takes place in the process of social intercourse, this implies that this intercourse and its most systematized form, the teaching process, forms the development of the child, creates new mental formations, and develops higher processes of mental life. Teaching, which sometimes seems to wait upon development, is in fact its decisive motor force.

(Quoted in Forman and Cazden, 1985)

We have already stated that Vygotsky regarded development as a synthesis between biological and socio-cultural processes, internal drives and external forces, which lead to the acquisition of cultural tools, attitudes, values and ways of thinking, acting and learning. The notion of teaching as a decisive force implies a reconceptualization of some aspects of early years practice. It calls into question the role of adults in children's play, their teaching and interactional styles and their approaches to curriculum planning. It is evident that early childhood educators can create the conditions which support learning and development in proactive rather than reactive ways. This still maintains the importance of learning by discovery, exploration, first hand experience and enquiry-based approaches. But children may need some support with understanding what they have discovered, or learning strategies for exploring, enquiring and investigating which make these processes educationally more powerful. Educators need to be aware of what and how children learn, what they can be assisted to learn, where that fits with their existing knowledge and understanding, and what connections can be made between areas of learning. This links closely with the idea that educational settings can become zones for proximal development.

Vygotsky's theories about teaching and learning and the ways in which they have been interpreted by subsequent theorists provide a model of learning which involves a wide range of complex processes. But for these theories to become meaningful to practitioners they need to be linked to an appropriate curriculum and pedagogy in early childhood. As with Piaget's theories about assimilation and accommodation, Vygotskyian theories about scaffolding and zones of proximal development are broad and general. Educators need a much more specified understanding of the processes of learning both in the three main developmental domains (cognitive, affective and psycho-motor) and in the subject areas. They need to observe and make sense of learning in ways which enable them to make assessments and diagnoses which inform curriculum planning and facilitate progression. It is unlikely that teachers will talk in terms of children assimilating and accommodating, spiralling, scaffolding, restructuring or accreting, although these are useful broad-brush terms which characterize the models of teaching and learning outlined here. In the context of play, more informed perspectives are needed which enable teachers to go beyond assumptions and intuitions, particularly if we accept Guha's (1988) distinction between play 'as such' and play in schools with the implication that play in an educational context should be qualitatively different. The following section explores the fourth key theme – Vygotsky's theories about play.

Vygotsky's theories of play

As we have argued, the assumption that play is the predominant feature of early childhood has been reinforced by the ideological tradition and continues to be an important educational tenet in the early years. Vygotsky wrote very little about play and his theories are more evocative than definitive (Newman and Holzman, 1993). However, his work does offer some different perspectives, particularly if we relate these to his theories about learning and development, the ZPD and the role of instruction.

Play for Vygotsky is mainly role play and he was concerned with its function as developmental activity. He regarded play as the leading source of development in the pre-school years, but not the dominant form of activity. Thus we can link the concepts of play leading development and learning leading development to explore possibilities for curriculum planning, the role of the teacher and to understand more fully the processes which link play and learning.

Vygotsky challenged the view that play can be defined simply on the basis of pleasure since there are other things which may be pleasurable for the child and equally there may be some forms of play which may be unpleasurable. The main characteristics of play are:

- imaginary situations
- subordination to rules
- the liberation from situational constraints
- the definition of roles

Like all other higher psychological functions, play is social in origin, is mediated by language and is learned with other people (peers and adults) in social situations. He believed that all forms of play have imaginary elements and that all play is necessarily rule-bound by the presence of these imaginary elements. In combining the 'what if' and 'as if' elements, children automatically suspend real world behaviour and rules in order to enter into the imaginary situation (although the imaginary situation may contain real world elements). A further characteristic of play is the ability to dissociate the meanings of objects and actions from the real objects and actions. This creates early experiences of complex, abstract thinking in which action increasingly arises from ideas rather than from things. This challenges Piagetian notions of stages, hierarchies and transitions from simple to complex and from concrete to abstract forms of thought.

Vygotsky considered that the developmental course of play is characterized by the changing relationships between imaginary situations and rules in play. In free play, children create an overt imaginary situation with covert rules. These are sometimes implicit and sometimes explicitly negotiated at the onset of play or during the development of a play sequence. Children establish rules about roles, props, actions and behaviours. They are to a large extent dependent on the play context and are the preconditions of successful play experiences. For example, a child pretending to be a Dad may dress up in appropriate clothes, adopt a deep voice, a strong walk, possibly a domineering part in the play to convey personal understanding and interpretation of that role. Samir, age four, liked to play this role repeatedly after his own Dad left home. He always selected a tie as the indicator of his role in the play with the announcement 'I've got the tie so I'm the Dad'. One day Samir could not find the tie, but went through his usual ritual and made the same announcement, this time just patting his neck to signify he was 'wearing' the tie and hence taking on that role. This symbolic gesture was accepted by the children and thereafter Samir did not depend on the tie as a prop.

In contrast to free play, games have overt rules with a covert imaginary situation. Vygotsky used the example of chess where one has to abide by clearly defined rules but at the same time imagine that the pieces are able to move in specified ways and be capable of certain actions (1978, p. 95). Similarly when playing football children assign their positions according to the established rules of the game but also often decide which of their favourite players they represent. They not only play the game of football but frequently role play behaviours of current sporting heroes, including exaggerating injuries, disputes with the referee and ecstatic reactions to goal scoring. Play is linked essentially to the fulfilment of the child's needs, motivations, incentives to act and affective states. Vygotsky considered that any analysis of play should take into account these factors.

In contrast to Piaget who distinguished between practice play, symbolic play and games with rules, Vygotsky linked play and imagination with rules in terms of gradual, qualitative shifts from an emphasis on the imaginary situation to the dominance of rules: 'where there is an imaginary situation in play there are rules. Not rules which are formulated in advance and which change during the course of the game but rules stemming from the imaginary situation' (1976, p. 542 in Bruner, Jolly and Sylva).

Newman and Holzman (1993) have argued that this theory has created a paradox in our understanding of play and its role in development. On the one hand, imaginative or free play liberates children from everyday rules and situational constraints. A cardboard box can become a delivery van, a racing car, a secret den. But at the same time the context of play which children create carries implicit rules which are necessary to establish and maintain the imaginary situation.

For example, Umesh brought a large cardboard box to the nursery and planned to make a space shuttle, having seen a launch on the television the previous day. He asked for assistance with cutting holes for the windows, then selected pieces from the junk box to represent controls, booster rockets and other features he had evidently discussed at home. He organized his fellow astronauts, assigning roles and giving information about how they should behave. Their journey started and ended with the box in the same position, but spatially and temporally the play context developed in complex ways. As the astronauts landed they walked with slow, exaggerated movements and then pretended to explore the moon and find creatures (soft toys from the home corner). On their return to earth, Umesh explained that they had been 'a long way away for a very long time' but then enquired whether he had missed snack time!

Vygotsky argued that these rules of imagination both liberate children from everyday constraints but at the same time impose other constraints – another paradox of play. Children know implicitly that they must control their desire to act spontaneously outside their assigned roles in order not to destroy the play sequence and the shared fantasy. This is not a hard and fast rule as children often change or renegotiate their roles during the course of free play, but if too much disagreement occurs the play is likely to disintegrate. Equally, if children cheat or ignore rules in game play such as snakes and ladders part of the meaning and pleasure of the game is destroyed as is the chance to win fairly. It appears that subordination to rules and restraining spontaneous action are a means to pleasure and success in play. Both derive from inclusion, negotiation, cooperation and the construction of shared meanings.

The concept of subordination to rules is itself intriguing in the context of early childhood. Often children create quite elaborate, clearly defined rules to sustain and develop play and they will, for the most part, abide by these rules for the pleasure gained, the satisfaction of inclusion or for the power it affords. They often use sophisticated (and sometimes quite ruthless) self-determining and self maintaining strategies. In contrast, teachers sometimes have to wage a continuous battle to maintain externally imposed rules such as lining up, not running indoors, sitting still for story. Perhaps this tension between resisting externally imposed rules and subordination to self-imposed rules tells us something about the anarchic nature of childhood and the ways in which children view themselves in relation to more dominant and powerful others. Play gives children the opportunities to be powerful, dominant and to exercise control in an adult-dominated world. This also indicates how play can change the nature of power relationships within educational contexts as the locus of control is with the children rather than with the adult. This can make play, especially free play, difficult to accommodate and manage beyond the pre-school years.

For Vygotsky the value of play is related to both cognitive and affective development through the fulfilment of a child's needs, incentives to act and motivations. The maturing of new needs and new motives for action are a dominant factor in development. Through play, children satisfy certain intrinsic needs so that in order to understand play we need to understand the special character of these needs, inclinations, incentives and motives. This links with Vygotsky's ideas about learning and motivation. Through play children are motivated to learn, so the learning that occurs in meaningful contexts becomes a spur to further motivation and hence to further learning:

> Though the play-development relationship can be compared to the instruction-development relationship, play provides a much wider background for changes

in needs and consciousness. Action in the imaginative sphere, in an imaginary situation, the creation of voluntary intentions and the formation of real-life plans and volitional motives – all appear in play and make it the highest level of pre-school development. The child moves forward essentially through play activity. Only in this sense can play be considered the leading activity that determines a child's development.

(1978, pp. 102–3)

The notion of the formation of 'real-life plans' is interesting, particularly in the context of imaginative play. Children do not step from the real world into an imaginary world but maintain a continuous dialogue between the two. This was shown in the example of the space shuttle play. Umesh could become an astronaut in his imagination but in order to sustain this fantasy he drew on a wealth of knowledge gleaned from the real world. Play thus reveals the unity of children's development, the myriad sources of knowledge they draw upon and the novel, creative contexts they construct. Umesh used internal motivation to transform the box into a space shuttle and to develop the imaginative qualities of the play. Constructing the play was not just about using the imagination since it depended on logic, reasoning, memory, recall of factual knowledge, communication, organization and the ability to negotiate shared meanings. The richness and quality of the play were influenced by self-restraint and self-determination. Again there was the element of paradox – the props, roles and actions simultaneously being real and not real with children making transformations and abstractions in their play. This shows how imagination and creativity are related to both cognitive and affective development and are therefore intrinsic to education, and how play is a powerful vehicle for learning (and for learning leading development), thinking, generating ideas and communicating. Play thus creates a zone of proximal development in which 'a child always behaves beyond his average age, above his daily behaviour; in play it is as though he were a head taller than himself' (Vygotsky, 1978, p. 102).

Vygotsky argued that in play children's actions and behaviour are influenced by contexts and situational constraints. As we have seen, this is both limiting and liberating. Children use two strategies to overcome limitations. First, thought can be separated from an object as in the example given above where a box became the space shuttle and an egg carton represented the control panel. Second, action arises from ideas rather than things which allowed the children to believe they were astronauts and to behave accordingly. They did not need heavy suits or to have experienced lack of gravity to role play with such accuracy.

This demonstrates the interaction between external influences (interpsychological) and internal processes (intrapsychological): 'The child in wishing carries out his wishes; and in thinking, he acts. Internal and external action are inseparable: imagination, interpretation and will are internal processes to external action' (1976, p. 549 Bruner, Jolly and Sylva).

Through play children both manipulate and change their relationship with reality. This presents another paradox since children do not just play to escape from reality, they actually get closer to reality, particularly in their role play. In acting out roles they can experience what it is like to be a Mum, Dad, police officer, doctor, patient, but these roles are dependent on their interpretations of real-life behaviour and hence are rule-bound. Thus imagination in play is not trivial or frivolous since it can be linked to the development of consciousness and awareness of reality. Vygotsky argued that the relationship between realistic thinking and imagination is complex and can lead to higher forms of cognition in adulthood (Newman and Holzman, 1993).

This process can be seen as children become increasingly adept at separating thought from an object and developing action from ideas rather than things. The paradox here is that different actions arise from the ideas and meanings constructed by the children – hence the view that play is both liberating and constraining. Skilled, experienced players free themselves from the need for props and will often improvise in quite theatrical ways. For example, Bobbie and Jamel were regular, experienced play partners who often repeated similar themes based on karate style play fighting. One morning Jamel was waiting for the nursery to open and saw Bobbie approaching some distance away. They both immediately adopted a karate position and gradually advanced towards each other using these movements. As they drew nearer, they circled each other with karate chops in mock aggression. There was intense eye contact, but no body contact and no dialogue other than sound effects for the karate chops. The play became more energetic and Bobbie intentionally fell to the ground in a defensive position to signal his 'defeat'. Jamel placed his foot lightly on Bobbie's abdomen and raised both hands in a victory salute – both boys were smiling at this point. Bobbie then got up, dusted himself down and said 'OK, what shall we play today?' Both boys were intensely engaged in this episode and blocked out all the activity going on around them.

The combination of mime, drama and movement had a choreographic quality and can be seen as some of the tools of play which children manipulate to their own ends. Bobbie and Jamel could literally play with their play because it was so well practised that intentions could be communicated through symbolic gestures rather than through verbal negotiation. In play children are capable of abstract levels of thinking and often reveal themselves as keen observers and intuitive interpreters of other people's actions, characteristics and behaviour which goes far beyond simple mimicry and imitation. Teachers often report that young children playing school can represent teacher behaviours with alarming accuracy!

As we have seen, although Vygotsky did not eulogize play, he did invest it with profound significance for children's learning and development. However, he also noted a familiar problem with play which has dogged early years practitioners and theorists alike, namely that play bears little resemblance to what it leads to, at least in its most productive forms. He argued that only a profound internal analysis makes it possible to determine its role in the pre-schooler's development (1976, p. 544, Bruner *et al*). This point is echoed by Bruner from a different standpoint: 'Deep play is playing with fire. It is the kind of serious play that tidy and even permissive institutions for educating young children cannot live with happily, for the mandate requires them to carry out their work with due regard to minimizing the chagrin concerning the outcomes achieved. And deep play is a poor vehicle for that' (Woodhead, Carr and Light, 1991, p. 270).

As we have argued, Newman and Holzman's (1993) interpretations of Vygotsky's theories regard play as revolutionary activity because it involves imaginary situations and is concerned with meaning-making which is often novel and creative. Children also move towards higher levels of cognitive functioning thus changing their knowledge, skills and conceptual frameworks. These perspectives reveal some tensions which are of central concern to educators in their attempts to make sense of play. Bruner argues that deep play is indeed serious and significant but that it is difficult to control or assess in terms of outcomes. Vygotsky's theories indicate that outcomes are not immediately visible through what we might term surface features, but can be accessed through internal analysis. This is an important issue which will be explored fully in the following chapter. We have already seen that profound internal analyses of play have begun to delve beneath the surface actions of children's play to reveal their learning, patterns of thinking and understanding. Research by Athey (1990), Gura (1992) and Meckley (1994) is helping to demonstrate the relationships between play and learning in different settings and contexts. These studies have concentrated on content, processes and outcomes and contradict Bruner's pessimistic standpoint. However, such analyses must be concerned with all areas of development, not just the cognitive domain. Vygotsky warned against a 'pedantic intellectualization of play' if children's affective aspirations were ignored (1978). This warning still has relevance for practitioners today as they are coerced into narrowly intellectual justifications for play, particularly in terms of the National Curriculum. Many teachers have stated the view that this is often at the expense of children's affective development.

There is one further perspective which has challenged our own thinking about play and has informed some lively debates with teachers. As we have seen, Newman and Holzman (1993) have argued that play can be seen as revolutionary activity because it is concerned with learning leading development and meaning-making, either in individual or collective zones of proximal development. This has led us to question whether play is inadequately represented in the curriculum partly because its significance is not fully understood but partly because we are wary of its revolutionary nature. Play changes the nature of power relationships within educational settings because children are in control and it can be difficult to manage, to predict outcomes and to interpret its educational significance. This presents a dilemma since play can be limited in many different ways by educators who may strive to control outcomes through structures which constrain deep play and revolutionary activity. Just as children must learn to adapt to adult-defined bureaucratic structures, educators must learn to work with children's internal needs, motives and aspirations so that there is meaningful accommodation between the two. Unchallenging environments can be disempowering for children and will fail to harness the educational potential of play.

In the detailed analysis of different theories of children's learning which we have presented in the previous two chapters, it is interesting to note some distinct changes in this discourse. Previously, early learning and development were characterized in the 'secret garden' metaphor where children were likened to growing plants which needed nurturing conditions in which to flourish. The image of the child as unfolding and blossoming into maturity fails to capture the complexity of learning and development or the fundamental role of the educator in these processes. The dominant metaphor now is that of building which, as we have seen, characterizes learning as an incremental process which can be scaffolded by a more knowledgeable other. In the process children acquire tools for thinking, learning and playing which they then use in their own ways and for their own purposes.

On the basis of the models of learning and development explored in Chapters 3 and 4 we consider that social-constructivist perspectives on play, teaching and learning demand a reconceptualization of how play/learning environments are organized and, in particular, how educators might develop their roles in children's play. In the following chapters we will examine the practical implications of the theoretical perspectives which have been presented here.

5

Understanding and Developing Play

We have argued that a more informed understanding of play can be developed through examining the processes which link play and learning. This can be achieved by a critical analysis of children's play which goes beyond the surface features (behaviour and actions) to what is happening inside children's heads when they play. This raises questions about what play involves and what it does for the child. And, more critically, how play can be integrated into the curriculum in order to develop its educational potential.

We have shown that, in order to understand play, we need deeper insights into how young children learn and develop. Multi-theoretical perspectives have been explored which now beg the question: so what does this mean in practice? There are three levels at which we can understand the relationships between play, learning and development which can inform curriculum planning.

First, at a broad level, play is seen as contributing to the development of the 'whole child'. This includes the three domains of development – the cognitive, affective and psycho-motor (Figure 5). At a second level, we can look at play in relation to the subject disciplines (Figure 6). These may be

---

Cognitive: All the skills and processes involved in learning, thinking and understanding.

Affective: All the skills and processes involved in learning a repertoire of appropriate behaviours, making relationships, social interactions, expressing and controlling emotion, developing a sense of self, understanding the needs of others.

Psycho-motor: All aspects of physical development including
Fine motor skills – use of hands, fingers, hand/eye co-ordination.
Gross-motor skills – large body movements such as sitting, turning, twisting, balancing, controlled movement of head, trunk and limbs.
Loco-motor skills – large body movements involving travelling and an awareness of space such as crawling, running, climbing, walking, hopping, skipping, jumping.

Figure 5 Areas of development

Nine areas of learning and experience (HMI, 1989)
High/Scope key experiences (Hohmann *et al*, 1979)
Gardner's forms of intelligence (Anning, 1994)
National Curriculum core and foundation subjects (DfEE, 1995)

Figure 6   Subject disciplines

described differently but essentially add more depth and specificity to what children may be learning in their play and how that may be identified as, for example, mathematical, scientific, geographical or linguistic and literary. Such perspectives also indicate how play can integrate discipline-based learning. It is important to acknowledge such connections and gradually make these more explicit to children in order to support and extend their rapidly developing understanding. For example, small world play, block play, train sets and road mats encompass many geographical skills and concepts. But these may remain implicit in the activity without the support of a knowledgeable educator to focus the children's learning and activities in distinctly geographical ways or to make connections between teacher-directed and child-initiated activities. This reflects Bruner's contention that there is an appropriate form of any skill or knowledge that may be imparted at whatever age one wishes to begin teaching – however preparatory that version may be (1966, p. 35). Play as an integrating mechanism potentially has an important part in this process as children weave together their knowledge, skills and understanding and move between real, imaginary and play worlds.

At a third, deeper level, we can look at the cognitive processes which link play and learning (Figure 7).

As we have seen, learning and development depend on cognitive structures which are complex both in their origins and subsequent evolution. Processes such as exploration, practice, repetition, mastery and revision are important in forming, extending and connecting cognitive structures. Play can be seen as a means whereby children try to impose some structure or organization on a task and make sense of their world, and as a continuous rehearsal of these cognitive processes. Teachers often express concern that children's play is sometimes repetitive but a closer examination often reveals subtle changes in play themes and patterns as children revise and extend what has previously been played at and played with. This process of refinement, pruning and editing through rehearsal and practice is an important component of cognitive development leading to increased complexity in thinking, learning and understanding.

The cognitive processes outlined here are also fundamental to learning through the subject disciplines. Characteristics of children's play such as exploration, investigation, making and testing hypotheses and taking risks are also integral to learning in, for example, science, mathematics and history. Children's learning becomes increasingly focused and refined through the distinctive methods of inquiry, key skills and conceptual frameworks which the

Cognitive processes and skills
- attending, perceiving, observing, recognizing, discriminating, imitating, exploring, investigating, concentrating, memorizing, retaining, retrieving and recalling information, scanning for information, integrating knowledge and experience, categorization, classification, making connections and relationships, transferring knowledge and skills, developing transfer-ability
- making intelligent use of past experience to formulate a plan of action, reflecting on action, noticing causes and effects
- making choices and decisions, acquiring knowledge, making sense, creating meaning, understanding
- creativity, imagination, flexibility, making novel connections using metacognitive strategies – awareness and conscious control of one's own learning, using metamemory, metacommunication and meta-awareness
- creating, recognizing and solving problems
- convergent and divergent thinking, practice, repetition, rehearsal, consolidation, retuning, accretion, mastery, interpreting, communicating – through language, signs, symbols and artefacts
- making and testing hypotheses, predicting, innovating, combining, re-combining, reasoning, extrapolating.

Attitudes to learning
- curiousity, motivation – intrinsic and extrinsic, open-mindedness, flexibility, engagement, interest, enthusiasm, originality, creativity, independence, interdependence, willingness to take risks, ability to struggle, cope with challenge and failure, perseverance.

Influences on learning
- mood states, home background and experiences, parental pressures and expectations, social skills, learning environment – home and school, quality of educative relationships.
- self-systems – self-concept, self-image, self-esteem, self-worth, self-efficacy.

Figure 7 Cognitive processes linking play and learning

subject disciplines represent. These three levels of understanding play provide a framework for curriculum design which takes into account breadth, balance, relevance and continuity between phases.

Curriculum models

There is a variety of curriculum models which provide structure and define content. How these are interpreted in practice depends on the knowledge and expertise of educators in school and pre-school settings. Each of these models has different features which can be combined or adapted to individual settings and all can integrate play as an essential component of the curriculum.

HMI nine areas of learning and experience

The nine areas of learning and experience defined by HMI (1985) have been recommended as a useful framework for the planning and analysis of the curriculum for children under five. They are:

- Aesthetic and creative
- Human and social
- Linguistic and literary
- Mathematical
- Moral
- Physical
- Scientific
- Spiritual
- Technological.

This framework was endorsed by HMI (1989) and in the Report of the Rumbold Committee (1990). Evidence from local authority guidelines and nursery practice indicates that the nine areas have been widely adopted to inform curriculum planning (Smith, 1994). This model provides a strong validation for 'planned and purposeful' play and emphasizes the involvement of adults to maximize its potential. As was shown in Chapter 1, play is not regarded as a wholly free or unstructured activity but as the means by which educators' intentions for children's learning are translated into practice.

There is potential overlap between this model and Key Stage 1 of the National Curriculum as it was designed to promote continuity between phases. It argues for high quality planning which supports planned interventions through organization of the learning environment, structured play and a balance between adult-directed and child-chosen activities. The nine areas of learning and experience are intended to promote breadth and balance and recognize that much of what children learn at this age connects directly with the subject disciplines. This acknowledges that from an early age children are real world geographers, historians, scientists and mathematicians. Their interactions with more knowledgeable others as conveyors of knowledge and culture ensures, as we have seen, that children learn the tools of their own and other cultures and move gradually towards disciplined ways of knowing.

However, this framework should not be seen merely as providing a head start into Key Stage 1, and should not be based on formal, sedentary tasks. The guidelines for the inspection of settings for children under five (OFSTED, 1993b) adopted the nine areas of learning and experience as a framework for examining children's achievements and the nature of the educational provision. There are frequent references to different types of play in this document as an indicator of the quality of teaching and learning.

Gardner's forms of intelligence

Anning (1994) argues that there are alternative and superior models to the National Curriculum which use play and creativity as the basis of an early years curriculum. She proposes Gardner's more radical standpoint that a curriculum should be designed around the need to educate eight 'forms of intelligence':

- Linguistic – dealing with language and words
- Logical/mathematical – abstraction and numbers
- Musical/auditory – rhythm and sound
- Visual/spatial – patterning and imagery, knowing the environment
- Kinesthetic – physical skills, reflexes and timing
- Interpersonal – sensitivity to others' emotions and needs
- Intrapersonal – self-knowledge and inner-focusing
- Intuitive/spiritual – flow states and feelings

Anning argues that in the context of schooling most information is passed through the *auditory* mode whilst little emphasis is placed on the *visual and kinesthetic* modes of learning (1994, p. 71). She also confirms the rhetoric/reality divide in early childhood education with teachers paying lip-service to the value of play whilst concentrating on literacy and numeracy activities. Hence the emphasis on the auditory mode takes precedence over the visual and kinesthetic, which shuts down potential areas for growth. Gardner's forms of intelligence are seen as informing a curriculum which aims to empower children with tools for thinking, giving them the capability to explore a whole range of ideas, experiences, feelings and relationships (1994, p. 75). It incorporates a knowledge base that integrates the cognitive, affective and psycho-motor domains and values the cultural tools and social interactions that Vygotsky and Bruner regard as essential to learning and development.

Play provides relevant and stimulating contexts for integrating and learning disciplined ways of knowing. Educators need to think flexibly about the content of the curriculum. For example, during in-service courses many Key Stage 1 teachers have expressed concerns that the National Curriculum reduces time for personal and social development and have subsequently integrated Gardner's forms of intelligence with the National Curriculum to overcome these problems. One teacher described how this had 'totally enlightened' her practice and gave her more confidence in making the curriculum more relevant to this age group.

The High/Scope curriculum

Another curriculum model which has influenced practice considerably during the last fifteen years is the High/Scope curriculum. This originated in America and is based on a defined theoretical base, a set of principles and detailed guidelines concerning curriculum content, planning, routines, with systems and strategies for assessment and record keeping (Hohmann *et al*, 1979; Brown, 1990). Curriculum content is based on 'key experiences' which represent eight areas of children's learning:

- Active learning
- Language
- Representation
- Classification
- Seriation
- Number
- Spatial relations
- Time.

Active learning is seen as the foundation of the High/Scope approach, that is learning initiated by the child rather than predetermined by the teacher. The curriculum is planned around the interests and ongoing cognitive concerns of the children and can be adapted to different age groups, settings, to children with special educational needs and from different ethnic groups. It centres on a plan-do-review system which involves children in setting their own goals and choosing their activities within a structured environment. This does not embody a *laissez-faire* approach since the environment is structured to provide key experiences in these eight areas. Educators have a clear idea of the forms of knowledge which can be accessed through, for example, construction, sand and water play. The children usually have more freedom to combine materials according to their intentions. The role of the adult is to act as facilitator in supporting the children's decisions, monitoring their activity and providing ongoing support.

Review time is seen as an important element of this curriculum model where children come together to discuss what they have done, made or learnt. They are encouraged to ask questions of each other, to share information and to think about future extensions. At its best, review time can encourage the development of metacognitive skills and processes. At its worst, it can degenerate into a repetitive ritual. It really depends on the size of the groups and the expertise of the educator in enabling children to make the most of this experience. Originally it was designed for an adult:child ratio of 1:8, so implementing this model with larger groups can be problematic and can negate the benefits of this approach. Teachers who have experimented with High/Scope have reported that with large groups planning takes up too much time with the result that others in the group become restless. This has led them to question whether sitting still for sometimes up to thirty minutes was a valuable and active use of children's time. However, early years practitioners are frequently creative and pragmatic and many have reported that they use small planning groups on a daily basis so that during the course of a week all children are able to experience greater choice, autonomy and independence. Teachers have also indicated that they use review time frequently and constructively so that children can feed back what they have been doing in their self-initiated activities, including play. This helps to value such activities and provides a feedback loop into the curriculum to inform further planning.

There is an underlying assumption in this model that what children choose is what they need. However, feedback on this model from teachers suggests that some caution should be exercised here. Some children may endlessly repeat what is safe and known and educators have to make decisions based on their professional expertise about breadth, balance and progression for each child. Therefore they have to trust children to some extent but also trust their own judgments.

The National Curriculum

This is based on three core and seven foundation subjects. Following the Dearing review in 1993 a revised version was implemented in 1995 (DfE). The original statements of attainment in each of the subject orders were clarified and reduced and were replaced by ten level descriptions which were seen as the basis for making judgments about pupils' levels of attainment. Whether this is the most appropriate form of curriculum organization for young children is still the matter of considerable debate. As we have argued, the extent to which the National Curriculum was conceived on the basis of political imperatives rather than sound educational considerations has created considerable angst within the teaching profession (Anning, 1991; Blenkin and Kelly, 1994). Not only did this model appear to run counter to long-established methods of integrated, topic-based approaches common throughout the early years, it also threatened to promote approaches to teaching and learning which appeared to be directly at odds with teachers' understandings and the established theory and knowledge base. Moreover, as we have already seen, play was threatened with even greater marginalization in schools.

The adoption of a subject-based structure has been perceived as an attack on progressive, child-centred methods. The primacy of subject expertise is characteristic of the secondary sector. The working groups which produced the original subject orders contained very few members with any experience of teaching in the primary sector, let alone in the early years. The rallying cry of 'we teach children, not subjects' expressed the concerns of many early years practitioners that they were being forced to teach in ways which were incompatible with how young children learn. We have shown that early years practice was seen as being based loosely on ideological principles rather than on clearly defined organizational and pedagogical strategies. Some of the basic tenets of early childhood education such as educating the whole child, providing a curriculum based on needs, interests, play and talk, lacked clarity in the new era of accountability with an emphasis on subject knowledge.

Part of the difficulty faced by teachers in implementing the full range of the core and foundation subjects has been that there was relatively little research on the development of children's understanding in subject-specific domains to guide their practice. There was a lack of information about progression, particularly in science and the foundation subjects. Consequently, the tensions which teachers faced were both practical and ideological. The original statements of attainment did not adequately reflect the complexity of young children's learning or the qualitative differences in their intellectual processes, with the result that many teachers found it difficult to match up children's attainments to these statements. Blenkin and Kelly (1994) argue that the National Curriculum backward stepped to a rather simplistic, behaviourist approach to teaching and learning.

Early years teachers had to get to grips with curriculum content, testing and assessment procedures across all the core and foundation subjects. Unlike their secondary colleagues who develop expertise in one or two subject areas, primary teachers needed to understand more fully the structure, content, skills and processes within every subject area. The notion of primary teachers being 'generalists' tends to have pejorative undertones. However, they specialize in being generalists and, in terms of how children learn, there is merit in being able to make meaningful connections between the subject disciplines. Although the National Curriculum defined content it was up to teachers to find the most appropriate ways of making that relevant and accessible to young children. This did not automatically mean that play should be rejected or marginalized further although, as we have seen, this was a perceived threat. Clearly teachers needed to think more critically about play and its relationship to the curriculum. They also needed to consider the nature of children's learning in subject specific domains and how this could be represented in play.

Subject matter knowledge

These problems stimulated wider debates about the importance of subject matter knowledge and, in particular, its relevance to young children. The insistence by some early years practitioners and educationists that children do not learn in subject compartments seemed to deny the relevance of any subject-matter knowledge. Again there was some entrenchment in polarized positions which did little to clarify issues or move the debate forward. There was an assumption that children-centredness and subject-based planning were incompatible:

> a curriculum divided into subjects is, potentially, the most alienating form of curriculum for young children because it formalizes experience too soon and, in doing so, makes it distant from the everyday common-sense knowledge and learning that the young child is familiar with and responsive to.
>
> (Blenkin and Kelly, 1993, p. 58)

This view is echoed by Nutbrown:

> Young children cannot be taught effectively if planned learning is divided into man-made compartments called subjects. Children will explore science, learn about maths and develop language skills through activities and experiences which are planned to encompass these and many more elements of thinking and learning.
>
> (1994, p. 3)

Whilst we do not disagree with these perspectives, they lack specificity. Describing the curriculum and children's learning in terms of activity, experience, exploration, needs and interests is vague and inadequate. It does not provide a sufficiently rigorous underpinning for describing what goes on in early years settings in terms of how the curriculum is designed, planned and implemented and how that is received by the children. Nor does it reflect adequately the complexity of the teacher's role. Such descriptions beg important questions such as: what elements of thinking and learning are significant? Where do they derive from? What are children learning when they explore science or develop language skills? Which activities are worth while? What are children's needs and interests? If they love learning, what are they learning that is valuable to them and inspires motivation? The answers to some of these questions lie in a more objective appraisal of subject matter knowledge and its relevance to young children.

Part of the problem which is central to this debate has been the limited frames of reference used about subject matter knowledge. The sledgehammer approach adopted by the National Curriculum Council, and subsequently by the School Curriculum and Assessment Authority, seemed to place factual knowledge at the heart of the curriculum on the narrow and simplistic assumption that what was taught was learnt and could easily be tested. The reality is much more complex. Teachers need more than just subject-matter knowledge. As Alexander *et al* have argued, the subject disciplines represent the most powerful tools for making sense of the world which human beings have devised (1992, p. 64). Each of the disciplines is characterized not just by its knowledge base, but by key skills and processes – ways of learning, knowing, doing and understanding. These particular skills and processes are a framework which provide essential 'tools for thinking'. They are, in Bruner's terms, part of the scaffold which allows for incremental learning.

Teachers need to understand the knowledge, skills and processes which characterize each discipline for several important reasons. First, it enables them to identify which elements are discrete and distinctive and which are interdisciplinary. This understanding creates a frame of reference which supports teaching and learning. Bruce's assertion that 'learning is not compartmentalized, everything links' (1987) gives only a partial view. Teachers need to know what these links are, how they occur spontaneously as part of children's 'everyday common-sense knowledge and learning', how they can be planned intentionally, and how they can be presented in ways which are compatible with children's understanding.

Second, knowledge of the subject disciplines needs to be related to teachers' pedagogical knowledge. This enables teachers to focus their teaching, select resources, refine their questions and explanations. They can plan activities and environments in which children both create and solve problems and, in the process, learn to select appropriate strategies and use flexible, creative modes of thinking. Subject-matter knowledge must also be related to pedagogical knowledge so that it can be represented to young children in relevant, appropriate ways and can be adapted to their understandings. Teachers also need to identify the qualitative changes in the development of concepts, skills and knowledge which are, for example, distinctively scientific, musical, artistic, mathematical or historical. In this way, they not only understand how children's thinking and learning are developing, they can then connect them with increasingly refined 'tools for thinking' or disciplined ways of knowing which help them to make sense and create meaning. This is compatible with the models of learning outlined in Chapters 3 and 4, which show that learning is influenced by social, cultural and historical factors. A social-constructivist approach recognizes the importance of forms of knowledge as the building blocks of understanding.

This does not imply didactic approaches, nor does it focus the planned or received curriculum narrowly into subject compartments. And it certainly does not marginalize or trivialize play. Moyles takes a pragmatic stance on this issue:

> because play is a process rather than a subject, it is really within subjects that one should look to play as a means of teaching and learning rather than as a separate entity. Because of the relevance and motivation of play to children, play must pervade how teachers present learning activities, not sit as an uncomfortable and somewhat suspect activity in itself.
>
> (1989, p. 86)

It is also important to remember that children find it exciting and challenging to connect with knowledge and learning which goes beyond the 'everyday common-sense'. As Tizard and Hughes (1984) show, children frequently demand knowledge which is well beyond their understanding but still within their realms of inquiry, wonder or imagination. Part of the art of teaching is responding to children's questions and interests since they are an important indication of their attempts at making sense and creating meaning. We cannot just connect children with subject matter knowledge in narrow, prescriptive, deterministic ways. But we can and should draw upon the subject disciplines in order or create or respond to opportunities to develop knowledge, skills or understanding which are relevant and appropriate. This does not contaminate childhood innocence. Children need tools for thinking (processes) as well as something to think about (content). This links with the work of Athey (1990) and Nutbrown (1994), who argue that children's developing schemas or patterns of learning need to be nourished with worthwhile content. By these means, teachers can engender positive attitudes towards learning.

This is not to deny the importance of teaching which responds to children's ongoing cognitive concerns which can be identified in their play. Part of the art of teaching lies in transforming these, assisting performance and leading children from informally acquired concepts to more formalized concepts. We do not mean formalized in relation to level descriptions, but in stimulating different ways of learning, thinking and understanding. In this sense, responsive teaching can also be intentional. Adults spontaneously mediate between children's everyday, common-sense learning and more abstract, formal, school-based learning (Donaldson, Grieve and Pratt, 1983). It is the styles of mediation and interaction which influence the quality of learning. Tharp and Gallimore have argued that the shifting of goals by an adult is the fundamental reason that a profound knowledge of subject matter is required of teachers who seek to assist performance: 'Without such knowledge, teachers cannot be ready to promptly assist performance because they cannot quickly reformulate the goals of the interaction; they cannot map the child's conception of the task goal onto the superordinate structures of the academic discipline that is being transmitted' (1991, p. 50).

Integrated and subject-specific approaches to teaching and learning are not mutually exclusive. They are co-dependent. Imparting knowledge by itself and for itself, particularly as prescribed in the National Curriculum subject orders, is of little use unless it is embedded within children's frames of reference and in meaningful contexts, including play. Knowledge of the subject disciplines is important for early years teachers because they are able to access and interpret the knowledge children acquire in a variety of contexts. As we have seen, all forms of play provide valuable contexts for revealing the form and content of children's thinking, their ways of knowing and understanding. Play provides a window into their minds and can reveal how they are emerging as scientists, writers, geographers, artists and mathematicians. Teachers know that children need to make sense and construct meaning at a personal and human level, not just at an intellectual level. Although teachers may prefer to view the curriculum as integrated from a child's perspective, this does not mean that they are incapable of planning and evaluating work in terms of the subject areas (David, Curtis and Siraj-Blatchford, 1993, p. 18).

The point is that, however we choose to describe frameworks and models, teachers must still pay careful attention to the knowledge, skills, concepts, ways of thinking, attitudes and values which are embedded within them. All curriculum models reflect a set of beliefs and values about what is considered to be educationally and developmentally worth while in terms of children's immediate needs, their future needs and the wider needs of society. Knowledge is not value-free. Each of the models outlined here gives status to different kinds of knowledge and modes of thinking. But whichever model (or combination of models) is favoured by educators, they have to make informed decisions about curriculum content, how that will be presented to young children, through different types of play as well as other activities, and to monitor how that is received and interpreted. They also have to create learning environments in which children can express and represent their developing knowledge and understanding and use these to design further worthwhile activities and experiences.

The following examples demonstrate how two teachers in a nursery school and a nursery class had radically different conceptions of children's learning, curriculum content, play and the place of subject matter knowledge. The observations were carried out on the same day which happened to be Shrove Tuesday and pancake making was planned in both settings.

In the nursery school the kitchen area was devoted to making pancakes. A group of children had been involved in identifying and buying the ingredients. The groups that chose this activity first set out the ingredients and equipment under the guidance of a student teacher. Recipe cards were available with writing and pictures to encourage reading. The children weighed the ingredients and although they did not fully understand the use of standard weights, they were able to balance the scales or 'make both sides the same'. They contrasted wet and dry ingredients, sweet and sour tastes and observed how the mixture changed from liquid to solid through the cooking process. The richness of language and variety of activity generated was impressive. Children were able to make choices and decisions and were supported by an adult who sought to interact rather than control. To link this activity with play, children were printing with circles and making circular patterns. There were frying pans in the home corner with pancakes cut from vinyl floor covering for the children to toss. A nursery nurse had designed a board game to see who could catch the pancake first. They learnt the rhyme 'mix a pancake' and, of course, read the story of The Big Pancake. There were other activities available but every child chose to make a pancake. Engagement and enjoyment were evident. Several children 'copied' the recipe to take home and one boy was so pleased with his pancake, he went to put it in his coat pocket to give to his granddad. A nursery nurse intervened to wrap it up!

In the nursery class observed the same afternoon, all the children sat on the floor. The teacher put out the ingredients and equipment on a table. She weighed and mixed the ingredients, telling the children what she was doing and showing them each stage of the process. The mixture was then taken into the kitchen by the nursery nurse, who made two dozen pancakes and presented them to the children at snacktime when they were able to choose whether they wanted lemon or sugar. Some did not seem to connect the previous activity with the finished product and there little interest in the pancakes. During the session the children had participated in a variety of play activities which were self-chosen but the experience of making and eating pancakes was entirely separate.

These examples demonstrate how teachers can conceptualize their practice in radically different ways in relation to subject matter knowledge. In the nursery school, the activities had been planned in relation to the nine areas of learning and experience. These were reinforced through different play activities so that the processes and content of children's learning were embedded in meaningful contexts. The story of The Big Pancake was used subsequently to develop spatial awareness and mapping skills. In the nursery class, the activity was little more than an annual ritual and the potential breadth of learning was not harnessed. This was reflected in other areas of the curriculum. The nursery environment was devoid of print on the displays and the children's coat pegs only had a picture on them as the teacher believed that the children needed lots of play before they could learn to read and write. The teacher thought that as they couldn't understand print, it was considered to be unnecessary and inappropriate in a nursery environment.

Educators can help children to mediate between the known and the unknown both in play contexts and in teacher-directed activities. Therefore they can choose to expand or limit children's learning and development through the curriculum models adopted and environments created. Meadows has argued that it may be educationally effective to teach strategies for learning and domain relevant (subject matter) knowledge at the same time in order to link both content and processes:

> many strategies need an extensive and well-organized base of factual knowledge on which to operate. Some are specific to domains of knowledge . . . It seems that having efficient cognitive strategies for use in a particular domain will enhance both the acquisition and the organization of factual knowledge within that domain so that the knowledge base and strategies improve together.
>
> (1993, p. 340)

As we have argued, just as children need tools for thinking, they also need something to think about. We have seen how children weave into their play the knowledge gleaned from the real world and how experience and activity can lead to demands for new knowledge and skills – the process of transition to what Vygotsky termed higher levels of cognitive functioning. This leads to consideration of how children's learning can be best promoted in early years settings through play.

Curriculum design

If we reflect on the multi-theoretical perspectives outlined in Chapters 3 and 4, we can see that play can be a compelling force which provides a context for learning and development in early childhood. In this sense, play can create zones for proximal development (both individual and collective). We need to look at both the structure and content of the curriculum so that educators can build secure pedagogical frameworks for play. Figure 8 shows the structure of the curriculum. The activities and experiences which educators design and provide, including play, provide the mechanism whereby educators' intentions are translated into practice.

• planning:	defining aims and intentions
• organization:	space, resources, time, adults' role
• implementation:	activities and experiences, intended and possible learning
• assessment and evaluation:	feedback loop into planning

Figure 8 The structure of the curriculum

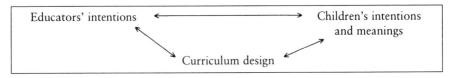

Figure 9   Creating play/learning environments

In defining aims and intentions we do not mean that those of the teacher should predominate in a transmission model, or that play can only take place if it is meeting fixed outcomes. Educators can also create play/learning environments which reflect their own intentions for children's learning but at the same time are responsive to children's intentions (Figure 9).

Awareness of children's intentions can only come about through a curriculum model which encourages them to express those intentions and to fulfill them. It also demands sensitivity on the part of educators to the meanings which children communicate in their play and how these then inform further curriculum planning. They need a dual perspective here as well as a two-way flow of information which is dependent on observation of children playing, supportive interactions in play where appropriate and a feedback system for children to relate and reflect on what they have been doing and learning. These structures enable educators to understand patterns of learning, emerging schemas, ongoing cognitive concerns and the meaning of play to children. It also enables them to consider carefully what additional input is necessary, either through resources, reorganizing the environment or enrichment activities in adult-directed contexts. Many early childhood practitioners shy away from the word structure since they tend to see it as embodying forms of control in children's play which deny the importance of free play in particular. But we argue that structures can be enabling and empowering to children, particularly where there is a continuum between work and play and between teacher-directed and child-initiated activities which provides feedback and feedforward on how the curriculum is received and interpreted (Figure 10).

Where enabling structures are used, play can become more than just an occupational activity which is relegated to the margins of the school day. Educators can make valuable connections between children's ongoing cognitive concerns and the forms of knowledge which serve as an organizing structure for curriculum content. For example, early literacy activities can be embedded in children's play so that they are able to play with the underlying concepts and purposes of literacy in our culture. Children play their way into reading and writing but only where this is recognized and valued as an integral part of the curriculum. In the example given above, the nursery class teacher acted as a barrier to such knowledge because she believed it was irrelevant to young children. In the nursery school the children were familiar with the tools

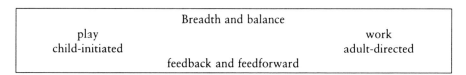

Figure 10   Creating an enabling structure

and conventions of literacy and engaged in a range of literate behaviours in their role play which included reading and writing letters, stories, messages, prescriptions, menus, orders for food in a café, appointment cards, taking registers. The children were not just playing at becoming literate members of society – they believed that they were readers and writers which is an important distinction. They knew that these activities were authentic and were given status within the nursery. This was extended through the provision of supportive resources and other teacher-directed activities such as reading stories, using information technology and drawing children's attention to the range of information and the ways in which it can be conveyed.

Providing a structure for the curriculum and defining the content is a complex process. Educators then have to make it work. The best-resourced learning environment will not support children's learning if they cannot make full use of the potential it offers. First there have to be ground rules about accessing and taking care of resources. Where children have some freedom of choice, there has to be responsibility. The plan-do-review approach outlined above demands a high degree of responsibility in order to support independence, decision-making and autonomy. These should not be seen as exclusively individualized or individualistic processes as children will often plan collaboratively. Interdependence should be encouraged as much as independence. Children have to learn these skills and how to operate effectively within such a framework otherwise there is a danger that the approach will deteriorate into anarchy. This puts the onus on educators to be clear about what skills need to be taught and how (Figure 11). These are relevant to both play and work contexts.

In line with the social-constructivist model of teaching and learning outlined in this book, we can see that these skills and concepts embody interdependence, collaboration and cooperation. They also enable children to develop confidence, motivation, the ability to take risks, consider alternatives, to struggle, to succeed and to identify failure as a learning experience. Teaching such skills to adults is difficult enough and may seem beyond the capabilities of young children. However, from our own work with children from three to eight we know that given careful guidance and input this is not only possible but highly desirable, although it does take time and practice. Children who are able to function at these levels are less dependent on the adults around them for managerial trivia which actually liberates time for involvement, interaction and observation.

- Speaking and listening in a group.
- Understanding the concepts of planning and making decisions.
- Being able to implement a plan.
- Selecting and knowing how to use materials and resources.
- Acting independently and collaboratively.
- Asking for assistance from peers or adults.
- Specifying the assistance needed to implement a plan or carry out a task.
- Paying attention to the activity.
- Creating, identifying and solving problems.
- Remembering how the plan was carried out.
- Reflecting on action – raising and answering questions.
- Representing knowledge and experience.
- Processing information and communicating the meaning and purpose of an activity.
- Conscious awareness of learning processes (metacognition).
- Making and sustaining relationships with peers and adults.

Figure 11   Skills that need to be taught

Extending play contexts

Within such a framework, the learning environment supports this type of curriculum organization. So the resources selected, where they are located and how frequently they are changed are an integral part of the balance between children's and teachers' intentions. For example, children may want to make different combinations of materials such as using small world play resources in the sand and water trays, so that they can be 'world weavers' and make miniature environments. Or the teacher may structure a learning experience which the children then take over and play with. For example, as part of a history topic a PGCE student simulated an archaeological dig with a Year 1/2 class by burying artefacts in the sand tray. The children unearthed them, cleaned and then investigated them. Subsequently their play followed this theme. Martin, age six, created a whole town using Playmobil which he buried, 'discovered' and made up stories about how the people escaped from a volcano. This provided a valuable context for extending skills in historical enquiry. Another teacher with the same age group changed the role play area to a science laboratory. His underlying intentions were interesting since they derived from observations that the children had gender typical roles and expectations for their adult lives. The laboratory enabled both boys and girls to play at being scientists and provided the context for some authentic experiments which linked directly to the National Curriculum.

In both these examples, the teachers were providing direction and enrichment without controlling the children's play. It allowed them to access 'the fascinating world of adults' (Smilansky, 1990) and maintained the paradoxical nature of play in that, by liberating themselves from reality, they got closer to reality. In a curriculum which allows for a two-way flow of intentions, such interventions are both desirable and legitimate. If children only play with what they already know, can do and understand, there is little opportunity for progression. It is also important to identify opportunities to 'go with the flow' of children's ideas. In a nursery class, a teacher told the children she would be having a day off to move house. One of the boys asked 'Where are you moving your house to'? – an understandable misunderstanding! When the teacher explained what it meant a group of children decided spontaneously that they wanted to move house by moving the home corner to a different area of the nursery. The teacher and nursery nurse followed and supported this unplanned development which led to a great deal of discussion, planning, negotiation and cooperation. The children also looked at real maps to show where the teacher was moving from and to, made a map of the nursery, talked about packing up valuables and even suggested that her daughter's cuddly toys should not go in a packing case because they wouldn't like the dark.

In the same class the children were involved in planning a new garden area in the playground. The teacher saw this as an authentic activity which again involved a lot of planning and decision making. She was surprised when the children transformed it into a play situation. The children had to use real tools and barrows to remove old soil and replace it with new prior to planting. They organized roles and responsibilities and played out the task as real workers. This raised some interesting gender issues as John insisted emphatically that girls were not strong enough to push heavy wheelbarrows so they could plant the flowers instead. Again this view was challenged during the activity and was addressed subsequently through relevant stories and images of men and women in non-stereotypical roles. The real-world-play-world nature of this activity continued for some time as the children took responsibility for selecting, ordering and planting bulbs and shrubs. The role play area was changed to a garden centre so that they could follow up some of these experiences in this context.

The value of providing sufficient flexibility to support the work-play continuum with older children is shown in the following example. A teacher in a mixed Reception/Year 1/2 class took in a selection of Victorian artefacts to stimulate historical investigation and extend the children's knowledge base. Among the artefacts was a shop bell. Following the teacher-directed input, the children spontaneously created a role play context using the bell as a stimulus. They organized other children to make playdough cakes to sell in the shop and gathered other items to sell. The historical content of this activity was negligible and the teacher decided to structure the role play to create a Victorian shop. The older children carried out some research and they all planned to make different artefacts to sell. These were supplemented by some original artefacts which were sufficiently robust to withstand the usage. The children's and the teacher's intentions were balanced and the role play provided valuable insights into children's developing historical knowledge and understanding.

We argued earlier that this type of deep or revolutionary play can be challenging because it may appear to threaten the traditional autonomy of the teacher. But in fact, it creates a different role for teachers which demands high levels of pedagogical expertise in creating a challenging curriculum, responding to and transforming children's ongoing cognitive concerns. In each of these examples, the teachers and nursery nurses were aware of the disciplined ways of knowing, forms of knowledge and learning processes which were embedded in the children's play and which provided the building blocks for further learning.

It must be remembered that children need to play with materials and resources in order to learn how they can be used and combined. This reflects the continuum between epistemic and ludic play defined by Hutt *et al* (1989) and pure play and non-play. For example, a child may plan to paint a picture, but if all that is available is pre-mixed, drippy paints with thick stubby brushes and poor quality paper this task will become repetitive and unchallenging. In our experience children benefit from learning to use a variety of brushes and paints as well as a wide range of media in their efforts to become real world artists. They are capable of mixing paints and using thin brushes and benefit from being able to decide consciously which media are appropriate for a task. In learning to use these tools creatively and efficiently, children then go on to play with the media and develop new uses and combinations. This is a far cry from screwed up tissue paper, sticking on cut out shapes and presenting parents and caregivers with immediately recognizable but frequently identical products. A curriculum which denies and constrains children's play in a range of contexts limits their creativity, their ability to experiment, take risks, test out possibilities, reflect on action, and make connections between areas of learning and experience. It also prevents them from becoming successful learners.

As we have argued, children play with materials, resources and roles and, in doing so, integrate their real world knowledge into their imaginary and play worlds. But they also play with ideas and concepts, moving from concrete to abstract, from reality to fantasy, from the known to the possible or even the impossible. This quality of thinking is highly valued in society as people increasingly need transferable skills, the ability to become lifelong learners, to be flexible and creative in response to shifting patterns of employment and expectations. As educators, we need to value the kinds of thinking and learning which play promotes in the children's own terms and for their immediate needs. But it is also useful to bear in mind what this might potentially lead towards.

Planning for progression

As we noted earlier, there is little research on how children's play changes as they get older which can guide practice. The examples given in this book indicate that children's play preferences change and develop in line with their developing skills. Hughes (1991) argues that the major development beyond the pre-school phase is that the child's thinking becomes more orderly, more structured and more logical. Play therefore tends to become more realistic and rule-oriented and reveals a developing need for order, a need to belong and a need for industry. Increasingly their play is centred on cognitive activity as opposed to sensory exploration and physical manipulation. This enables children to use increasingly abstract forms of thinking so that, in Vygotsky's terms, symbols and language can convey ideas. The need for order reflects progression in their cognitive development.

As their patterns of thinking and learning become more refined along with increased competence in language, they are able to predict, reflect, plan, organize, structure and control in their play, whatever forms it takes. For example, in constructive play seven and eight year olds generally need less time exploring new equipment and are more likely to make decisions about what they are going to make or represent. They reveal higher levels of cognitive functioning as well as greater confidence in their skills and abilities. They may become less dependent on an adult for support as they are more confident about sharing ideas and tasks within a group. The nature of the adult's involvement may change. For example, a group of seven year old boys cooperated well to produce a complicated model of an airplane with LegoTechnik. When it came to review time they had a dispute about who was going to show the model to the group. In the ensuing argument, the model got broken leading to anger and frustration. The teacher intervened to help them resolve the dispute and repair the model as well as bruised egos. Later they reflected with the teacher on the design problems. She was able to focus their thinking and enable them to consider alternative designs and strategies which they then went on to use.

In terms of their socialization and a need to belong, older children begin to orientate more towards peer group affiliations and away from the family unit. Increasingly they construct their identities in relation to their peers and will become concerned with demonstrating skills, expertise and talents which define their status:

> The peer group is a major socializing agent in middle childhood. It is from their peers, not from parents or teachers, that children learn about the nature of childhood. Peers will teach children quite effectively, and sometimes very harshly, about social rules and about the importance of obeying them and establish a moral order which may differ from that established by adults.
>
> (Hughes, 1991, p. 100)

In early childhood education there is a tendency to regard all that children do in their play through rose-tinted glasses. The reality can be rather different. Children's affiliations are located increasingly in a distinct childhood culture which is governed by its own rules, codes and hierarchies. These may be invisible to adults if children's play is increasingly confined to the playground and often include both prosocial and antisocial behaviours such as bullying. Inclusion and exclusion from friendships and groupings are powerful forms of social control within this culture and can be based on gender, class, race, physical characteristics, abilities and possessions. As we have shown, children are popular if they are good players, even where other children may have to suppress their will and intentions to the more dominant, powerful player in order to enjoy the inclusion. Generally this is a positive experience which may boost the status of the group and individuals within it and develop their self-confidence. For those who are excluded, the reverse can be true. They may feel rejected and incompetent, which can lead to a negative sense of self. In planning for progression in play, educators need to be aware of these changes so that play environments and related learning experiences can be designed to encourage more complex forms of play but also to address the developmental issues regarding socialization and emergence of self.

Hughes (1991) states that the developing need for industry is apparent both in children's work and in their play as children need to be productive, to achieve a sense of mastery and a feeling of accomplishment. This is related to their social status as it can bring either positive or negative validation from peers. We have argued that play and work can be congruent as children sometimes work very hard at their play, showing concentration, perseverance, determination and attention to both means and ends. Their conscious awareness of their skills and abilities leads to greater control of both processes and outcomes and play continues to provide a context for exercising volition – their will, choices and intentions.

Brostrom (1995) argues that for older children there is a growing awareness of the purposes of play which influences its content and complexity. There is a gradual shift from play with objects to play which is more structured, rule-bound, and which involves taking on a role. Where older children are given opportunities for engaging in socio-dramatic play they are more likely to spend time negotiating the plot, story line, defining roles and directing the action. This is also a conceptual framework in which the dramatic structure and content shape the play which is then more like a performance. Brostrom calls this 'frame play' and argues for adult involvement in the planning of the collective fantasy. This involves organizing the play environment to support the chosen theme with appropriate props and input from the educator, who interacts with the children on their terms and in response to the meanings they construct. Frame play can be constructed around children's own 'real world' experiences as well as around stories and movies. The educators aim to inspire and enrich children's play, but not to limit or deny the children's childlike ways of playing.

Older children also enjoy games with rules such as board games and, increasingly, computer games where they compete against a partner or a character in a game. They enjoy the success of winning, particularly where it contributes to their self-esteem and standing in their peer group. Increasingly children's identity becomes defined by what they are perceived to be good at, particularly in the context of games such as football or chess which demand skill and expertise. In an increasingly consumer-oriented society, their identity is also defined by what they own. For older children, their hobbies may structure their play and may be centred on collections of toys, games or spin-off products from the latest movie and television characters. Again this enables them to get closer to the adult world. In a mixed Year 2/3 class, the children's play revealed some quite sophisticated real world economic understanding. The children became obsessed by collecting conkers and used them as a form of currency for barter and exchange. High and low values were assigned to a variety of personal possessions according to their scarcity and desirability. This all took place without the knowledge of the teacher until a parent complained that her son was missing a large quantity of items. She did not assign the same status or value to his vast collection of conkers!

It is evident that children do not outgrow play but their preferred modes of play change. Therefore, this needs to be considered in planning the curriculum. The activities and experiences provided should continue to reflect a balance between teachers' and children's intentions. For example, older children may need specific input from an adult to master the rules and conventions of board games. They particularly enjoy the chance to compete with adults and peers in a rule-bound activity. Booth argues that teachers are instrumental in shaping the progression from spontaneous socio-dramatic play in early childhood to more structured forms of drama based on their own or familiar dramatized stories:

> Dramatic role-playing helps the children go one step beyond identifying and empathizing with the story; they begin to use the story elements to structure their own thoughts, reacting and responding personally, entering as deeply as they wish into the new world of meaning ... Through such externalized representations as drama, children's perceptions are altered and extended. As children grow in dramatic ability, they improve their communication skills – grappling with experiences, playing out problems and learning to use the conventions of the medium.
>
> (1994, p. 19)

In constructive play, there are many opportunities for progression. There is little point in children continuing to encounter the same equipment from one year to another when progression can be structured by thoughtful selection of resources. Much of the constructive equipment now available is technologically sophisticated and, in some cases, can be linked to computers. Such equipment can continue to integrate playfulness and industriousness as children are enabled to use their skills and knowledge to solve complex problems and extend their creativity and imagination. In doing so, children draw increasingly on disciplined ways of knowing and reasoning so that play continues to provide contexts for extending and integrating subject matter knowledge.

Children's rates of development vary significantly, as do their abilities and preferences. Planning for progression in play should take into account differentiation for children with special educational needs. Play/learning environments, both indoors and outdoors, need to be designed to promote the optimum development of children's abilities:

The lack of appropriate physical surroundings to play in, the failure of adult supervisors to help them plan and carry out their play routines, and the unavailability of suitable playmates all conspire to foster an impression that handicapped children suffer from basic play deficits. In fact, this impression may be completely false: the observed play differences may be environmental in origin.

(Hughes, 1991, p. 144)

This involves consideration of what kinds of play are important for and appropriate to children with a variety of special educational needs in order to ensure full participation in the curriculum offered. For example, Peter had cerebral palsy and had difficulty controlling his body movements. His physiotherapy programme included a lot of repetition to improve control and coordination. The teacher designed a variety of experiences which promoted this in a variety of contexts. Peter was supported by specialist equipment, such as grippers for pencils and brushes and a plastic mat to secure objects and materials, which enabled him to engage in writing, drawing, constructive and small world play. Jennie was partially sighted and needed a sensory-rich play environment. The teacher also reorganized the nursery layout and added additional spotlighting to key areas. In both these instances, all the children benefited in their social skills by learning to play to accommodate the needs of these children. Again the role of the educator is critical in designing experiences, structuring the environment and encouraging enabling conditions not just for play but for the development of a positive self-image for the children.

By developing an informed understanding of the relationship between play,

---

Children need . . .
- Time, space, and varied, good quality resources.
- A curriculum which is culturally diverse and relevant, includes a wide variety of play experiences and a balance between teachers' and children's intentions.
- Appropriately matched activities and experiences with opportunities for hands-on and brains-on activity. These can be self-selected as well as teacher-provided for balance and enrichment.
- Opportunities for practice, mastery, consolidation and transferability.
- Opportunities to perceive relationships between areas of knowledge and experience.
- The support of more knowledgeable others – peers and adults.
- To make connections between learning and experiences at home and in school.
- To develop confidence and self-esteem.
- To learn to take responsibility for their learning and their behaviour. This includes making choices and decisions, formulating and carrying out plans, acting independently and interdependently, knowing when to ask for and give help.
- To be valued, listened to and taken seriously.
- To be with highly skilled, knowledgeable educators.

Figure 12   Implications for teaching and learning

learning and the curriculum, the status and meaning of play to children can be extended beyond the pre-school years and can continue to provide powerful contexts for both teaching and learning (Figure 12).

The theoretical perspectives presented in this book emphasize consistently that the educator has a crucial role in children's play. Just as children can create their own zones for proximal development, the examples given here show how these can also be created and extended by educators who take an active part in enriching and extending children's play. However, this is an area which provokes much discussion amongst early childhood specialists, who often have different views of play and their role in it. This will be explored in the next chapter.

6

The Role of the Educator in Children's Play

Mari, age three and a half, asks the teacher to join in her play. She has for some time been watching a group of children playing together, but evidently does not have the skills or confidence to join in.

Mari: You come on my bus. I'm the driver, you're the Mummy. (Sits in driver's seat and pretends to drive the bus. Holds imaginary steering wheel and makes engine noises.)
Teacher: Where shall we go?
Mari: Shall we go to Portland?
Teacher: Is that a long way?
Mari: Not very far, it's not very far. I've been there, we go to the zoo.
Teacher: That would be good. I'd love to go to the zoo. How long will it take to get there?
Mari: I don't know, it's not very far.
Teacher: Will it take a few minutes or half an hour?
Mari: What time is it? You look at your watch.
Teacher: Ten o' clock.
Mari: It's not very far. We go to see pandas. Oh we're there, it didn't take very long. You can come in as well.
Teacher: Do I have to pay any money to get in?
Mari: Yes.
Teacher: How much does it cost?
Mari: (crossly) I don't know, you've got the watch. (Mari then turned away and lost interest in the play.)

We have opened this chapter on the educator's role in children's play with an example of what not to do and when not to do it. At the outset, Mari had the confidence to approach the teacher as a play partner as an alternative to joining in with a larger group with an established theme. She was able to assign roles, communicate the pretence and define the action, showing abstract and symbolic thinking. Unfortunately on this occasion the teacher was more concerned with eliciting Mari's concepts of space, time, distance and money. The continuous barrage of questions eventually left Mari cross and frustrated – the teacher clearly was not a good player and failed to enter into the role, the flow or the spirit of the play on her terms.

is not knowing how or where to intervene

This illustrates some of the dilemmas which educators face when considering their role in children's play. It is not a straightforward issue and usually provokes heated debate amongst practitioners on in-service courses for very good reasons. Ideologically, educators may feel that children need to have 'ownership' of their play, and that it is their private world. Intervention may be seen as intrusive, particularly in dramatic and socio-dramatic play. At the other extreme highly structured play (as in the Montessori approach, for example) where apparatus is used for a specific purpose gives little space for the child's creative thought (Dowling, 1992). Alternatively, educators may have to focus on adult-directed tasks which are then perceived as having different status, intentions and outcomes to child-initiated activities. This is likely to be the case in school settings where there is generally a higher ratio of children to adults. There may be practical constraints which prevent teachers from becoming involved in children's play such as the pressures of the National Curriculum, time, space and resources.

There is a danger here that an over-emphasis on prescribed content coverage may not be congruent with the styles of learning and thinking which are characteristic of young children. Teachers in particular face real dilemmas in their practice. On the one hand, they know that some involvement in children's play is often desirable. In reality they may lack the time or skills to do this. It is perhaps inevitable, therefore, that under certain circumstances play in schools becomes little more than a holding activity or a reward for completing work. However, as we indicated in the first two chapters, in nursery and pre-school settings without these constraints play is not always of good quality. In order to give higher status to play and to liberate time for more adult involvement, educators may need to reconsider their role.

Meadows (1993) argues that in order for educational settings to become more effective, they need to adopt a Vygotskian model of teaching and learning. As we have seen, the role of the adult as a 'more knowledgeable other' (as well as peers) is central to this model. Meadows outlines research which supports this standpoint. The activities of parents and other adults are critical in supporting a child's cognitive development and achievement throughout infancy and childhood:

> The core is warm participation in socially and intellectually stimulating interactions, with adults showing reciprocity with children, being responsive to them, but also providing some structured, directed experiences with encouragement and praise. Possibly the child participant in such interaction derives an enhanced sense of being competent and effective as well as receiving good cognitive opportunities and helpful interpretations and support from an adult.
>
> (1993, p. 317)

If we accept the Vygotskian principles of teaching and learning outlined in Chapter 4, it follows that the role of educators is fundamental in supporting children's learning and development through play. This is particularly the case in the pre-school phase where play is likely to be a leading form of activity.

There is ample evidence to support this viewpoint. Smith (1994) argues that the attitudes and expertise of practitioners directly influence the quality of children's educational experiences in all forms of pre-school provision. Hennessy *et al* (1992) report that in day care settings the frequency and type of adult-child interactions are influential in promoting language development, particularly if they are based on real conversations and exchanges of information rather than just giving instructions. Responsiveness, positive interactions, access to stimulating toys and educational materials are also seen as helping to stimulate cognitive development. Meadows and Cashdan (1988) argue for adult support of children's developing language and cognition through 'real, rich conversations' and for more involvement in their play. Similarly Hutt *et al* conclude that claims that

> The key to the quality of children's learning experiences is adult participation. Just as the presence of an adult may increase a child's attention span and may present a greater conversational challenge than that of other children, so the adult's participation is an essential ingredient in any programme aimed at enhancing cognitive performance.
>
> (1989, p. 179)

Jones and Reynolds (1992) argue that becoming a master player is the height of developmental achievement for young children and that it is the skilful teacher who makes such play possible and helps children to keep getting better at it. The challenge to educators, therefore, is to ensure that they are aware of the many ways in which they can support these important processes. We emphasize that we are not proposing a curriculum model which advocates adult domination or control of children's play. But there needs to be a balance between the educator's management of the play/learning environment and children's choices in order to enhance the quality of educational experiences, including play.

In a Vygotskian model, the curriculum itself can become a scaffold for children's learning and, as we have argued, classrooms and other educational settings can become zones for proximal development. If we accept the distinction between 'play as such' and 'play in schools' we can see that in order for play to be valued it needs to be located securely within the curriculum structure and organizational framework. Clarifying the role of adults in this process is, therefore, essential. The word structure need not imply stricture. Indeed, structures and frameworks need to be complex, well-organized and clearly established for children's pre-school and school experiences to be enabling and empowering rather than disabling and disempowering. In the same way, intervention and interaction need not imply interference and control. In the context of play, educators need to liberate themselves from the notion that structures are undesirable with young children. In the next section we will show how the educator's role is critical in designing the curriculum and influencing the quality of experience and learning.

Designing the curriculum

The structure of the curriculum consists of five main elements (Figure 13).

planning
organization
implementation
assessment
evaluation

Figure 13   Elements of the curriculum

This is applicable equally to school and pre-school settings. At the planning stage, educators make decisions about their aims and intentions. These can be long-, medium- and short-term. This is not to say that defining aims and intentions reflects a fixed set of decisions which put the adults in sole control of what happens, where and when. In a responsive curriculum, educators' intentions can include responding to children's intentions and meanings as well as allowing for unplanned developments. This is important for organizing and developing play and creating a balance between teacher-designed and child-initiated activities. At the organization stage, educators will make further decisions about how the learning environment (both indoors and outdoors) will be organized, the resources available and their location, how much choice children have, whether materials and activities can be combined, and how the day or session will be structured. These decisions should support the established intentions and how these will be put into practice through different experiences and activities. As Moyles (1989) states, play itself does not constitute a curriculum. It is rather one of the means through which educators' intentions are enacted. Educators decide what forms of knowledge or areas of learning and experience help to shape the curriculum offered.

Bennett and Kell's (1989) model of classroom task processes provides a framework for evaluating whether there is an appropriate match between children and the planned curriculum. This depends on the nature of the tasks, the way they are presented to the children, how children then interpret and respond to the task, and whether this information is sought and used by the teacher to inform further planning. We have adapted this model to provide a useful analysis of the relevance and meaning of play to children and its role in their learning and development (Figure 14).

Bennett and Kell report that difficulties tend to occur in teachers' assessments or diagnosis of children's work:

> Our consistent finding is that teachers are adept at informal assessment, but they do not diagnose. Lack of diagnosis by teachers does, of course, mean that they do not ascertain what children already know, or perhaps more important, what they do not know, and therefore have insufficient knowledge to enable an optimum decision to be made about the next task.
>
> (1989, p. 29)

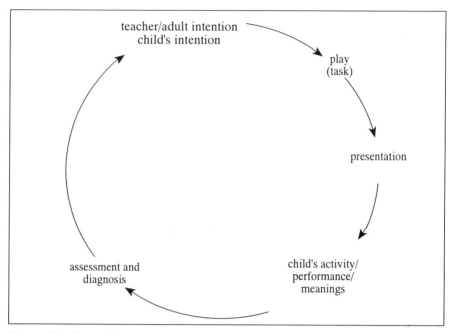

Figure 14   Play and classroom processes

The same problem may be found in this model if we apply it to children's play rather than just to teacher-set tasks. If there is little or no adult involvement in children's play, then there can be no effective assessment and diagnosis of learning and development, or of the relevance of the activities to the children. This means that there is no feedback loop into the cycle. Consequently educators will fail to pick up on children's schemas or patterns of learning, persistent cognitive concerns, skills, attitudes and dispositions as well as the processes and outcomes of play. Thus they will fail to capitalize on what the children themselves bring to the educational setting – what they already know, can do and understand – and will be unable to plan for transformation, extension and progression.

Assessment and evaluation, therefore, provide the essential feedback loop into planning in order to ensure that the tasks and activities are appropriate to the children, and the aims and intentions are being realized. This reflective cycle ensures that educators maintain a critical overview of the relationship between

- the curriculum that is conceived
- the curriculum that is enacted
- the curriculum that is received.

These strategies are relevant to all educators who work in different settings in the early years.

The educator's role is critical in each element of designing the curriculum. We now need to consider content. As we have shown in Chapter 5, there are numerous curriculum models which can be used to inform the activities and experiences which will be provided. Educators need to consider the questions of 'what, how, why and when?' as they look at the finer details of their provision. This will be guided by their understanding of the characteristics and capabilities of the age group as children's play changes as they get older. They need to be clear about the potential learning outcomes which are embedded in different play materials and activities to ensure breadth and balance across the three domains of development (cognitive, affective, psycho-motor) as well as discipline-based forms of knowledge. This enables educators to lead children from their informally acquired concepts to more disciplined ways of knowing, reasoning and understanding. For example, literacy can be stimulated by introducing a range of materials into play contexts which encourage children to become readers and writers, to understand the meaning and purposes of print and the contexts in which it can be used. Hall (1994, p. 114) argues that play can provide numerous opportunities for children to experiment with and use literacy in many different ways by enabling children

- to experience a wide range of different situations within which literacy is appropriately embedded
- to have holistic experiences of literacy
- to enable children to control the ways in which literacy is used and experienced
- to demonstrate what they know rather than what they can copy
- to cooperate in learning about literacy.

Booth (1994) sees drama as an extension of spontaneous role play in early childhood and argues that such experiences are formative in their literacy:

> Children who have had experience in creating their own dramatized stories bring a greater sense of expectation to print, since the speculative nature of spontaneous role-playing develops the ability to think creatively, to examine the many levels of meaning that underlie each action, and to develop the 'what if' element that is necessary for reading. Just as a story can affect the drama to follow, the learning experience in drama can increase the child's storehouse of personal meanings, thus altering any meaning he or she brings to the text.
>
> (p. 18)

There are other forms of literacy embedded in children's play. For example, technical and geographical literacy can be developed through encouraging children to draw maps and plans of their layouts, small world play and constructions. Such experiences have meaning and relevance for children where they are embedded in educationally powerful contexts. Similarly mathematics involves more than learning to count, match and recognize colours. The wealth of mathematical experiences embedded in children's play is far wider and more complex than has been assumed in the past. Children emerge as competent mathematicians through being encouraged to look for patterns and relationships, use signs and symbols and acquire relevant mathematical language and concepts through mediated experiences. This is not an argument for justifying play only as a means of paying into the National Curriculum. It is a realistic standpoint which reflects Vygotskyian views that children need and are capable of developing increasingly refined tools for thinking and learning based on disciplined ways of knowing which assist in their sense- and meaning-making. As we have argued, play provides an absorbing context for these processes and attitudes which should be supported through worthwhile content to form the building blocks of learning and development.

Educators can act as mediators in play and learning by providing a curriculum structure with guiding principles for the content, the underlying aims and intentions. They should also have a clear sense of the range of learning outcomes which are embedded in both child-chosen and adult-directed activities with an awareness of the relationships across this spectrum. Educators can also act as mediators in direct ways to enhance children's play and learning through supportive interactions.

Interacting in children's play

If, as Jones and Reynolds (1992) argue, educators can help children to become master players, they need to consider appropriate strategies which support learning and development but are not overly intrusive or domineering. Again this is a question of balance. In a predominantly *laissez-faire* environment children may miss out on the support and guidance a skilled educator can give. In an over-structured environment, children will not learn to be resourceful or creative in their play. Figure 15 shows the range of skills and strategies which educators may select to guide their interactions.

Skilled educators learn when to intervene in children's play, how to adapt to the play context and what strategies to use in different situations. This is important as the same activity can serve a variety of different purposes according to the age, skills and prior experiences of the children. The critical questions about involvement are when, how and with what intentions? Sometimes the initiative may come from the adult, sometimes from the child. For example it may be necessary to intervene directly to resolve a dispute, particularly with young children who may lack the necessary

---

observing, listening, questioning, responding to children's initiatives and directions, communicating, demonstrating, modelling, encouraging, praising, advising, guiding, suggesting, adopting a role, staying in role, playing on the children's terms, instructing, imparting new knowledge, prompting, reminding, extending, structuring, restructuring, transforming, directing, redirecting, managing, monitoring, assessing, diagnosing

Figure 15 Educators' skills and strategies

strategies. The intervention may provide opportunities to help children to recognize the problem that has arisen and to learn conflict resolution strategies for future use. We have already given several examples in this book which show that children who are used to enabling adults will readily contact them for support with a self-identified problem. With experience they are also more able to identify the support they need from an adult, which shapes the nature of the interaction. Skilled educators carry a memory bank of the children's patterns of learning and previous experience so that they can readily act as re-mind-ers, particularly where children's memories are less reliable (Wood, 1988). They can thus assist children to make connections between areas of learning and experience and make patterns of learning visible to the children.

Where children set themselves challenging problems in play, interaction with a more knowledgeable other may provide a bridge between what is known and what is being learnt or discovered which encourages conscious awareness of the skills and processes involved. As Meadows suggests, discovery will only take the learner so far:

> Discovery learning may have positive effects on motivation because of its encouragement of the learner's autonomy – the 'I did it all myself' boast will come more easily here – but may not encourage metacognitive analysis. Regimented instruction may serve neither motivation nor metacognition well if it bores the learner and omits space for reflection and generalization. Neither rote-learning nor self centred discovery are immediately compatible with socially co-operative learning, though they could alternate with it.
>
> (1993, p. 340)

Some educators may be uncomfortable with the use of direct instruction and imparting new knowledge. However, as we have argued, in a social-constructivist model children need tools for thinking and playing and something to think about. Therefore it is important that both the strategies for learning and the children's knowledge develop hand in hand. Direct instruction is appropriate where it is carefully matched to the child and where it involves the strategies of 'out-loud' thinking, talking through the task, modelling it for the child, then checking whether the child has internalized the new skills or processes. This is particularly relevant in constructive play, sand, water, art and technology where children may need some support with using tools and materials and creating new uses and combinations. Input of skills, concepts and knowledge enables children to play with their own ideas which assists in the processes of internalization and organization. Skilled educators encourage conscious reflection on action to promote consolidation, confidence and mastery.

Modelling is another important strategy to use as imitation is a powerful spur to learning in early childhood. Bruner (1991) calls this 'observational learning' and argues that it is much more complex than the term imitation implies. The educator can actively model skills, strategies, attitudes, behaviours and learning processes again using out-loud thinking, questioning, reflection on action and feelings. This assists the process of guided reinvention in which children internalize or actively construct knowledge and the tools for thinking and learning.

These strategies apply equally to children's social cognition – their understanding of roles, rules, relationships and their place in the world. Sometimes a play sequence may break down because children lack the skills of negotiation, cooperation or conflict resolution. At one level, the adult may need to intervene to resolve disputes and encourage the play to continue with minimal disruption. This is often done on a spontaneous basis with little follow through. It may then be useful in adult-directed time to allow the children to reflect on their feelings and actions and discuss strategies to guide appropriate behaviour. Children have a lot of learning to do in order to develop successfully and operate effectively as individuals in a wide range of contexts which make many different demands. Often they get conflicting messages about what is acceptable in different contexts. For example, in Superhero programmes, children watch the same themes being played out repeatedly with conflict being resolved through physical strength, interpersonal violence and moral superiority. Children often imitate these behaviours as they play out their own understanding of good and evil, weakness and strength. But in the real world, they have to learn that physical contact is unacceptable. For Nolin, this was a difficult problem. He experienced violence in the home between his parents and, in rough and tumble or Superhero play, he did not understand the boundaries between pretending to hurt and really hurting other children. His aggression upset his friends who excluded him from their play, thus leading to further problems which needed the intervention of the teacher. Here Nolin could not play with aggression or violence in a controlled way because they were a present reality in his everyday life.

So the skilled educator is an important influence in helping children to become master players. We have used the words interaction and intervention to describe complementary processes. Both can be either spontaneous or planned. Interaction may be characterized by sustained involvement which is led predominantly by the children. An intervention may be an opportunity for the input of new skills or knowledge to enable the play to continue and develop. Both processes will be based on reciprocity between the teacher and the learner and will be informed by knowledge of the child, the context and the curriculum. Hall (1994) gives several examples of how teacher intervention contributed to the quality of children's literacy experiences as they arose in structured play contexts. Here the play was enriched rather than inhibited so that it was not 'turned from a joyful children-initiated experience to a mournful teacher-led experience' (p. 124). Many forms of play involve sophisticated levels of abstraction and symbolism which educators may need to understand in order to inform their interactions and interventions. Unless they become skilled interpreters of children's play, they cannot offer the right kind of assistance at the right moment or make ongoing changes to the play/learning environment and the curriculum offered.

Educators also need to consider their role in different types of play. For example, constructive play makes different demands on children and creates specific learning opportunities that are not present in sand and water or socio-dramatic play. Many of the kits available today are quite sophisticated and need specialized manipulative skills, technical language, and understanding of concepts related to design and technology. As children get older and their competence increases they show increased skill in planning, designing and building which reflect many of the processes adults use. They also become more confident in problem creating and problem solving as the following example shows.

Joe, Helen, Katy and Martin are discussing their ideas for renovating an area used previously as a bank. They have decided to change it to an art gallery and want to put up black wallpaper to show up the paintings. They have already stripped the walls, removed the staples, cleaned it out and are now talking about the door which is old and has several holes in it:

Joe: We could take the old door off and make a new one.

Martin: We can't do that Joe cos if we cut the old door off we won't be able to get a new one back on.

Joe: We'll put some cardboard down cos there's holes in it.

Katy: Mmm, yes, it would be stronger then.

Helen: Yes, you can put string through the holes so it will open.

Katy: There's too many holes to do that. You'll get tangled.

Joe: There's a big hole in the actual door bit. You could put a door handle there.

Martin: I know how to make a door handle. You could get those screws like you use on a bath. You could get a screw and screw it on through the other side then you'd have a handle.

Katy: There's a lot of little holes. We could cover those up with cardboard and paint over them and the big hole could be where the handle is.

Helen: Yes, and you could use string to put round the handle and it would hold the door back like the hall door.
           (After this task was completed successfully the children moved on to papering the walls.)

Joe: We'll have to cut the shape there (where the paper overlaps the door), it's too big.

Teacher: Don't cut it. Instead of cutting it fold the paper under and staple it there. That will make the edges stronger than a cut edge and the edges will be smoother. If it's too big you can always fold it, if it's too small you can't make it fit.

Katy goes to stick the wallpaper up in the middle of the wall. The teacher shows her how to place it up against the corner and outside edge. Joe starts to measure the size of the paper needed by placing the metre rule down the centre of the paper. The teacher shows them how to measure the outside edge. The children have measured to find the size of the wallpaper they have to cut from a roll. They measure and cut one piece and stick it on. They need three whole pieces the same size for each wall.

Martin: Start at the next bit now. It's 1 metre 55 centimetres isn't it?
Teacher: That's right. How many pieces do you think we'll need for this wall?
Helen: Two.
Joe: Um, three.
Teacher: Yes, three I think, you'll need the same piece of paper how many times?
Joe and Helen: Three.
Teacher: How about this time then we cut the next piece, then roll out the wallpaper
             again and lay this piece on the top, mark it and cut it to the right size?
Martin: That'll be quicker.

The children are measuring another piece of wallpaper which has to be 1m
20cms long. They lay down a one metre ruler and get another one to continue
measuring. The end of the second ruler gets caught on a nearby cupboard.

Teacher: Do you think we need to measure the next bit with the metre ruler? We've
             got 1 metre, we need our paper to be how much longer?
Katy: 1 metre 20 centimetres we said – um—
Joe: Twenty more.
Teacher: Yes we only need twenty centimetres more. Would it be easier to use a
             smaller ruler? It has centimetres the same as the metre ruler.
Helen: They'd be the same wouldn't they? (doubtfully)
Teacher: Let's try.

Helen picks up the metre ruler and checks to see if her measuring is the same
as the teacher's and then uses the smaller ruler.

Joe: It will be the same, Helen.
Teacher: It's always a good idea to check if you're not sure.

In this example, the involvement of the teacher promotes the development of
new skills, thinking and understanding using the children's existing knowledge
in a meaningful context which has clear purposes and goals. The children were
skilled at such interactions and cooperated well. Some readers may wish to
question whether this activity counts as play since it seems more work-like
than playful. However, the children initiated the task, created the problems
and blended the pretence/reality features of this activity. The children were
'pretending' to renovate the bank and create an art gallery but at the same time
needed 'real world' skills and competences to sustain the pretence. Similarly the
teacher acted as a more knowledgeable other by demonstrating skills, using out-
loud thinking, prompting the children's own thinking and reflecting on action.
The children also assisted each other. Helen was clearly doubtful about the
process of measuring with two rulers and needed to check her understanding
that the metre ruler and the short ruler had the same units of measurement.
The teacher assisted here and Joe confirmed the outcomes to Helen. She was
responsive but not intrusive and the children accepted her presence on this
basis. They brought a lot of energy and motivation to this task and knew that
their efforts would be valued by the other children who were creating their own
works of art to hang in the gallery. This also shows how play and work can
be complementary as children move along a continuum between the two. The

children were transforming ideas, materials and their environment. Play acted as an integrating mechanism for knowledge, experience, social skills and as a spur to further learning.

It is perhaps easier for adults to respond to children's activities in this type of context where there are visible, ongoing opportunities for interaction. Those who are tuned in to children's responses will be able to provide appropriate interactions which help children to consolidate, reflect, refine and extend their competence. Socio-dramatic play poses different problems. Educators may feel most reluctant to intervene in this type of play because of its free flow nature. Probably we have all experienced awful moments when we have intervened in children's play only to kill it dead. Many teachers – both beginning and experienced – report that often they have seen good opportunities for adult involvement but have been constrained by their existing personal theories which dictate that they respect children's privacy and 'ownership'. Or they have forgotten how to play and feel that they need to rediscover these skills in order to enter into the children's play on their terms. This implies that educators need to observe socio-dramatic play to develop their understanding of what the children are playing with and playing at. This will sensitize them to ongoing themes, rules, conventions, groupings, play partners, children's preferences and their use of space and resources. It will also enable them to reflect critically on what kinds of interventions are desirable. These may range from becoming a successful player alongside the children, to helping them structure their own themes, to providing different contexts and resources or a combination of all three. The following example shows how an adult can enter successfully into children's socio-dramatic play. Jenny (age seven years two months) is playing as a nurse in the role play area which has been set up as a health centre. An adult has registered as a patient with an injured ankle:

Adult: Ow, ow, my poor ankle, what shall I do nurse?

Jenny: I think that you should stay in for two days and calm yourself down and stop rubbing it.

Adult: Is it broken nurse? Can I sit down? Ow, ow.

Jenny: Yes, you'd better sit here. I'll go and get the X-ray . . . no you have sprained it. I'm going to bandage it before I water it.

Adult: You're going to water my ankle? Why are you going to water my ankle, nurse, it's not a flower?

Jenny: No I'm going to dab it and then I'll put this bandage on.
       (Begins to put the bandage on over the adult's shoe.)

Adult: Ow, ow. Do you think I should take my shoe off?

Jenny: Oh yes. Nurse come and help me (to another child) . . . you hold the safety pin and give it to me when I've done this.

Adult: Can I walk on my ankle or should I rest it?

Jenny: I'll give you some crutches and when you get home you've got to put it on a stool or table or something soft.

Adult: Do I have to take any tablets for the pain?

Jenny: I'll give you a 'scription (asks for help with writing here).

(Later – to another child who has had a car crash):

Jenny: I'll put the bandage on your arm and you must never put it on the table like that or it'll get even more bad and you can still play football but try not to hit anyone with your hand and be careful you don't cut it when you're washing up. There now, come back in two weeks.

Here the adult's questioning acted as a prompt to reveal Jenny's wide understanding of a nurse's role and related activities. The role play continued for some time and provided the adult with a window into her learning and development. This allowed for some detailed interpretations and assessments of Jenny's skills, knowledge and understanding as the record sheet shows:

Emotional: Jenny is quietly confident and able to organize other children in role play. She showed perception of the caring role of a nurse and sustained this attitude throughout the play.

Social: Takes an organizing role, involves others in the play. Takes turns with equipment and demonstrates skills to others.

Attitudes: Motivated to write and continued in role for an hour. Much enjoyment evident. Sustained concentration throughout the play and was fully absorbed in her role.

Language: Used language for directing, explaining, talking on the telephone, questioning her patients in her role as a nurse. She listened to others before making decisions. Used writing for different purposes – making appointments and writing prescriptions.

Mathematical: Experience of writing appointment times with the help of an adult.

Scientific: Naming parts of the human body (pelvis, hinge joint), knowledge of X-rays and what they are used for.

Physical: Used props for bathing wounds (tweezers and cotton wool), fastening bandages, tying slings. Organized layout of health centre, set up equipment, led patients around.

Problem solving: Organizing one or more play partners, involving other children to help, thinking about caring for the patients and seeing to their injuries.

The teacher was able to identify that Jenny wanted to know more about X-rays and bones and how plaster is used to set broken bones. She needed to develop more confidence in writing for different reasons and in different contexts. This information provided vital feedback into the curriculum to support further learning. It enabled the teacher to see how the area was being used and whether any further resources were needed. The quality of the pretence was supported by the context and the props which had been provided. These were discussed with the children beforehand and the teacher introduced the correct names for the equipment and how it is used.

Jones and Reynolds (1992) identify a variety of roles in children's play. They see the educator as:

- Stage manager
- Planner
- Scribe
- Mediator
- Role model
- Player
- Assessor and communicator.

Adopting these roles enables educators to help children to set their own problems and find their own solutions within a carefully planned but flexible curriculum. They can then support the integrity of children's play with appropriate interactions and interventions rather than interrupt it through intrusive questioning and redirecting. They too need to become skilled players. This applies to all adults who work with young children. Teachers may need to train other adults, including students and parent helpers, how to become involved in children's play, to observe carefully and feed back this information to the team.

Going with the flow of children's ideas will mean accepting the irrational, anarchic and apparently chaotic nature of some types of play – particularly socio-dramatic play. However, as we have argued, there are often internal patterns and consistencies which, over a period of time, can reveal progression in knowledge, skills and understanding. As assessors and communicators, educators can discuss their interpretations with the children, thus assisting in promoting metacognitive awareness. This can be informed by the interpretations and meanings the children create. By these means educators can communicate to children that what they are learning and doing in their play is as valuable as their 'work' in teacher-directed activities. Again this is not an invasion of their private worlds. In this type of context children will readily share their experiences if they know they have an interested audience. Such attitudes can transfer between home and school enabling parents to understand the meaning of play and their role in it. This enables educators to be sensitive to the ways in which children master the cultural tools of school, home and society and how these are integrated in their play. These insights can then inform the recording and reporting process so that parents can see evidence of play in schools as a valuable tool for learning, not as the opposite to work.

In a responsive curriculum, educators will involve children in making decisions about the learning environment, allow them to make choices about the materials they choose to play with and the play themes they wish to develop. This does not imply a completely *laissez-faire* approach. On the contrary, it involves teaching children the skills of decision making, cooperation and metacognition – conscious awareness of their own learning and how they are using the learning environment. It also implies having trust in children's capabilities and potential as well as the confidence in oneself as an educator to experiment and take risks. The structure and content of the curriculum should allow for a balance between play and work, and between child-initiated and adult-directed activities. These should also inform each other so that equal status is given to the different activities. We know this is achievable in practice both from our own and other teachers' experiences of curriculum development. Some strategies for achieving this in practice will be discussed in Chapter 8.

Children learn quickly that educators who value their play and are interested in what they do are good players and will be invited to play in a variety of contexts. This was evident in a nursery class where the nursery nurse had developed these skills successfully. She entered into the children's play on their terms and accepted the roles assigned to her. However, at the same time she developed the ability to energize and inspire the children's play where necessary so that play themes were extended rather than repeated. Her interactional skills blended conversation with 'tutorial dialogue' (Meadows and Cashdan, 1988) which provided a model for the children. Over a period of time, they internalized ways of integrating new players, resolving conflict, planning new themes and making props and resources. These skills did not just emerge spontaneously under favourable conditions. They were an integral part of the curriculum which did not just pay lip service to developing children's autonomy, but provided the structures which enabled this to happen. The role of the adults in this nursery was clearly defined and articulated and was based on a belief in the value of their pedagogical expertise across a range of activities. They recognized the potential value of play as a medium for learning and assisted children in becoming master players. They also knew when to respect the children's privacy so that not intervening was a conscious decision and not a blanket approach. This contrasts with the supervisory and managerial roles which are sometimes adopted in pre-school settings and which can discourage any meaningful engagement with children.

Supporting progression

Hannikainen (1995) argues that the role of the teacher changes qualitatively along with the development of play. Pellegrini and Boyd (1993) state that the common forms of play for each period in early childhood should be the starting point for a curriculum which incorporates play since it is possible that the most common form of play for each period is the most effective instructional strategy. Therefore, as the content and modes of play change, so should the nature of tutoring and styles of interaction. With younger children, the educator may need to initiate, support and maintain the play, particularly where it is new or unfamiliar or children have not yet learned the requisite social or manipulative skills. This is often the case in the home as parents and caregivers teach children how to play in different contexts, what tools and materials are for and how they might be used. They may also create motives and engage interest by playing alongside the child with sensitivity to the child's intentions as well as awareness of the processes involved in peer tutoring.

As we argued in Chapter 4, adults can lead children ahead of their development through sensitive mediation. In this sense they can also model the tools for playing in a variety of contexts. For example, children usually learn how to play board games with a more knowledgeable other since they involve rules and conventions which need to be understood and practised for the game to be successful. For older children these games become increasingly sophisticated as they have to learn to combine strategies, to predict and remember opponents' moves and play to more complex rules.

Similar patterns of learning and development are evident in children's sociodramatic play. Both Hannikainen (1995) and Brostrom (1995) distinguish frame or plot-based role play as a qualitatively different kind of activity from other forms of play. Taking a Vygotskian perspective, they argue that the educator is still important in this type of play, even where the motives arise from the children and much of the negotiation and management can be carried out by them. The main motives for this kind of play are seen as the development of relationships and moral consciousness and the exercise of will. In frame play the teachers and children plan together and the adult is involved in the play activity. The planning stage may include deciding on a play theme, negotiating rules and roles, constructing a plot or text and locating that in a context. The props and accessories may be made in advance and designed by the children and the motive for the play shifts towards the results of the play activity. The educator has a significant role to play here:

> In the arrangement of the frame play the teachers are responsible for encouraging and supporting the children and for promoting a good atmosphere. The children have to formulate the frame themselves. The teachers should support and guide, but they have to be very gentle in the way they make suggestions and introduce play scenarios and ideas for the frame of the play activity. In order to inspire the children to play, the teacher has to take an active part in the play and be genuinely involved. The teacher's role is to support, enrich and expand the play but without exceeding the zone of proximal development.
>
> (Brostrom, 1995, p. 26)

The role of the adult is to respond to the children's initiatives, largely on their terms, and not to take over, direct or control the play to the extent that it loses its spontaneity and becomes teacher- rather than child-centred. This can be problematic for adults who are uncomfortable with a shift in power relationships. On the one hand if this kind of play is seen as a leading activity and, therefore, as revolutionary activity in early childhood it has potential for learning and development. On the other hand, it can be difficult to predict the flow of play, let alone any outcomes. Educators who have forgotten how to play may feel self-conscious about this kind of role and may worry that they might not be able to enter into the play without spoiling it for the children. Using frame play supports progression across a number of domains whilst still allowing for the development of shared meanings derived from the children's imaginations.

As a starting point, it may be useful to set up experimental situations just to see what happens. For example, a student on final teaching practice changed the role play area into a hospital and used group times to introduce the resources, talk about adults' roles, share experiences of going to hospital and read stories. She began one session lying in the hospital with her arm bandaged and in a sling. This simple stimulus enriched the play as the children questioned her about what had happened, discussed what they needed to do and assigned roles to structure the play. The student recognized their competence in this area and did not need to offer support. However, she was able to extend their language and, in terms of their social cognition, noted that they held stereotypical views of girls as nurses and boys as doctors. She challenged these views through inviting visitors to the nursery to talk about their roles and organizing a visit to the local hospital where the children were genuinely surprised to meet male nurses. They were then able to develop their role play with greater accuracy within a curriculum which genuinely tried to incorporate equality of opportunity. Here there was some accommodation between intended learning outcomes and unplanned developments.

Informed structures and interactions will ensure that the children's creativity, imagination and originality are not diminished. Significant opportunities will also be provided for the development of language through play experiences. which Booth (1994, p. 26) regards as essential to language growth:

> Dramatic play takes place in an imaginative frame that depends upon language for its existence. The talk of play shapes and develops themes, encourages cohesion and provides opportunities for meeting individual needs. The interactive feedback by the participants helps them bring together experience and create knowledge as they plan, discuss, support, reject and clarify. The feeling and the challenge of playing roles give the players new ways to gain experience, perception and insight, and enriched language skill is not just a by-product; it grows from the play, because of the play, and structures the play all at once.

Supporting progression is also dependent on the informed choice of resources, not just for children under five but throughout the primary school (including Key Stage 2). We have seen that children develop a need for order, a need for industry, a need to belong. This implies that educators should provide the requisite scaffolding to make this progression possible. This can be achieved in a variety of ways, including play, preferably through a whole school approach which enables children to develop and transfer skills throughout the primary school. Younger children will need a wide range of sensory experiences and tactile equipment as they tend to use exploration and investigation more extensively. Older children will have developed patterns of learning and expectations which will enable them to use, combine and transform materials and ideas in increasingly sophisticated ways. Children between the age of around two to three may need realistic props to develop their dramatic and socio-dramatic play. From around four or five years old children will attach and convey their own meanings through gestures and other symbolic expressions which may or may not be dependent on props. Sensitive resourcing will ensure that all children can progress in their skills as players.

Educators also need to observe how children use resources and what kinds of play themes they act out in their dramatic and socio-dramatic play. Young children engaged in dramatic play may use self-speech to take on a number of roles. They speak and act as if in role and will verbalize the action and plot of the play. This can be seen as a rehearsal for socio-dramatic play in which children have to develop the more complex skills of managing themselves and others in a play sequence. Children will step in and out of the shared fantasy in order to structure, define, negotiate and direct the play sequence. This involves conscious perspective-taking and distancing the need for management and order from the fantasy. Educators need to observe patterns of action and interaction in order to determine which children need help with their social skills to enable them to participate in this type of play and benefit from the learning processes involved. These patterns can also reveal information about friendships, dominant or passive children, who is included or excluded and why. Educators need this information to determine whether all children are experiencing breadth and balance and to ensure equality of opportunity.

Access and equality of opportunity

These are significant issues in early childhood as stereotypical assumptions about race, gender and special educational needs can develop at a young age and persist if not challenged. The National Curriculum is an entitlement curriculum which means that all children should have access to the breadth, balance and relevance it is intended to incorporate. In promoting the spiritual, moral, cultural, mental and physical development of all pupils it reflects the role of schools as major agents of children's socialization. The different curricula offered in the pre-school sector should also reflect these principles. Here we have to acknowledge some limitations. As Smith (1994) argues, both the quality and quantity of pre-school provision are uneven and children may be effectively denied access on the grounds of socio-economic status, ethnicity or special educational needs. If the curriculum offered in different settings is not culturally relevant then children may be further alienated by experiences which reflect a predominantly white culture rather than representing diversity. All educational settings should reflect the fact that we live in a pluralist society and should enable children to function effectively as active citizens both in their present and future lives (Siraj-Blatchford, 1995).

These issues are relevant to young children because from an early age they begin to develop stereotypical and sometimes prejudiced views and attitudes which influence their behaviour towards other people. We know that play provides a means by which children come to understand and master the cultures of home, school and society. So where children are developing negative or stereotypical attitudes, these will be manifested in their play. We also know that children play with powerful concepts such as strength and weakness, good and evil, justice and injustice. Often they use socio-dramatic play in order to feel powerful in an otherwise adult-dominated world. On this basis they include and exclude children on the grounds of race, gender, physical appearance and capabilities. Our belief in childhood innocence is sometimes misplaced since children can be quite cruel in this respect. A group of teachers and nursery nurses on an in-service course were asked to record any discriminatory comments they had heard in their settings. They were surprised to find that many of these arose in children's play and might otherwise have been out of the hearing of an adult. For example, a three year old girl told a friend not to play with the black baby doll because it was dirty.

Some of these attitudes and behaviours may have been acquired at home and many educators feel that it is difficult to challenge them. For example, in looking at gender in the early years, some educators have reported that both boys and girls create 'no-go' areas. Often it is the girls in the role play area who exclude the boys, particularly if it is only resourced as a home corner. Similarly technological and constructive play is sometimes dominated by boys. This is not surprising since, as Garvey (1991) points out, preferences for sex-stereotypic toys and activities begin to appear during the second year of a child's life:

> Despite differences in the values and organization of diverse communities and cultures, these tendencies are virtually universal. Children generally play in same-sex groupings, in childhood a 'best friend' is usually of the same sex, and those who have imaginary playmates even tend to create them in their own image.
>
> (p. 148)

Creating an ethos which promotes access and equality of opportunity obviously requires what Garvey (1991) calls 'the intentional curricular and environmental engineering of caregivers and teachers'. This can be done implicitly in a number of ways through the curriculum, resources and the role modelling of the staff. However, it will sometimes be appropriate to make explicit challenges to comments and behaviour where they may have a negative impact on the self-worth of others or limit children's views of their potential. In socio-dramatic play, for example, children represent their existing knowledge of their own and other people's roles. The type of provision here can either limit or broaden children's perceptions of these roles and their expectations of their future careers. Again the role of the educator is to be sensitive and responsive, to monitor provision and to establish areas where some engineering is both necessary and desirable as the following example shows.

In a primary school with a majority intake of British-Asian children, the teachers noticed that they did not appear to play in the home corner very much. One teacher thought that this was due to cultural differences as the children were encouraged in their homes to value work rather than play. Following an in-service course, they realized that their resources did not reflect what was used in their homes for everyday activities. This led to the teachers buying a range of cooking and serving equipment, recipe books, dressing up clothes and books which were more representative of the children's experiences at home. The quality of the children's play improved dramatically and there were other benefits as parents became more involved in the school and extended teachers' understanding of their culture. As the majority of these children were growing up to be bi-lingual, their early attempts at literacy reflected their ability to learn two different styles of writing. The teachers then came to see this not as a deficit but as a range of competences which needed to be valued and represented in all areas of the curriculum.

It is important to reflect the pluralist nature of society in all school and pre-school settings. In areas where there are few children from ethnic minority groups racism through ignorance is likely to emerge if different cultures and lifestyles are not represented in the curriculum through a wide range of resources. Educators can ensure that they provide positive images of men and women of different racial origins in a variety of roles so that children begin to develop a sense of possibilities rather than limitations for both themselves and others.

This is equally valid for children with special educational needs. In a nursery class, Paul was diagnosed as having dwarfism. Whilst he was with three and four year olds, he did not particularly stand out as different from the others. However, once in the reception class, his short stature became more noticeable. The boys who had been good friends in the nursery started to call him a baby and excluded him from their play. Paul found it increasingly difficult to run and keep up with their playground games. Alternatively, he did not like being cast in the role of the baby by a group of girls who wanted to mother him. Paul had to deal with the knowledge that he was unlikely to grow much taller than 1.5 metres, that his condition would cause decreasing mobility and that he might eventually need a wheelchair. This was quite enough to cope with at the age of five without the negative, isolating comments of peers. The teacher used a variety of strategies to challenge the children's attitudes and to change their negative perceptions of children who appear to be different from the majority. Paul needed to be seen in terms of his capabilities rather than his disabilities. Gradually the children restructured some of their play themes to include Paul. He emerged as a skilful player and often led the play with his vivid imagination and good organizational strategies.

Another child, Lina, arrived at a nursery unable and unwilling to speak, with few social skills and an inability to play. She had been seriously neglected by inadequate parents who left her for long periods of time in a cot with little stimulation. She was quite passive and would just sit watching the other children. The teacher and nursery nurse embarked on a long programme to encourage Lina to play and take part in all the activities in the nursery. This involved some play-tutoring from the adults first in a one-to-one context and then gradually involving other children. After a shaky start Lina gradually learned to communicate and began to interact on her own initiative. It took about a year for her to learn all the social skills which the other children used so competently such as joining a game, taking on and staying in a role, and being able to pretend. Children like Lina show the complexity of learning which is required to become a master player – it is not inevitably the natural prerogative of all children. Often we need to think in terms of small, manageable steps which help children to learn and build their self-confidence at the same time. Moyles (1989) outlines a variety of play contexts which can help to meet children's individual needs. The resources and strategies recommended are dependent on the adult's role in structuring the learning environment, providing materials and creating situations where children can learn to play successfully, cooperate, use imagination and creativity and develop positive attitudes towards themselves and others.

As we have argued it is advisable not to view play through rose-tinted glasses as children can exhibit many anti-social behaviours including insults, threats, bribes, bullying and name-calling. As children get older, they use play to exert their dominance and control and, sometimes, to establish a reputation which may be positive or negative. They also use play to explore the power of language and action to create worlds and transform situations. In some contexts, children can reveal discriminatory behaviour through ignorance of its anti-social nature. But in others, the discrimination can be intentional and may be designed to hurt or to reinforce the dominance of one group or child over others. In Kelly-Byrne's (1989) study, Helen's play revealed themes of fear, aggression and violence as she played out battles between good and evil, beauty and ugliness, smartness and dumbness. Like other children, she was making sense of her own sexuality and relationships within families, between friends and between the sexes. These are powerful feelings and behaviours which some children may not always learn to control and understand in pro-social ways. The lack of opportunity to articulate these feelings in a supportive context can result in behavioural problems which lead further into a negative cycle of difficulties for the child which then impact on peers and adults alike.

For example, on the day that William started nursery he decided that everything in it belonged to him and was for his sole use. He recruited a fellow conspirator, Tom, to help him exclude other children from the activities they wanted to dominate. When playing in the shop they wanted all the money and goods, put them into bags and hid with them under the climbing frame. Similarly in the sand tray they would pile all the sand into one end then protect it with their arms or a pile of equipment. The water tray posed different problems which they surmounted by filling all the available containers, stacking them together at one end and again protecting them from other children. William was protective of his own space, but invasive of other children's space. This extended to hitting, thumping and pushing where he felt threatened. These anti-social behaviours were persistent and, on occasions, extreme and led to William being isolated as the other children disliked his aggression and need for control. This necessitated a home-school programme which involved some play tutoring for the parents and for William so that he received positive attention and reinforcement.

Supporting socio-affective development through play

For a variety of reasons, not all children spontaneously develop understanding of the rules that govern play and social relationships. We have argued here that all school and pre-school settings should be enabling and empowering for children and adults and that there should be a balance between play and work in which child-initiated activities are equally valued. This requires a well-designed curriculum and careful organization so that there is time to attend to children's socio-affective development. Some teachers report that this is an area which they feel is neglected as the National Curriculum focuses predominantly on the prescribed content coverage. Feinburg and Mindess (1994) suggest that there are three main areas which educators need to attend to in order to develop a cognitive approach to the socio-affective domain:

1. Helping children to deal with their own and others' feelings
* encouraging children to express their ideas about affective issues
* focusing children's attention on negative as well as positive feelings
* accepting children's comments
* encouraging children to listen to one another
* recording children's reactions
* developing plans that elicit children's expressions of feelings
* observing and listening to children's spontaneous comments
* structuring neutral discussions; deflecting attention from particular children
* helping children generate many alternative suggestions
* helping children recognize the importance of feelings in making decisions
* engaging children in hypothetical decision making
* providing opportunities for children to label and express feelings

2. Helping children to understand similarities and differences among people
* deliberately planning experiences that call attention to differences as well as similarities among people
* setting up an environment in which children can discover and raise issues about similarities and differences
* integrating into all aspects of the curriculum a focus on the ways in which people are similar and different
* continually expanding their understanding about differences within the group and sharing this understanding with children in a variety of ways

3. Encouraging the development of friendship-making skills by helping children to
* listen to and observe others
* be able to read the behaviour of others
* know how to join an ongoing activity
* be able to negotiate conflict
* initiate contact

- handle rejections
- sustain a relationship
- express empathy
- give feedback
- provide ideas or build on the ideas of others
- engage in discussion of specific behaviours and social skills.

This model is based on negotiation and reciprocity between teachers and learners which help to build an ethos of trust and respect. Many of the skills which Feinburg and Mindess see as essential can be embedded within play, particularly where there are opportunities for children to feed back what they have achieved in play or what problems emerged which need to be resolved. These problems may be of an interpersonal, social nature and require conscious reflection on action, feelings and behaviours for resolutions to be formulated.

The strategies outlined here provide a framework for educators to use their observations of children's socio-affective skills, behaviours and dispositions to structure experiences which can provide a bridge between play and adult-directed activities. These can take place within circle time, at story time or during dance and drama sessions where children can learn to express their feelings through different media. Stories (both fact and fiction) and poems can be selected to explore feelings and situations and to encourage children's emotional literacy. These can also be used as a theme for structuring role play. For example, a reception class teacher noticed that the home corner was used in a repetitive, stereotypical way, mostly by girls. She used the story of Jack and the Beanstalk to extend and enrich the children's play. They were involved in planning the new setting, designing and making some of the resources, making suggestions for representing ideas in the story. The giant's treasure chest was filled with milk bottle tops and a variety of things that the children brought from home. A three dimensional beanstalk was made which wandered up the walls and across the ceiling. The teacher added many other resources such as different sizes of clothes and cooking equipment to contrast Jack's home with the giant's home. Because the children were involved in planning and decision making, interpersonal skills were developed such as negotiation, cooperation, establishing rules, taking responsibility for looking after the props and resources. Time and opportunities were made for adult involvement, though not as much as the teacher would have liked, and the children were encouraged to talk about their play, add further resources and develop the theme as they wished. This model was both enabling and empowering. It allowed children to have 'ownership' of their play but at the same time the teacher felt that they were enjoying higher quality play with many opportunities for learning that were embedded in a meaningful context.

Extending play

Many educators on in-service courses express some dilemmas about intervening in children's play in order to move it forward. On the one hand we know that practice, repetition and rehearsal are important cognitive processes which assist in learning, memorizing, consolidating and making connections. On the other hand, children may get into a repetitive rut because they do not know what else to do, what other combinations to develop, what further possibilities exist. We cannot take it for granted that all children develop rich and varied imaginations which they are able to use spontaneously in their play. Again some scaffolding by the adult may be necessary to form the building blocks of creativity and imagination. In one school which used a modified High/Scope approach, six year old Paul had planned to use the Lego every day for five weeks. Moreover, he invariably chose to play on his own and frequently made similar models on a space/Star Wars theme which he acted out by himself. The dilemma for the teacher here was respecting Paul's choices and independence, but at the same time recognizing that there were other valuable activities which he was not experiencing. This was further complicated by the underlying High/Scope philosophy which argues that what children do is what they need. In Athey's (1990) terms, Paul may have been working through a number of connecting schemas.

Here the teacher's expertise led her to intervene in a variety of ways. Paul was encouraged to bring in his collection of Star Wars resources which immediately attracted the interest of other children. This led to designing space ships and space stations and using other resources to create a miniature world. These were used as the stimulus to developing fantasy play themes so that Paul was gradually drawn into socio-dramatic play and learnt to share his ideas and resources. However, another dilemma arose for the teacher as this group consisted exclusively of boys. She was prepared to accept this as a valid means to an end for Paul but ensured that other aspects of provision were used by both boys and girls.

The problem of repetition can arise for children with special educational needs. Where there is some form of learning impairment, repetition may be necessary to form and consolidate internal cognitive structures and pathways. Often children will feel safe with the known rather than the unfamiliar. Too much challenge may lead to distress and inhibit learning. Here educators should try to ensure that similar skills can be practised in a variety of contexts.

There is a tendency to assume that the need to play declines beyond the age of five. Many of the examples we have used in this book are based on observations of older children and indicate how the richness and complexity of their play develops rather than diminishes as they gain greater confidence in their skills, knowledge and a sense of their own competences and identities. Far from assuming that children outgrow the need to play, we need to assess carefully how we can support their development as master players.

We have argued that play in school and pre-school settings should be qualitatively different from play as such. The role of educators in this process is fundamental to developing high quality play experiences. This requires conscious planning, organization, observation, reflection and a willingness to be flexible and responsive. If early childhood practitioners make claims for the potential of play as a learning medium then the onus is on them to demonstrate this through their practice. If, on the other hand, other pressures mean that play can only be used as a time-filler with little or no connection to the curriculum then this should be stated honestly. Alternatively, the curriculum could be redesigned to ensure that play becomes more closely integrated in the curriculum using the structures and strategies outlined here. In the next chapter we will examine how assessment, recording and reporting can be used as a means to developing play and communicating its role and value to parents and other professionals.

7

Assessing Children's Learning in Play

The processes of assessment and evaluation provide the feedback and feedforward which are essential to understanding children's learning and development and the effectiveness of the curriculum offered. In any educational setting these processes apply equally to play, particularly where it is a leading source of activity and experience in the pre-school phase. Assessment and evaluation can be seen as complementary processes by which educators make judgments and interpretations about learning and development which then provide information about the effectiveness of the curriculum. For all children play can provide a window into their minds which reveals structures, patterns and meanings that may not be evident in more formal or adult-directed contexts. The information gleaned from children's play can assist educators in the fine tuning process which enables them to interpret the relationship between the planned curriculum and how it is received by the children. This awareness provides educators with a framework for evaluation through which they can explore strategies for improvement and development. These structures promote reciprocity between educators and learners and create a curriculum which is based upon informed perceptions rather than uncritical assumptions.

In Chapter 1 we argued that there are certain problems in assessing children's learning through play. First it may not be taken seriously by educators who fail to realize its potential as a medium for learning, or by those who relegate play to the margins of the school day and regard it as an occupying activity rather than as an integral part of the curriculum. Second, play bears little resemblance to what it may lead to in later childhood, although there is increasing evidence which indicates some of these important connections. Third, deep and serious play is 'playing with fire' and tends not to sit comfortably in school contexts. Much of children's play is unpredictable, which can make it difficult for educators to define precise learning outcomes. Finally there are hierarchies of good play or bad play which reflect adults' value judgments about what is educationally worthwhile. We cannot resolve these tensions and dilemmas through the arguments presented here as educators have to address their own beliefs and values about play. But we can offer strategies and insights which may enable educators to develop and improve their practice. In this chapter we will look at the rationale and strategies for assessment and evaluation. Case studies of children's play will show how these strategies can be used, the range of information which can be obtained through observation and interaction and how this can be recorded and reported to parents and other professionals.

The assessment process

In all pre-school and school settings, assessment needs to be formative, summative, diagnostic, evaluative and informative. The purpose of formative assessment is to provide educators with information about a child's progress so that decisions can be made about learning styles, aptitudes, interests, needs and any emerging problems. Diagnostic assessment goes a stage further and enables educators to identify matters for concern and to plan future tasks which are carefully matched to a child's learning styles and existing strengths. Summative assessments give a snapshot of evidence of attainment at a particular point in time such as a baseline assessment on entry to school or through Standard Attainment Tasks at the end of Key Stage 1. The evaluative and informative aspects of assessment provide the essential feedback and feedforward which can be used to promote critical reflection on practice and provide evidence for recording and reporting to parents and other professionals.

The role of the educator is critical in the assessment process since it can be argued that this is the starting point for curriculum design. This is complex in relation to play as its unpredictable, free-flow nature creates certain dilemmas for educators. First, they may set up a play activity with specific learning outcomes in mind. For example, the water tray may be resourced with equipment to develop understanding of floating and sinking. Or the role play area may be designed around a theme such as a hospital, different types of shops or a café. Children may be expected to play in certain ways, to use the resources as anticipated by the educators, to apply and develop their existing skills and knowledge.

These are all legitimate approaches as long as educators strive not to control children's play according to narrowly defined outcomes but to extend and enrich it. The problem is that research evidence suggests that children do not always play according to the adult's intentions. In a study by Bennett, Wood and Rogers (1996) reception class teachers selected episodes of play to be video-recorded and then reflected on the action observed. In many cases, the teachers were surprised to find that the children did not play in the ways that they had anticipated or intended. For example, one teacher set up a shop to extend the children's understanding of money in a meaningful context. She reported that the children played burglaries which resulted in the cops and robbers chasing around the classroom. This reflects the reality that when role play begins the structure of play changes as the children determine the theme, assign roles, and attach meanings to props and actions. The dilemma for the teacher here was that the children's ongoing interests and cognitive concerns were at odds with her perceptions of what was educationally valuable This is exactly the sort of play that Bruner identified as being in conflict with teachers' outcomes since it is not easy to accommodate in an organized setting where a range of activities have to co-exist within enabling but realistic frameworks.

Clearly educators have to maintain a balancing act between their intentions, children's intentions and children's meanings. As we have shown, Reception and Key Stage 1 teachers also operate within different constraints from their pre-school colleagues. Hence, as we have argued, the nature of play 'in schools' will be qualitatively different from play 'as such'. The assessment process can enable educators to track learning and development and to provide valuable evidence for reporting and recording which demonstrates how play is qualitatively different and in what ways it can be perceived as educationally worthwhile.

In determining the relationship between play, learning and development, the critical questions are: what actually happens inside children's heads when they play? How do they become 'master players' and successful learners? What are the children doing which is of value and interest to them in the immediate term, and may be of relevance in the longer term? We have seen that play is a complex activity which integrates many different processes and, potentially, has a wide range of possible outcomes. Sometimes the outcomes can be enjoyment, peer group affiliation or status, rehearsal and repetition leading to mastery and control, or just fun and relaxation. In our experience it is not unusual to identify tangible instances in which children learnt or realized something new in their play. Clearly both processes and outcomes are important indicators of the value of play.

Educational settings make many demands on the educators' skills and time: 'The very conditions of classroom life, the complexity of classroom events, the interconnectedness of context and curriculum, of teaching and learning, all make it harder for us to look at learning as closely as we would wish' (Drummond, 1993, p. 17).

Therefore the challenge for educators is to create a framework in which they can make sense of play and learning through careful analysis and interpretation of the children's actions, interactions, choices, preferences, repeated play themes and ongoing cognitive concerns. Good home-school links will also enable educators to make connections between wider experiences. This valuable information can then feedback into the cycle of curriculum planning through effective diagnosis of children's abilities and difficulties. Collecting evidence of learning in play can also serve the purpose of demonstrating to colleagues and parents the value and purposes of play experiences and their relationship to other areas of the curriculum. In striving to promote play as an indicator of quality in early childhood education, this must be seen as a pragmatic and desirable direction for practitioners. It implies responsiveness and reciprocity, rather than an instrumental exploitation of play as a means to fulfilling narrow educational ends.

Guiding principles

Because play reveals patterns of learning, thinking and understanding in the three domains of development as well as in the subject disciplines, it needs to be brought within the framework of assessment, recording and reporting. In this way, educators have an ongoing record of learning and development which can be shared with parents and caregivers and can provide the basis for informed statements about a child's progress. At a broad level, Cleave and Brown (1991) suggest the following strategies for four year olds in school which could be applied to all settings:

- Monitoring and record-keeping procedures should take account of the whole child: physical, social, emotional and cognitive.
- All schools should have procedures for monitoring progress throughout the school with a shared common language.
- Monitoring procedures must take account of the diversity of young children's development and pre-school experience.
- Monitoring should be a continuous process, carried out by observation during the course of children's normal activities.
- Monitoring should be team-based involving nursery nurses, ancillary helpers, the parents and the child.
- Good record-keeping is essential both to evaluate the curriculum and to assess the children's progress; the emphasis should be on the child's own progress rather than on the child's position in relation to other children.
- The purposes of records, who will have access to them and the uses to which they will be put, should be made clear to all involved.

(1991, p. 251)

Setting up an integrated system which is based on sharing and communicating perceptions requires a great deal of effort and indicates how assessment has to be planned for as an integral part of the ongoing daily activities, including play. Some schools have adopted a whole school approach, sometimes with the support of LEA guidelines. Many have also made valuable links on their own initiative with feeder nurseries and playgroup settings to establish a common language, share perceptions and enhance continuity of learning and experience. However, such initiatives are by no means uniform and there are settings which do not make any provision at all for assessment, evaluation, recording or reporting. Where this is the case, the daily activities may do little more than keep children occupied and contained. One teacher described the private nursery in which she worked as little more than a 'dump and run' establishment where parents paid little attention to the quality of the curriculum offered and did not expect any feedback of the children's experiences or development.

At a more detailed level Dowling (1992) suggests that educators need to set up situations for assessment which look at the child's abilities and transfer-abilities. In the fast-changing complexities of pre-school and school settings, it is all too easy to become bombarded with an unmanageable amount of information. The following strategies may help to deal with this problem:

- Look at the context for assessment. What possibilities exist and what types of assessment are going to be made?
- What is the best way to gather evidence of learning – through observation, interaction, video- or audio-recording?
- What, if any, are the intended learning outcomes for the activity? Focus on these at first in order to assess if there is a match between intentions and outcomes, where appropriate.
- What are the possible learning outcomes? Be aware of the scope for divergence, for example in role play. This will be informed by the educator's understanding of the nature of the activity and the prior experience of the child/children.
- How did the activity develop and what opportunities for assessment were presented as a result?
- Track evidence of learning across a variety of activities in order to check how the child is using, applying and transferring knowledge and skills between different contexts.
- Track evidence of learning over a period of time in order to understand patterns of learning and ongoing cognitive concerns.
- Share observations with other team members, including helpers and students, to share, validate or challenge perceptions. Share observations with parents and caregivers.
- Use assessments for summative, formative and diagnostic purposes – where is this child at and where might he or she usefully go next?
- Feed this information back into the next cycle of planning (short-, medium- and long-term).

By using formative, summative, diagnostic and evaluative approaches to assessment across a range of activities the underlying processes of learning can be identified. The three levels of understanding play presented in Chapter 5 can provide a useful framework for looking at the detailed content of children's play. Educators can also attend to the form and content of their thinking, as suggested by Athey (1990) and Nutbrown (1994). The nature of children's thinking and learning, their areas of strength and weakness can be analysed to provide information about their capabilities, interests, attitudes and dispositions. This holistic approach to assessment enables educators to provide challenging activities and experiences and to plan for continuity and progression.

If assessment is to serve these purposes, educators need to make time and liberate themselves from the guilt of standing back and observing, where necessary. Skilled observers will do this whilst interacting with children but will still need time to reflect on and make sense of the observations, and then discuss these within the team. Looking at the progress of each individual child is also important. For example, Peter, who had cerebral palsy, often made small but steady advances in his physical development as he struggled to control his involuntary movements. Yet these small steps were immensely significant and represented a great deal of effort and concentration. When Peter was four, his child development profile from the hospital showed up mainly what he could not do in relation to standardized assessments based on 'developmental norms' for 'typical' four year olds. But his detailed nursery profile, supplemented by videos, gave a different picture of Peter's capabilities, as well as the strategies and willpower he used to overcome his disability. This assessment was ipsitive – based on Peter's individual rates of progress.

Although we have shown here that learning is both recursive and incremental, characterized by Bruner as a spiral, the processes involved are not even, inevitable or predictably sequenced. Children have difficulties and setbacks, fallow periods, or may even appear to regress, especially if experiencing stress. The framework for analysis which Moyles presents is useful for building up a profile which links the child, context and curriculum and provides valuable evidence of attitudes and dispositions:

- child's activity
- attitude to the task
- self-initiation and responsibility
- learning – concepts, skills and processes
- application of earlier learning
- communication
- cooperative learning
- teacher intervention.

(1989, p. 101)

She also argues that assessment can provide information about the balance of activities which links with Norman's model of learning outlined in Chapter 3. Educators need to ensure that their provision allows for:

- incremental tasks
- restructuring tasks
- enrichment tasks
- practice skills
- revision.

(Moyles, 1989, p. 102)

Tracking the nature and purposes of teacher intervention can provide information about the effectiveness of the adult's role.

If educators have a coherent, shared framework for assessment it can make the process easier and more meaningful, and can provide the evidence on which to base further planning. This means establishing overall aims and underlying principles for assessment, as well as clarifying intended and possible learning outcomes for a variety of play situations. This can provide evidence of learning, progression and whether there is an accurate match between the children and the curriculum offered. A critical question when considering the assessment process is – does it do justice to the children? And, in the context of play, does it do justice to their self-initiated activities? In order to answer these questions, educators need to engage in participant and non-participant observations across a range of play activities:

1. When children are playing alone.
2. When they are playing together.
3. When they are involved with an adult.

They need to be sensitive to:

1. How individual children are spending their time.
2. The children's interests and attitudes to learning.
3. The knowledge, skills and understanding that the children demonstrate as they are purposefully engaged in self-initiated activities.

Drummond (1993) suggests that assessment should be part of an act of understanding and that, rather then being confined to what the children say and do, it should be informed by deeper questions and a broader vision: 'Starting to ask questions about children's learning, however precise or trivial they may seem, is always the start of something big. It may even be the beginning of a life-long enquiry into teaching, learning and the curriculum' (p. 16).

Regarding assessment as a process of enquiry can stimulate reflective approaches to teaching and learning which help educators to improve the quality of the curriculum offered.

One of the problems when assessing children's learning through play is that it is often difficult to be sure whether the play activity itself has stimulated new learning, whether it is providing a context for mastery and revision, or whether it enables children to reveal what they already know, can do and understand. There is no easy prescription to resolve this dilemma other than through sensitive adult interactions, careful observation and a framework for discussing observations within the team (where possible), raising questions, and sharing interpretations. Just as educators have to be sensitive to children's meanings in their play, they have to attend to the meanings and interpretations they then construct and their implications for further planning. Through these processes, educators will track patterns of children's interests and learning but will also become more knowledgeable about the value of different types of play to different aspects of learning and development. If we accept the argument that play changes as children get older, then educators need to plan for change and progression. Sand and water trays may not be necessary for six and seven year olds, but a variety of challenging games, puzzles, technological construction kits and opportunities for socio-dramatic play will be desirable. Curriculum planning should be informed through insights and reliable predictions of potential learning outcomes across the domains of development and the subject disciplines.

Recording and reporting

If assessment is to serve these important purposes, there needs to be some way of recording educators' observations and interpretations of children's learning and development through play. Recording enables educators to:

- collect evidence over a period of time
- look for patterns, meanings, interests and ongoing cognitive concerns
- identify learning processes evident in play
- identify learning that connects children with subject matter knowledge
- develop understanding of how these processes can be extended through a range of activities which challenge children's thinking and action
- share these insights with team members, parents, caregivers and other professionals involved with a child
- use these insights to design further activities and experiences
- provide evidence for reflection, evaluation and curriculum/staff development.

The problems here are: how much should be written down, what forms of evidence should be collected and how can adults' interpretations be reliable and informative? These issues need to be resolved so that assessment and recording can be seen as ongoing, integral processes which contribute to a meaningful dialogue at the reporting stages. Where educators work as part of a team, all should be involved in collecting evidence of the children's learning. Parent helpers, students and teaching assistants can be encouraged to contribute. These strategies have been used successfully by practitioners.

- Slips of paper or sticky 'post-it' labels for writing down notes of significant events which are then put into a folder or on a display board and analysed at the end of the day or week.
- A daily diary for the same purpose. In both cases, fuller notes are written into a child's developmental profile or record of achievement.
- Summary accounts of significant events and developments with an action plan to inform further provision.
- Selected examples of the 'products' of children's play – layouts, drawings, paintings, emergent writing, constructions, plans, photographs of dramatic and socio-dramatic play, both indoors and outdoors. These should be annotated to indicate their significance again with a view to sharing them within the team and with parents.
- Audio and video recordings where possible. These can be particularly useful for children with special educational needs where detailed evidence is needed for further reflection. It can also be interesting for children to watch videos of themselves playing and to give their own account and interpretations. Again this information can be shared with parents and caregivers.
- Tick lists to provide a summary of what has been covered and achieved by each child. These should always be supplemented by written notes to

provide more detailed evidence of the contexts in which children are able to use and transfer their skills, knowledge and understanding. They can also be used to identify any significant gaps in a child's experience to ensure breadth and balance.

- A statement of intended outcomes for each area of learning, for example, literacy, mathematics, science, social/emotional development, psycho-motor development.
- Records of planning to show how these learning outcomes are integrated in play.
- Children's planning books. It can be useful to annotate these occasionally to record how the plans were implemented and what were the outcomes.

We are not advocating a system in which adults constantly maraud around children's play in ways which are invasive or destroy its spontaneity. Sensitive educators will learn to recognize and respect children's rights to privacy. Even observation can be intrusive and make children self-conscious about their play. Audio and video recordings may be useful in some situations as they extend the possibilities for assessment without the presence of an adult. Insights can be gained into children's thinking and learning while they are actively engaged in play without an adult's support. These can be contrasted with play with adult support where educators can reflect on their roles and interactive skills. These holistic forms of assessment and recording reveal information about children's attitudes and dispositions, motivation, creativity, imagination, interests and interpersonal relationships as well as their ability to transfer skills and knowledge within and between different contexts. Educators need to build up and communicate a clear, accurate picture of children's competences across a wide range of activities and social situations to create a developmental profile. This will enable them to make meaningful connections between child-initiated and adult-directed activities so that work and play are not seen as separate or differently valued. Such evidence will also enable educators to identify where children are connecting with disciplined ways of knowing so that a profile can include information about learning in the subject disciplines. For example, a good literacy profile will track learning and development in speaking, listening, reading and writing and will identify significant stages across the early years age range. Similarly Wood and Holden (1995) outline a pre-school profile for the development of young children's learning in history and give examples of how this can be supported through play.

Most schools now have a ringbinder for each child's record of achievement. Children often select which pieces of work should be entered with their own comments about why it was particularly significant. This could easily include examples of the products of children's play which we noted above. In our experience, the children also enjoy looking through their profiles as an *aide mémoire* to what they have achieved in their play during the year and how they have developed. This activity can help to promote metacognition as the children can often see progression in their learning, skills and interests. These folders could be started at the pre-school stage and transferred between settings. They can also provide a link between learning at home and in school with parents and caregivers making contributions. This system can help to sensitize educators to any cultural differences which need to be represented in the curriculum and can help parents and caregivers to value their role in children's play.

Any annotations need to indicate the significance of the examples included. The language used should refer specifically to learning processes, attitudes and dispositions and subject matter knowledge where these can be identified. For example:

Jodie *investigated* the water wheel. She *discovered* that she could make it turn fast or slow with the amount of water poured. She *inquired* whether it would work with sand. She *tested* her idea and *described* to the group what she had *learnt*.

Kamal *decided* to *design* a board game. He *drew* a plan and *wrote* some rules. He *discussed* his idea with a friend and they *collaborated* to achieve a joint goal. They *decided* on appropriate materials and *planned* the sequence for making the game. They used pictures and writing in the game and to convey the rules to the players, *showing awareness of purpose and audience*. They *persevered*, showed *intrinsic motivation* and *concentration*. They *tested* the game, *evaluated* it and *revised* the design in response to suggestions from peers.

Andrew *enjoyed* playing in the post office. He *pretended* to be the postman. He *sorted* the parcels into different sizes and *learnt* how to weigh them. He *learnt* that heavy parcels cost more. He *decided* to send letters to his friends and *requested help* with writing their names. He *referred* to the dictionary to help with spellings. He *stayed in role* throughout the session. He *identified a need* for a larger post box and *planned* to make one next session.

Sean and Joanne *played cooperatively* with the playdough. They both rolled out sausages and *used comparative mathematical language* (fat/thin, fattest/thinnest, long/short, longest/shortest). They *transformed* the sausages into shapes – triangle, oblong, square. Joanne said 'This is a round'. Sean *told* her it was a circle. Joanne *applied* the word subsequently. They *transformed* the shapes into wiggly worms and *decided* to mould different sized 'houses'. They *matched* the worms to the houses and spontaneously *created* a story about them.

Focusing attention on the quality of language used in framing assessments and diagnoses can enable educators to avoid banal descriptions and to give more rigorous accounts of the breadth and complexity of children's learning and development through play.

Collecting and interpreting evidence

The following examples indicate the type of evidence which can be collected through different methods and how it can be recorded. The observations were carried out in a local authority funded Play Project in a nursery and infant

Name:	DoB	Date
Child		
Context		
Curriculum		
Emotional		
Social		
Language/literacy		
Mathematical		
Scientific		
Physical		
Manipulative		
Problem solving		
Drama/role play		
Attitudes and dispositions:		
Concentration		
Motivation		
Curiosity		

Figure 16   Recording evidence of learning

school in the south-west of England (Attfield, 1992). These were supplemented by tape recordings of children's play with and without an adult present. The intention was to demonstrate the opportunities for assessing children's learning and development through a wide variety of play activities. The record sheet (Figure 16) was adapted from Manning and Sharp (1977) and was designed to show evidence of learning in the three core subjects of the National Curriculum as all the children in the study were in Key Stage 1. It also includes information in other domains of learning and development which contributes to a holistic picture of each child. This format could be adapted to include other areas of learning and experience or subject disciplines.

VERNON (1)
Child: Vernon is seven years old, quiet, self-contained, knows the rules and works calmly and methodically. He considers problems thoughtfully.

Context: Play in the café with a group of Year 1 and 2 children. The teacher participates for some of the time. Vernon organizes the area, prepares food, serves customers, clears away and stays for the session (one hour).

Curriculum

Language: Initially very quiet. Responds to the teacher, joins in and begins to participate in talk. Needs encouragement to talk to customers and ask for their orders. Writes the menu competently.

Maths: Very able and becomes animated when dealing with money. Adds and subtracts in his head. Makes sure transactions are correct, attends to all the money handling rather than serving the customers. Practises known skills. Teacher observation shows he can work out change from 50p in his head and add amounts totalling £2.05. Knows concept of half but unsure of quarters.

Science: Food preparation – cheese grating, noticed spreading, heating, melting. 'It's not easy to grate, it's a bit soft and squidgy'. Washing up – noticed bubbles and the effects of soap on grease which he discussed with the adult present.

Problem solving: Sandwiches are 10p. How many can Helen have for 30p? Gives correct answer. Teacher extends – There are three sandwiches left and four customers so what are you going to do? Vernon answers 'Cut them in half'. Clearly enjoys money and mathematical problems.

Social skills: Vernon comes to the café alone and then is joined by two other children. Doesn't become involved with them and attends to tasks alone. Social interaction develops while preparing food with teacher and children, and when serving customers. Seemed to need the support of the teacher to become involved. Engages in role play towards the end when he takes on the role of manager at a child's suggestion.

Attitudes/dispositions: Well-motivated to organize the money and add up the profits at the end. Shows concentration by involving himself in the money transactions. Likes helping others with problem solving involving money and is encouraged by the teacher. Shows curiosity about other foods – grating apples – 'they'd be hard'. Is well organized, independent, lays the table correctly and clears up afterwards.

Intervention and extension: Teacher participates and encourages social interaction, extends money/problem-solving/thinking skills directly from a meaningful context and in response to problems set by Vernon – 'If we cut a whole sandwich into four pieces we call each piece a quarter'. Needs further experiences in these areas, both child-initiated and teacher-directed.

VERNON (2)
Context: He chooses to play in the post office. The teacher participates for some of the time. He then becomes an assistant in the toy shop.

Curriculum

Language: Speaks clearly and confidently in role and out – 'You need more money than that for the café'. Listens to what customers say. Re-labels two parcels. Gives directions and explanations to Sally in the toy shop.

Mathematical: Experience of units of weight extended with teacher in the post office. Familiar with kilograms, needs help with accurate weighing of parcels – 'I haven't done this yet'. In the toy shop he adds up the total cost of four items in his head correctly to 23p, gives correct change from 50p. Can count in 2s, 5s, 10s. Enjoys giving change, counts on, shows Sally how to do this, then gets stuck with change from £1.

Problem solving: Sally gets stuck with money skills and a queue forms outside the shop. Vernon first helps Sally, then asks customers to make two queues – 'I can serve them quickly . . . my Mum gets cross if she hangs around'.

Attitudes/dispositions: Vernon is well-motivated. His maths skills are valued and praised by the teacher and other children. This makes him even keener to use them to help others. His concentration is consistent. Vernon remembers and recalls his own skills with money and uses these in a meaningful context. Able to connect his own knowledge of weight to a new context with teacher support. Shows curiosity about weighing parcels. He acts out the role of a shop worker but stays as himself. He organizes the area well, sorts money efficiently and plans space for a display of toys in the shop.

The following accounts are based on the observations carried out by the teacher and give evidence of the children's learning on which the assessments are based. This format could be used to build up a child's profile, supplemented by check lists or reference to the National Curriculum level descriptions.

1. Account of play

Vernon and John choose to play in Mr Fixit's Repair shop. They use screwdrivers to undo the top part of a record player and examine it, take the face and back off a clock and examine the cog wheels and gear teeth. Very enthusiastic and interested in movement. Teacher intervenes to continue the development of interest and knowledge about cogs, then directs them to a construction kit – Capsela – where the movement of the parts depends on gear wheels and cogs. Vernon and John explore the apparatus and make a simple model. They talk about this at review time.

Indications of understanding

The boys have some knowledge and experience of wheels and cogs. Vernon explained how the meshing of teeth created movement. Development of speaking and listening with extension of vocabulary. They designed their own model with Capsela and, through practical activity, gained experience of putting together a working model using cogs and wheels. Able to investigate:

Teacher: Why does the propeller on your model go round without touching it?
Vernon: The handle moves this wheel and the cogs are all touching it so it moves
the next one. The teeth have to touch each other to make them move.

2. Account of play

Vernon plays alone with the construction kit 'Lasy'. He is making a Thunderbird car. Alec asks to help. The collaboration of ideas leads to a large model
which has many functions. They play with the materials, language and roles.
Vernon and Alec become Thunderbird characters, transform the model to a
spaceship, then become astronauts and pilots. The final model is a vehicle
which they show at review time and explain its functions.

Indications of understanding
Development of language – speaking and listening skills. Free play allowed,
exploration and experimentation with materials and development of creativity
through language and representation. Vernon talked a lot, offered ideas, information, knowledge of materials, suggested alternatives, asked Alec questions,
acted out fantasy situations. Showed competence with problem solving, able
to evaluate and adapt a design to suit a particular purpose. They both used
mathematical terms – shape and size – confidently. Extension of vocabulary:

Vernon.   This is where the look out stands. He looks through a watcher.
Teacher: Do you mean a telescope?
Vernon: Yes, a telescope.

3. Account of play

Vernon makes a model car from Capsela. His friend James has made one
from Ludoval. They push the cars along the floor to see which one will
go furthest. The teacher participates to extend thinking and observe the
investigation, to assess measuring skills and their understanding of the concept
of a 'fair test'. They investigate which vehicle goes furthest. They are joined by
two more children with different vehicles and discuss the outcomes.

Indications of understanding
Development of speaking and listening, explaining, reporting, discussing,
questioning. Use of mathematical language in context including length, shape,
size, weight, comparisons between vehicles. Vernon chose to measure in
footsteps, James suggested cubes. The teacher accepted the non-standard unit
of footprints but raised questions about whose footprints should be used and
was it a fair test. This led to the suggestion that a standard metre rule should be
used. Vernon indicated his understanding of a fair test and shared ideas about
factors affecting the movement of vehicles.

The following transcript shows the evidence on which the teacher's assessments
were based.

Teacher: Are you going to find out something?

James: We're seeing which one goes the further. Mine's a rocket car, it keeps stopping though, Vernon's just crashed.

Teacher: Let's go over here where there's more space. Now, which one goes the furthest? How can we be sure it's fair, do you think? Where shall we start them from?

Vernon: It's got to be the same place. They've got to be level.

Teacher: Yes, good, otherwise it wouldn't be fair, would it, if one started in front of the other? Shall we make a start line with something? . . . What would happen if I pushed it?

Vernon: It would go more further.

James: Cos you're bigger.

Vernon: Your hand's bigger, you can push harder.

Teacher: So would that be fair?

James and Vernon: No.

Teacher: How about when you push your cars? Do you think you push the same as each other?

James: Vernon's a bit bigger than me. I don't know.

Vernon: I know, I could push his car and he could push my car and then we could see.

It was decided that to get a fair test Vernon could push both cars and then James would do the same. They also checked they were using the same hands as they thought a left hand and right hand push might make a difference. The teacher then suggested that they test to see which car goes further starting off from a ramp.

Teacher: Suppose we run the cars down a slope this time and see which one goes the furthest.

James and Vernon: Yes.

Vernon: Make the board go up more. Mine will go a long way.

Teacher: Do we need to push the cars?

James: They go more longer.

Teacher: Let's just start by letting them go, then it will be fair because no one is using a push. Make sure the back wheels are at the top and just let them go down. Will that be fair?

James and Vernon: Yes.

Other children then joined in so that there were four different types of cars to see which one went furthest. Through testing, observing and talking the children suggested factors that might affect the distance the cars travelled.

Sally: Mine won't go straight.

Kevin: The wheel's loose.

Vernon: I think it's all the weight.

James: It's the clipper on the rockets at the back, they're touching the floor.

Vernon: Mine's got more weight.

Kevin: Sally's got faster wheels than mine.

Vernon: They're bigger . . . got more plastic.

James: This wheel's sticking out, it needs a stopper.

Vernon: Put the smooth tyres on.
Kevin: We could put a technic motor on then it would go furthest.
Sally: My Dad's Landrover's got bumpy tyres.

This activity continued for some time with the teacher extending the children's understanding of concepts of friction, forces and fair testing. On the basis of the evidence collected of Vernon's play experiences, the teacher was able to make ongoing formative and diagnostic assessments as well as a summative assessment at the end of the year which indicated his levels of attainment in the core subjects of the National Curriculum.

HELEN
Child: Helen is six years seven months.

Context: Street play – vegetable shop and cottage.

Curriculum

Language: Talked about money with Claire, the shopkeeper. Helen corrected Claire, who was overcharging her. Talked with teacher about parks for children and made a list of the play equipment she would like in the park.

Maths: Handling money, counting, giving change. This was extended by teacher intervention.

Science/design technology: Suggests ideas for making play equipment, relates to materials, safety and weather. Dresses doll appropriately for a cold day.

Problem solving: Defines a need for a park in the Playproject where toddlers can play. Suggests areas which could be used and identifies suitable apparatus for making a climbing frame. Suggests that the park should be separate: 'Put flowers in pots around the edge so they don't fall over. People won't trip over them.'

Social/emotional skills: Did not seek a friend to play with. Interacted with Claire in the shop. Invited teacher into the cottage as she wanted to talk. Confident in her role as mother looking after the baby. Took on a caring role and showed awareness of the baby's needs.

Attitudes/dispositions: Well motivated to develop the idea for a park. Takes this back to the class and develops it further. Fully involved in the role play. Maintained enthusiasm, concentration and motivation to develop her idea further. Was keen to put her ideas into practice and to test if the climbing frame would work.

Manipulative skills: Dresses doll competently. Able to tie bows and fasten hooks and eyes.

Drama/role play: Started as mother then customer. Stayed in role. Came out of role when she instigated teacher involvement.

Account of play: Helen dresses up as a Mum, then dresses a doll in winter clothes to take her out in the pushchair to buy vegetables from the shop. She plays alone. Interacts with shopkeeper and teacher in the shop and invites the teacher back to her cottage. Tells the teacher that they need a park in the Playproject for toddlers. They discuss suitable materials to make play equipment, the effects of weather on the equipment, safety issues. Helen writes a list of possible safety equipment which she later develops in class.

Indications of understanding: Initially solitary play but this became cooperative through interaction with a peer and adult. She read the price list, corrected the shopkeeper, added up to twenty and needed help with change. Teacher interaction ensured she understood the concept of change. Helen can give change from 10p and from 20p and can add two amounts in her head. Invited teacher involvement which developed speaking, listening skills and identification of a need. Able to write a list and generate a design proposal. Adult involvement needed to extend thinking.

Account of play: Helen is playing in the café with a parent helper and two five year olds, Jane and John. She lays the table, prepares jam sandwiches, writes the menu and discusses prices. Clears away afterwards, washes up, replaces plates, cups and cutlery.

Indications of understanding: Social and cooperative skills. Used language to inform and direct other children, practised writing skills. Practical mathematical experiences – using and developing number skills, handling money. Required help from an adult with making amounts of money to 15p and giving change. Developed physical and manipulative skills with washing up and clearing away. Extension of vocabulary – talked about properties of jam, identification of halves and quarters when cutting sandwiches.

Helen:	When your customers give you the money you have to be sure they give you 15 pence. What does 15 pence look like? Come and show me. (Jane picks up a 50p coin.)
Helen:	That's 50. (Jane picks up a 20p coin.)
Helen:	That's 20.
Jane:	I can't find one.
Helen:	It's less than 20.
Jane:	Can we make it like that? (Picks up 50p and 2p coins.)
Helen:	52 that would be. Our sandwiches are going to be 50p aren't they? (Helen picks up a 50p and 10p coin and starts counting on from 50. The adult intervenes.)
Adult:	We can make 15 pence from what we have here. (Helen picks up 50p.)
Adult:	Is 50 more than 15?
Helen:	Yes, so we don't want that. (Picks up 10p coin.)
Adult:	Yes, 10, what else do we need? Is that 10p?

Helen: No and four ones, 10, 11, 12, 13, 14.
Adult: Is that enough?
Helen: There isn't any more here.
Adult: There aren't any more 1p coins so what can you use instead?
Helen: Take that one away and put the 2 pence there instead, 10p, 1p, 1p, 1p, 2p.
Adult: That's right, let's count it with Jane.
(They count from 10p.)
Adult: There's another way of making 15 with the money. You could use a 10p and a 5p coin together. 10 and 5 make?
Helen: 15.
Adult: That's right.

Here the girls are engaged in an authentic situation – making sandwiches for children to 'buy' at snack time which provides a meaningful, play-based context for using and applying a range of mathematical skills and knowledge. At first, Helen is playing with the role of the 'more knowledgeable other' but seems to lack the requisite knowledge to scaffold Jane's learning in the way she originally intended. Her interactions with Jane are confident and 'teacher-like'. The teacher intervened to focus Helen's thinking and model the processes of solving the problem of how to make 15p. Subsequently when the customers came to the café, the girls adopted their roles in serving the children but maintained the authenticity by counting out the correct money and giving change.

Account of play: Teacher-initiated based on the need to make some beds for the teddies. Fifteen minute discussion with the teacher about the properties of the beds – they have to be firm, the right size for the bears, and have legs. Helen worked with John, Mary and Alison. The class teacher interacted with the group, observing and assisting. The construction of the bed was a success and provided motivation for future play. Helen identified that she wanted to make a bed cover next time.

Indications of understanding: Cooperative skills were developed to achieve a joint goal. Helen was able to listen to others and share her ideas. Developed language skills – reasoning to select size and shape as well as discussing the suitability of the materials and tools. Used language to describe her own experience of beds. Discussed and predicted the results of their actions. Problem-solving, reasoning, judging, estimating. Development of manipulative skills.

Account of play: Child-initiated. Helen asked to make a bed cover and pillow for the teddy bear's bed with Alison. They collected materials independently, worked well together and did not ask for assistance. They succeeded in making a cover and pillow which they showed to the group at review time.

Indications of understanding: Cooperative skills, speaking, listening, reasoning, giving directions, following instructions. New vocabulary – the word valance was introduced. Developed skills in selecting materials suitable for a task –

their choice was successful. The girls were being challenged and had to work hard at thinking through strategies to solve the problems they had created.

Helen: I'll get the bear. Right, first test it on the bed. Give me the cover. Yippee it's good. Now put the bear in . . . it's not quite long enough, it doesn't go down the sides, we can add a bit on each side. Get the pillow. I think the pillow's still a bit high.
Alison: It isn't, it's just right.
Helen: Mmm. The cover . . . look at the other side. I think we should have made it a tiny bit bigger.
Alison: Oh no, we'll have to start all over again.
Helen: Not if you do my idea.
Alison: What?
Helen: We can make another two little ones like that, look, and stick them on the side to make them bigger. Yes?
Alison: With different material cos we're doing patchwork?
Helen: Keep it all white cos we're doing little squares with the tissue paper and doing little pictures, remember? And then you do lines round it in brown so it looks like stitching.

Here the children were evaluating their ideas as they progressed with Helen identifying a problem and suggesting a solution. They followed through Helen's idea and made extra frills which they attached to the cover to make it longer and achieved success. Alison's idea for the patchwork was overruled by Helen, who later told the teacher that she didn't think they would have time to sew the patchwork. She showed skill in selecting the appropriate materials to make the patchwork successfully by sticking tissue paper squares on which the girls drew pictures on the top of the cover, and drawing on stitches with black felt tip pen. The girls required extra time to finish their work. They worked creatively and cooperatively to achieve a joint goal, showing evidence of their thinking and learning processes. The availability of materials and extra time allowed by the teacher contributed to the success of this activity.

This evidence shows that Helen is a confident child, bordering on the domineering perhaps. She directs the cover making activity and overrules Alison's suggestion for the patchwork. But Helen is a successful player and Alison is prepared to accept her lead. This activity may seem more like work than play but if we look at both definitions outlined in Chapter 1, we can see that it fulfills many of the criteria. The activity is intrinsically motivated, provides satisfaction to the players, the goals are self-imposed, self-controlled and the activity is dependent on the active engagement of the players. As Pellegrini (1991) suggests, it can therefore be categorized along a continuum from 'pure play' to 'non-play'.

The examples given of Vernon and Helen's play both indicate how they moved along this continuum. They also show how older children tend to become more goal-oriented in their play since they are more adept at using tools and materials, can formulate and implement plans and predict the outcomes. As we noted in Chapter 5, play in older children tends to reflect a need for order, a need to belong and a need to become more industrious (Hughes, 1991). In terms of their socialization, their self-concept becomes defined by their skills and competences as players, organizers, tool users and imaginative thinkers. In looking at progression in children's play, educators need to be aware of these factors and to plan for appropriate play experiences.

The evidence presented here shows how the processes and outcomes of play can provide evidence of children's learning which relates directly to the Level Descriptions of the National Curriculum for Key Stage 1. Whilst this is not the only justification for play, making these links can provide particular types of evidence such as whether children can use, apply and transfer their knowledge, skills and concepts between different activities. This can indicate how children are actively making sense and creating meaning from the curriculum offered, as well as continuing to integrate their real world knowledge with their play worlds. Educators need to be sensitive to the intended learning outcomes as well as the potential learning outcomes in a wide range of play activities. For example, they may anticipate that certain types of constructive equipment will demand specialist technological skills, language and knowledge of how parts fit together and interrelate, and what kinds of design features are incorporated. Some of this will need to be scaffolded by an adult through the variety of strategies outlined in Chapter 6. What children then make is entirely due to their own ideas and creativity. The assessment process helps educators to understand the meaning of such activities to the children and to identify their value in educational and developmental terms. The three levels for understanding play outlined in Chapter 5 (areas of learning, subject disciplines, cognitive processes) can provide a framework of analysis which can guide what educators look for in different types of play.

Of course, it is always difficult to prove that a child learns something new as a result of either a teacher-directed or a child-initiated activity. As we have argued it is often the case that different contexts provide opportunities for children to reveal what they know, can do and understand. Play is particularly valuable here because of its open-ended, free-flow nature which enables children to integrate their knowledge and experience gleaned in a wide variety of contexts. It also reveals children's ways of knowing, reasoning and understanding. This is often located in the continuum between sense and nonsense, logic and absurdity, fantasy and reality. Children literally play with their knowledge, especially where they use language, symbols, gestures and signs to communicate their meanings and intentions. In Vygotsky's terms, play thus creates zones for proximal development and contexts for revolutionary activity. Through symbolic and abstract thinking, they make novel connections and combinations, reversals, and create shared cultural contexts which simultaneously reflect and subvert the adult-dominated real world. In doing so they raise the cognitive demands on themselves and on others since they are both using and transforming what they know.

In summary, assessing children's learning, development and achievements through play can enable educators to:

- establish clear principles for curriculum planning which define the role and value of play
- identify the processes of learning evident in play
- enhance understanding of how these processes can be built into activities which challenge children's learning and thinking
- provide evidence which forms part of each child's record of achievement and provides meaningful information to children, parents, caregivers and other professionals
- provide evidence about the quality and effectiveness of play in the wider context of the curriculum
- obtain a different perspective of how children operate as learners in self-initiated activities
- ensure that activities are carefully matched to the abilities and interests of the children across the play–work continuum
- understand the nature and effectiveness of adult interaction in children's play.

The model of holistic assessment presented here takes into account children's achievements across areas of learning and experience and subject disciplines. It provides evidence of children's attitudes to learning, social skills, their interests and capabilities, some of which may not be evident in more formal, teacher-directed tasks. Holistic assessment enables educators to observe how children take responsibility for their own learning, create sense and make meaning, tackle new challenges and to notice factors that are affecting each child's progress. Time given to assessment is well spent where it provides an integrated model which informs planning, evaluation, reporting and recording.

Content, products and processes in socio-dramatic play

Vygotsky argued that we should not subject play to pedantic intellectualization, but at the same time considered that only a profound internal analysis could contribute to our understanding of the meaning of play to young children. In assessing children's learning and development through play, educators need to know what potential exists within a variety of activities. This enables them to specify more clearly the intended and possible learning outcomes and to know what they are looking for in their assessments. In the following section, we have chosen to focus on socio-dramatic play because it is a predominant feature of early childhood and because it reveals the unity of learning and development. We intend to show how this reveals evidence of children's learning in the three developmental domains, across subject disciplines and in terms of cognitive processes. A framework for assessment will also be presented.

Socio-dramatic play

We have adopted Smilansky's (1990) definitions of forms of social play activity to distinguish between dramatic and socio-dramatic play (Figure 17):

Both types of play involve imitation, make believe, imagination and are heavily dependent on verbal interactions:

> Children derive satisfaction not only from the ability to imitate but also to form make-believe play, which provides unlimited access to the exciting world of adults ... Make-believe in dramatic and socio-dramatic play, as opposed to other circumstances where it serves as a means of escape from the real world, extends the scope of the imitative activity and provides a comprehensive and comprehensible context that increases the realism of the behaviour.
>
> (Smilansky, 1990, p. 20)

Garvey (1991) argues that this type of play has a number of defining characteristics which reveal how complex it can be and how much young children have to learn in order to engage successfully in such activity. This is an important point, particularly as curriculum models which focus too directly on the acquisition of subject matter knowledge in predominantly teacher-directed activities may fail to appreciate the cognitive and socio-affective demands which play can make of young children. Smilansky (1990) defines six elements of dramatic and socio-dramatic play which can be used as a framework for assessment, diagnosis and evaluation:

1. Role play by imitation.
2. Make believe with objects.
3. Make believe with actions and situations.
4. Persistence in the role play.
5. Interaction.
6. Verbal communication.

The richness of the play depends on the extent to which these various elements

Dramatic play	involves pretending to be someone else, role taking, imitating a person's speech actions and patterns, using real and imagined props, using first and second hand experience and knowledge of characters and situations.
Socio-dramatic play	involves cooperation between at least two children, interaction between players, verbal interactions and acts are performed.

Figure 17: Forms of social play activity

are used and developed. Thus evaluation of the richness depends, not on the content of the child's episode or on the type of role being played, but on the degree to which each of the elements is developed and used as a play skill (1990, p. 21).

These insights indicate the complexity of children's thinking, actions and interactions which characterize socio-dramatic play. When children organize socio-dramatic play they may initially recall what has been previously played in terms of characters, plot and sequence of activities. This serves to define the play frame (Garvey, 1991; Brostrom, 1995) and often includes certain rituals which begin the play. As they establish the play theme they may revise, repeat or extend previous themes, combine and recombine ideas, negotiate rules, perhaps accommodate new players with different perspectives and contributions to make. Once the play is underway, children will step in and out of the frame to reformulate or elaborate plans, renegotiate rules, reconstruct the plot, reason about cause and effect, direct actions and behaviour, rehearse dialogue and roles. They may do this in and out of role according to age and the complexity of the play. This reflects the metacommunicative and metacognitive aspects of this type of play as children show conscious awareness of their actions and communications. Younger children may become more absorbed in assigning roles and arranging props (Garvey, 1991) as, at this age, action tends to arise more from things. Even in solitary dramatic play, children may use self-speech or out loud thinking to communicate the pretence, provide a commentary on the action and perhaps use different voices and actions as they play out a number of roles. Self-speech provides an important regulatory function as children verbalize their cognitive processes. Themes that are rehearsed in this way may be transferred to socio-dramatic contexts as children gain confidence in themselves as players and progress from simple-cooperative to complex-cooperative play.

With age and experience, action arises more from ideas and children become increasingly adept at both negotiating the play frame and predetermining the actions and interactions. As experienced players, older children can more readily formulate goals which they can realize through cooperation and reciprocity. They can both exercise their will and at the same time control it in order to engage in successful, sustained play – another paradox of play. This is of course dependent on the skills, dispositions and mood states of the group of players at any one time. The benefits to the child are inclusion, enjoyment, shared control, peer-group identity and self-efficacy. As Johnson (1990) argues, it is through such processes that play enables children to build conceptual frameworks to understand, interrelate and integrate different areas of experience. Understanding these frameworks enables educators to examine the meaning of such play to children and to appreciate its educational and developmental significance. Gradually they learn to understand and integrate the perspectives of others in their play. In taking on or assigning roles, they interpret their knowledge of how other people behave but at the same time coordinate each other's interpretations.

Negotiating a play frame provides some direction and internal consistency to the actions and interactions. This enables the players to make transformations and reversals, and create paradoxes so that a wide variety of imaginary situations can be played into the action. Imagination and creativity are essential as children invest objects and actions with new meanings and intentions. In socio-dramatic play children negotiate a text for their play and locate it within a context. The text reveals their often sophisticated knowledge of plot, characterization and sequence of events. The children create a text and context for play and action which depend on a range of cognitive processes for successful implementation. This generally reveals a progression from concrete to abstract in their use of signs and symbols to convey meaning and their ability to take on the perspectives of others. This defines both a play frame and a psychological frame (Bateson, 1972).

Negotiation is not always essential as children will often accept paradoxes and symbolic transformations as they occur spontaneously. For example, a group of children were playing in a café. Five year old Kati brought plastic bread rolls to the table for the others to eat. Li-li paid Kati for the food by handing her a bread roll to signify money, then Kati put it to her ear as she pretended to take a telephone booking for the café from someone who wanted to know if there were any chips left. This sequence happened quickly and spontaneously and the literal-nonliteral transformations were accepted and understood by the other children. It reveals children's implicit acceptance of the paradoxical nature of play – the 'what if' and 'as if' qualities that allow children to accept that something is simultaneously real and not real (the bread roll as money and telephone). This involves quite a sophisticated level of thinking and mental processing as children communicate multiple meanings through language, gestures, symbolic and iconic representations. This challenges Piaget's notion that play progresses from the simple to the complex. On closer examination, children's play is infinitely varied, often abstract and highly complex.

In another example, some children were playing cops and robbers in the home corner. They seemed to have a clear idea of roles and actions until Wayne (a policeman) started putting things in a bag and looking furtive:

Ben: Hey, you're not supposed to take that. You're not a robber, you're a cop.

Wayne: No, but I just pretended to be a cop so I could get in the house. Really I'm a robber and you don't know. And you catch the other robbers but you don't catch me cos you think I'm a cop but really I'm a robber. And I get all the stuff.

Ben: OK then but I'll have to catch you later when all the others are jailed up.

Again, Wayne's rather subtle transformation seemed entirely plausible and was accommodated by the group. It did not destroy the play sequence and justice was seen to be done in the end as Ben changed the rules in response to Wayne's change of role. The triumph of right over wrong and the meting out of punishments was a repeated and central component of this play theme.

Socio-dramatic play provides a dynamic context in which children learn and extend their skills in language and communication. They have to understand the implicit and explicit rules of different social situations in order to operate successfully. They can only do this by becoming experienced master players. In the ongoing discourse between sense and nonsense, logic and absurdity, fantasy and reality, children play with ideas, roles, concepts and language. In verbalizing their planning, children use metacognition and metacommunication. For example, they may outline what the characters must say and what register to use. In this sense they both use and play with language as they search for and construct meaning, often in novel ways. Smilansky argues that verbalizations in children's socio-dramatic play are complex, highly developed, and reflect the patterns and content of adult verbal interactions. Children

- set the scene for speaking
- make behaviour understandable
- provide proper interpretation and direction for the activity
- provide the means of management and problem-solving reflecting child-reality and child-interaction (1990, p. 20).

Creativity and imagination are both important cognitive processes which serve to direct, influence and generate the complexity in the role play. The roles which children create do not just involve actions and speech, they also generate feeling states which link both affective and cognitive processes. This reflects the argument that children use stories as a powerful means of making sense of the world. Egan (1991) argues that children need to connect with a wide range of human emotions in their play and story-telling such as love, hate, fear, anger, jealousy. These are often played out as opposing forces – good and evil, cruelty and kindness, strength and weakness, protection and abandonment, friendship and enmity – as children contextualize emotions and morality in their play.

The driving force for play is intrinsic motivation, the pleasure afforded by play and the ability to take control and exercise power in an adult-dominated world. The critical issue here is the need to understand play in the child's own terms. All too often we become bound up by the need to relate play to precise learning outcomes and attainment targets and perhaps fail to recognize the meaning and significance of play to children. In Vygotsky's view play has a central role in the transmission of culture through social interaction and communication. As we have seen these processes contribute to children's social cognition – their understanding of roles, rules, relationships, emotions, values, beliefs, how society is organized, how it functions, and children's own place in the world. As we have argued, far from being chaotic, children's dramatic and socio-dramatic play often reveals patterns and consistencies. Meckley's (1994a; 1994b) observations show that each play event has distinct, consistent, and predictable patterns of actions, objects and players: 'There was always a set sequence of actions for each play event which identified this specific event not only to the children enacting the event but also to those engaged in other activities in the room' (1994a, p. 293).

Sustained and systematic observation allowed Meckley to interpret the meanings which children constructed in their play. The children in the study actively communicated and interpreted their individual and collective social realities. They also created new play events to manage changes occurring in the social order of their culture (1994b). Such subtleties may be invisible to educators who are unable to spend time observing or involving themselves in children's socio-dramatic play. Meckley argues that

> Shared knowledge of the subjective and collective realities of child participants in this social culture can also be known by the adult participants through attention to metacommunicative signals which regularly occur during the play period. These signals include but are not limited to gaze or watching, body orientation or movement, specific actions with objects, specific sequences of action, imitation, language, and voice change. In fact, adults should note any attention-causing behaviour from play participants. Such behaviour reveals information concerning the play events and players' understandings about these events.
>
> (1994b, p. 47)

Socio-dramatic play also shows how, in Vygotsky's terms, children raise the demands on themselves which then create a zone for proximal development. They often go beyond the current contextual frame and, in 'what if' and 'as if' mode, appropriate the surrounding world and make unexpected, creative transformations. When socio-dramatic play begins, the structure of the play changes. Children progress from using gestures, imitation and play materials to formulating plans, plots, roles and imaginary situations. The play is determined by their understanding of real relationships which then structures their roles, which in turn requires intersubjectivity and shared understanding between players. This is characterized by fluidity which allows for the expression of motives, incentives and needs. As we argued in Chapter 6, adult involvement can be appropriate and desirable in supporting the processes of negotiating a play frame and helping the children to develop themes over a period of time. The adult can enrich, inspire and expand the play in ways which preserve the children's control, spontaneity and authenticity. This provides a context for assessment through observation and interaction and sensitizes educators to the patterns within the apparently chaotic nature of socio-dramatic play. As with other types of play, educators need to attend to the form and content of the children's thinking and learning as it is revealed in such contexts.

It can be seen that this type of play requires complex thinking and action. However, not all children have the skills and confidence to achieve this level of mastery without additional support. Educators may need to intervene sensitively, using a range of strategies which support children's efforts at becoming master players. Such interventions should be informed by wider knowledge of the children and conscious consideration of the right strategies to adopt. For example, a group of girls, age six and seven years old, created a text and context for socio-dramatic play which revealed their knowledge of plot, characterization and play sequence. They decided to perform a show in a theatre and began by discussing their ideas in a quiet area away from other children. The children argued about the plot, ending with one girl in tears. The teacher was able to help to resolve the dispute through discussing cooperation, ways of recording ideas and listening to each other. The teacher suggested using a tape recorder as an *aide mémoire* for the group's ideas and planning. Jenny and Betty wrote a list of events and characters in the play and the girls performed this later to a large group (Figure 18). The target child here for observation was Jenny, age seven years two months. The teacher was able to assess that she was developing confidence in speaking and listening, and performing to an audience through imaginative play. She had experience in social interaction and collaboration which revealed the need for teacher intervention in providing suggestions for cooperative strategies and turn-taking. The children realized the need for improved planning and organization as well as for clear diction and audibility whilst performing (Attfield, 1992).

In this example the energy which the children brought to the play would have disintegrated in conflict without the adult's support strategies. Subsequently, the teacher was able to observe Jenny in a variety of different contexts in which she demonstrated that she was able to use these social skills. This shows how learning leads development:

> Jenny and Sally decide to perform a puppet show. They use Frog, Snake, Mother, the Dog, and decide to tape their ideas and play them back as they go along. They need a wolf but the one in the puppet box is broken. They go to the toy shop and ask if there is one for sale. There isn't so they ask the teacher if they can make one. The teacher offers them the materials to make stick masks so they go to the art and craft area to make a wolf mask. This took up the remainder of the session. The teacher kept the audiotape to add to for next time and suggested that they wrote down further ideas. The children did this and performed it to an audience in the next session. This led to the development of speaking and listening skills. Jenny and Sally took it in turns to speak, offered ideas and then performed these in role. They showed independence in problem-solving and, once they had access to the materials, they made a mask without further help. Jenny had made a similar mask before and transferred her previous knowledge and skills into a different context. She showed Sally, who was unsure how to tackle the task, and used language for directing and explaining. She developed manipulative skills and creativity and used the materials (scissors, glue, sellotape) independently. This activity provided the motivation to produce a show for an audience.

> (Attfield, 1992, p. 81)

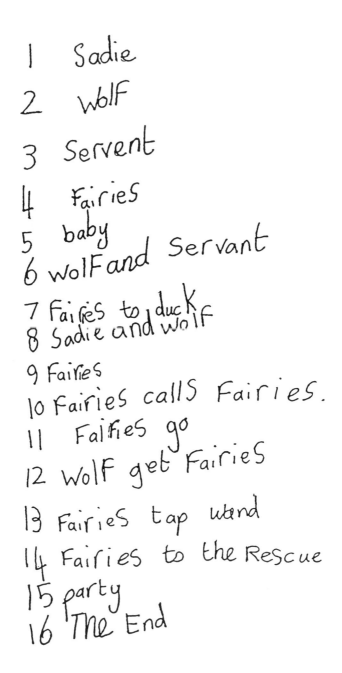

1 Sadie

2 wolf

3 Servent

4 Fairies

5 baby

6 wolf and Servant

7 Fairies to duck

8 Sadie and wolf

9 Fairies

10 Fairies calls Fairies.

11 Fairies go

12 wolf get Fairies

13 Fairies tap wand

14 Fairies to the Rescue

15 party

16 The End

Figure 18:   List of events in show

Here the children used the play/learning environment to move between a pure play and non-play situation to provide resources to support their self-initiated plans for a puppet show. The input of the adult in resolving conflict provided a model for further action and successful interaction with the children adopting the teacher's suggestions as part of their own planning. The play/learning environment actively supported their cooperative and interdependent activity and decision-making thus leading to successful outcomes. The teacher was able to make a range of assessments about Jenny, the play/learning context and her own role in scaffolding the children's learning.

Assessing socio-dramatic play

If early childhood educators had a National Curriculum style document which set out level descriptions and programmes of study for play, it is likely that it would need to reflect many complex forms of learning which are embedded in a range of activities and experiences. The framework in Figure 19 for the assessment of dramatic and socio-dramatic play is intended to sensitize educators to this complexity. Although there may be no end product in this type of play, we argue that it reveals the products or outcomes of children's thinking, learning, understanding and experience. Without systematic observation, these outcomes can be lost to educators, who then fail to appreciate the significance

- Uses memory and recall strategies.
- Defines a theme – plot, characters and sequence (text).
- Negotiates a play frame and establishes rules (context).
- Uses own ideas and listens to others.
- Able to negotiate and cooperate towards agreed ends.
- Transforms objects, materials, environment and actions.
- Communicates through language, signs, symbols and gestures (representational thinking).
- Communicates the pretence, defines roles and actions. Conveys meanings and intentions (metacommunication).
- Steps in and out of the play (distancing).
- Rehearses roles and actions, directs or manages the play.
- Can be directed/managed by others.
- Manages self. Manages others.
- Can maintain and develop a role.
- Uses imagination and creativity to combine and recombine ideas.
- Empathizes/understands the perspective of others.
- Creates, identifies and solves problems.
- Reveals motives, needs and interests.
- Listens, cooperates, revises and extends ideas.
- Uses metacognitive strategies – predicts, monitors, checks, reflects, evaluates.

Figure 19 Assessing socio-dramatic play

of this type of play to children's learning and development. Informed awareness of the patterns of learning which are integrated in such contexts can assist educators in fine tuning their provision to support the energy, imagination and creativity demanded for play to be enriched and extended.

The variety of cognitive processes embedded in dramatic and socio-dramatic play are both internal (what goes on inside children's heads) and external (what occurs in a social context). This gives educators a window into learning and development which may reveal levels of competence which are not evident in other forms of play and in adult-directed activities. Dramatic and socio-dramatic play can occur in conjunction with other forms of play. For example, children may use small world play resources to create miniature worlds in the sand tray where they then act out fantasies. Or they may make something from a construction kit which inspires further play. It can be seen that many of these cognitive processes and social skills are essential to a child's developing competence as a learner in a wider home and school context and contribute substantially to their all-round development as individuals. This framework of assessment could be supplemented by detailed descriptions of achievement in the subjects or areas of learning and experience so that educators can track the breadth and significance of learning that is possible in all forms of children's play.

8

Improving the Quality of Play

At this point we need to reflect on the assumptions that play is necessarily a good thing and that it implicitly promotes learning. There are many other activities which may not be classed as play but which can be stimulating for young children. The learning experiences which educators design and initiate are equally valuable if they are carefully matched to the children and are presented well. Adult-directed and child-initiated activities should be part of a continuum, not seen as opposites in terms of their educational value. A curriculum in which this balance is achieved will be relevant, meaningful and motivating.

We cannot assume that when children are playing they are automatically learning. Play takes many forms and serves different purposes, which can include relaxation, fun and enjoyment. Educators need to be clear about what purposes play serves in their individual settings. If claims are made about the educational and developmental value of play, then these should be substantiated by evidence to parents and other professionals. The three levels of understanding play presented in this book are intended to provide a framework for a more rigorous analysis of the relationship between play and learning. Play acts as an integrating mechanism which enables children to draw on past experiences, represent them in different ways, make connections, explore possibilities, and create sense and meaning. It integrates cognitive processes and skills which assist in learning (Figure 7). Some of these develop spontaneously, others have to be learnt consciously in order to make learning more efficient. We would like all children to become successful learners. Becoming master players can be an integral part of this process since it can harness motivation, encourage flexibility, creativity, imagination and transfer-ability. Such attributes are valued highly in adulthood as the need for lifelong learning is increasingly necessary with changing patterns of employment and expectations.

Educators need to address what happens when children are playing which is immediately visible and what happens inside their heads. These internal cognitive processes can be externalized through language, actions and interactions, transforming objects, materials and the environment, creating paradoxes. The outcomes of play can range from the enjoyment of inclusion in role play, the sense of being a skilful player, producing models, constructions, layouts, paintings and collages. Play can also give children the opportunity to become more powerful through making choices, exercising will and self-determination. This is an important feature as children are all too often powerless in an adult-dominated world. In combining the 'what if' and 'as if' characteristics of play they are able to access different worlds and experiences which are within the realms of their imagination if not within their direct experience. Here logic and reasoning become intertwined with their ability to transform and play with ideas, knowledge, rules, roles, conventions and skills. In Vygotsky's terms, play can enable children to raise the cognitive and physical demands on themselves and to explore different possibilities.

While we can remain enthusiastic about the potential of play, we perhaps need to be more critical about play in educational contexts. At the beginning of this book, we stated that the ideological tradition in early childhood education is strong on rhetoric, but less supportive in terms of realistic, manageable strategies to help educators develop their practice. The research studies and reports outlined in Chapter 1 indicate that the quality of play is not always as good as it might be in both pre-school and school settings. Clearly what is ideally possible is not always realistically achievable. Pre-school settings vary widely in their aims and approaches and some may not provide children with a stimulating curriculum in which play is regarded as a medium for learning and development. Once children make the transition to school they may experience a curriculum which devalues play and overemphasizes work, or fails to achieve a balance between child-initiated and teacher-directed activities. This can create learning contexts which deny choice and intrinsic motivation and cut off opportunities for extending creativity and imagination.

If play is to be regarded as a process which promotes learning and development, then it should be brought within the framework of the curriculum. Where play is integrated into the curriculum, it can serve a variety of purposes. Some educators may over-direct play, thus effectively relegating it to a teacher-directed activity. Here play may be made to pay in to narrowly conceived outcomes which again promotes an instrumental approach. Alternatively, educators may adopt a predominantly *laissez-faire* style in which they supposedly respect children's privacy but in reality often allow play to degenerate into little more than messing about. Both these extremes mean that there is little genuine opportunity for the potential for learning and development through play to be realized. Clearly improvements in the quality of learning through play can only come about by addressing the relationship between play, learning, teaching and the nature of the curriculum offered in pre-school and school settings.

Implementing change

The question which educators need to address is how might such improvements be made? Athey (1990) argues that not enough attention is paid to how children learn most effectively and consequently how teachers can teach effectively. She considers that early childhood practitioners are in a powerful position to create detailed pedagogical knowledge through becoming more conscious of their educational practices and the theories that inform them. Similarly Brown and McIntyre (1993) argue that the teacher is at the heart of improving the quality of teaching and learning in schools. This standpoint has been reinforced throughout this book. In our view, the role of the educator is critical in creating stimulating play/learning environments, with enabling organizational and managerial structures for children and adults which promote reciprocity and interdependence. The cycle of planning, implementation, assessment and evaluation maps the relationship between the curriculum that is conceived and planned and how that is received by the children. These are complex processes which involve a high level of conscious awareness of the underpinning values, beliefs and principles which shape practice and critical reflection on action. The process of changing, developing or improving practice needs to be informed by more than just ideology and rhetoric, particularly in the current educational climate where demands for quality, effectiveness and accountability are high on the agenda.

We consider that early childhood educators, particularly teachers, need to reclaim their pedagogical expertise. In order for educators to find a way forward, they need to analyse their current provision, what is actually happening and what they might like to improve, what is possible in the short-, medium- and long-term, how changes can be implemented and how goals can be realized. For some educators, this may mean building on existing good practice, whilst for others it may involve a wholesale reconceptualization of what they are doing, how and why. Implementing change can be a daunting process but if educators appreciate that it is in the best interests of the children and the adults involved, then both the processes and outcomes can be challenging and energizing.

It is important to keep the notion of reciprocity between teachers and learners in mind. Many early childhood commentators have consistently emphasized that the early childhood curriculum should be built on children's needs and interests. This is valid to a certain extent but it should be remembered that it is the responsibility of educators to design a challenging, high quality curriculum on the basis of their pedagogical expertise. This integrates many forms of knowledge which inform their practice. The nature of this pedagogical expertise needs to be stated clearly in order that early childhood practitioners articulate the complexity of their role and the demands it makes. Through play children reveal a great deal about their ways of thinking, representing, understanding and about their learning and development. This knowledge can be used by educators to inform their provision. Pedagogical expertise enables practitioners to identify where children are coming from but also to know the next educationally worthwhile experiences which connect them with new tools for thinking, learning and playing. This raises the question of whether the early childhood curriculum should be conceived or presented as a seamless web. We have argued that connecting children with disciplined ways of knowing through subjects or areas of learning provides these essential tools. Children's needs and interests are central to the curriculum, but transforming those needs and interests is what leads children forward in educationally powerful ways.

Skilled educators know that children's early experiences are of benefit to them in the immediate term as they strive to make sense of the world in which they live and their emerging sense of self. They are learning about learning, being and becoming. In the longer term, the quality of early childhood education can positively influence children's self-image and achievements in later life. If play is to be seen as an integral part of this process its relationship to learning and place in the curriculum have to be clarified and articulated to parents and other professionals.

It is not just the quality of play which needs to be improved, it is also the quality of learning through play that has to be addressed in educational contexts. This reflects the distinction between play 'as such' and play 'in schools' which we have maintained throughout this book. If this is accepted, then educators need to bring play within the framework of the curriculum through planning, organization, assessment and evaluation. They also need to look at the nature of teaching and learning in different settings and with different age groups and what are the pedagogical implications for integrating play successfully into the curriculum. As we have indicated, for some educators, this may mean a process of reconceptualization. That is, a complete re-think of their own values, beliefs and personal theories about the value of play and its relationship to learning and development. This may be followed through with a critical overhaul of the curriculum, managerial and organizational structures, aims and intentions, the learning environment, daily activities and experiences and the role of the adults involved.

Children can be motivated and challenged through play and can form positive attitudes to learning which can persist in later life. This can be supported by providing

- an environment which is organized to offer high quality, varied resources which allow for progression and extension
- experiences which promote self-reliance, cooperation, collaboration, responsibility and interdependence so that children are involved in their own learning
- educators who have the expertise and take the time to act as partners in children's play so that they can move them forward collaboratively
- managerial and organizational strategies which empower children as learners and develop their confidence as successful players and learners
- contexts which recognize the potential of play as a context for teaching and learning.

The curriculum

In order to support these principles educators need to define long-, medium- and short-term aims and to state how these will be achieved through different activities and experiences. A balance needs to be maintained between

• child-initiated activities	*and*	adult-directed activities
• play	*and*	work
• children's intentions	*and*	adults' intentions
• children's meanings	*and*	adults' interpretations
• potential learning outcomes	*and*	planned learning outcomes
• individual needs	*and*	group/whole class needs
• familiarity and security	*and*	challenge and risk
• flexibility and spontaneity	*and*	structures and routines.

Aims and intentions will be informed by decisions about content. These decisions will be made on the basis of the educators' knowledge of:

1. The three domains of development – cognitive, psycho-motor, affective.
2. Disciplined ways of knowing, reasoning and understanding. (Areas of learning and experience, forms of intelligence, National Curriculum core and foundation subjects.)
3. Cognitive skills and processes (tools for thinking, learning and playing).

Content will be based on the knowledge, skills, values and attitudes which educators consider to be worthwhile. The activities and experiences which are planned will embody those decisions whilst still allowing for spontaneous play and unplanned developments. Educators need to be clear about the range of possibilities for learning which are embedded in different activities and what kinds of support children might need for potential learning outcomes to be realized. Without these enabling structures, the notion that children learn through play is lost in the land of good intentions and uncritical practice.

The processes of assessment and evaluation will provide the essential feedback and feedforward which show how the planned curriculum is received by the children. Sensitive interaction and observation will allow educators to understand the meaning and significance of different types of play to children's learning and development. This knowledge can then be used to design further activities, often in collaboration with the children, which provide challenge, extension and progression. Evidence of children's learning and development through play can help to justify its place in the curriculum to parents, caregivers and other professionals. It can also inform progression and continuity in play between settings and key stages in the primary school. This can demonstrate how children's need to play does not diminish but changes according to age and how they gradually become master players.

The learning environment

The environment itself does not teach but can be an enabling structure within which educators' aims and intentions are realized. For example, if children's independence, decision making and autonomy are to be supported then they need access to a wide variety of materials which they can use and combine in novel, creative ways. It should be remembered that children need to play with objects, materials, resources and ideas in order for play to integrate cognitive processes and stimulate the imagination. The play/learning environment also indicates to children what they can and cannot do. For example, if paints are always ready mixed by the adults, it is unlikely that children will learn to be innovative in their use of colour. However, if a variety of paints is made available with mixing palettes, different sizes of brush and types of paper, children are more likely to develop a wide range of skills and positive attitudes to their own creativity, particularly if this is supported by interactions with adults who model, encourage and teach new skills. Thus educators are giving messages through the learning environment about expectations and possibilities. This enables children to experience success, but also gives them the motivation to struggle and the strategies to cope with failure.

Many early childhood writers believe that children should enjoy a fail-safe play/learning environment. Indeed many practitioners are uncomfortable with the concept of failure. But in the context of play is this either desirable or realistic? Children need to experience success, struggle and failure *en route* to achieving mastery and competence as players and learners. Making mistakes and even experiencing failure can, in the right environment, provide motivation for further learning, practice, revision or rehearsal, all of which are important cognitive processes. Children need the 'I can do this' feeling, but can also recognize how much effort, concentration, motivation and perseverance is sometimes needed when faced with a challenge. The play/learning environment should, therefore, enable children to take risks, create challenges, combine materials and generate ideas. In the process they may encounter frustration and even failure, but this can be a positive experience if there are skilled adults around to lend the right kinds of support at the right time.

The environment can reflect the educators' intentions and values through:

- the range, quality and availability of the resources
- children's access to the resources
- the ways in which the room is organized
- the space given to different activities
- the opportunities to combine different activities and materials
- the opportunities to support independence and interdependence
- space to display the outcomes of children's work and play
- the opportunities for solitary, paired and group play.

There is some debate about whether educators should organize discrete play/learning areas. This is a difficult issue to resolve as some educators believe that labelling an area as maths or technology and making available relevant resources instantly devalues play and makes it instrumental in relation to subject-based learning. It is difficult to label certain play materials as exclusively mathematical, scientific or technological, for example, as there may be many opportunities for learning embedded in one activity. On the other hand, is it fair to children to mask from them the distinctive nature of their learning and emerging understanding? In making decisions about the learning environment, educators have to be clear about how they can connect children's emergent understandings with disciplined ways of knowing through their play experiences. Dempsey and Frost (1993) argue that the materials and equipment provided strongly influence the types and qualities of children's play behaviour. The adult solicits and gets the type of play desired, not only by organizing the environment into learning centres, but also by the choice of materials and equipment.

We have shown that children move along the play/non-play continuum for a variety of reasons. Often they will make resources and artefacts to support their play based on an identified need, then step back into the play to make creative use of such props. In many of the examples of children's play given throughout this book, the children were well aware that they needed to use certain 'subject specific' skills, knowledge and understanding in order to solve self-created problems. They used language for reasoning about social problems, literacy for communicating ideas and intentions, mathematics for measuring, weighing, counting, sorting and ordering and technology for designing, making and evaluating. In moving along the continuum between work and play, children act as real world mathematicians, artists, dramatists, story tellers, geographers and so forth. In such circumstances, they need access to the tools, materials and resources which will support their emerging independence as thinkers and learners.

Managerial and organizational structures

These include

- the rules and routines
- the organization of the adults' roles
- opportunities for observation, interaction, assessment and evaluation.

The routines which shape daily provision are necessary to provide a framework for the curriculum. These can be either enabling or constraining. For example, too many changes of activity during a session can deny children the opportunity to develop and sustain long play sequences. In one nursery the children all had snack time together, which was taking up a good half hour of a two and a half hour session. The teacher decided to have ongoing snack time which allowed the children to help themselves to a drink and fruit as needed. This liberated time for more valuable activities as well as giving the children some choice, autonomy and responsibility. A lot of time can be wasted moving children between activities.

We have argued that educators as well as children lie at the heart of the educational process and that they have important roles to play in supporting children's play. Where adults adopt mainly supervisory roles, there may be lost opportunities to interact with children in their play in ways which are educationally powerful. Educators need to become master players themselves in order to combine the complex facets of their roles. By interacting in children's play, they can become more attuned to the meanings which children convey about their experience and knowledge.

Inevitably educating young children is a value laden process and educators may hold strong views about what is encouraged, tolerated or banned in the context of play. A particularly contentious issue which needs to be addressed is Superhero play.

Superhero play

This often provokes energetic debates on in-service courses as educators struggle to reconcile their views of what is educationally valuable with children's spontaneous interests. This type of play can be absorbing, stimulating, highly energetic and intrinsically fascinating to young children. But it is not always allowed by educators either indoors or outdoors for a variety of reasons which reveal a clash between adults' and children's perceptions of this type of play. There is considerable concern about the relationship between violence in the media, particularly television, and the development of aggressive behaviour in young children. This is seen variously as promoting anti-social behaviour and values and as commercial exploitation of young children. This has become more marked in recent years as films, cartoons and television programmes spawn a vast related industry in toys, clothes, soft furnishings, and school equipment. Children are encouraged to identify not just with the characters but with certain images which are reinforced through these spin-off products. It can be seen as seriously damaging to a child's credibility to appear with the wrong designer lunch-box. Dempsey and Frost (1993, p. 309) state that

> These television cartoons are little more than extended advertisements for the toys themselves, demonstrating ways to subdue one's enemies by violence. The combination of passive viewing of these incredibly violent cartoon sequences with one-dimensional, violence-connoting toys leads to an imitative form of play devoid of any active, creative aspects that might *allow* children to deal with their concerns about violence through the war-theme play.

The critical question here is whether children are working through emotions and behaviours which enable them to gain control over fear, anxiety, aggression, powerfulness and powerlessness. Or are they actually learning to be aggressive, invasive, to use interpersonal violence to solve problems or establish dominance and control? The central theme of Superhero programmes is that the good guys (they are invariably male) triumph over the bad guys, but it is always through conflict and might rather than through dialogue and moral reasoning. Does this implicitly provide children with a model which they then replicate in their play as well as in other aspects of their lives? It is undoubtedly the case that real conflicts occur in many types of children's play, especially where they have not yet learnt the skills of cooperation, sharing and negotiation which lead to conflict resolution. But most educators strive to make learning environments democratic and to teach children nonviolent ways of resolving conflict and solving problems.

Many practitioners consistently express their concerns about these dilemmas, usually on the basis of their observations of children's behaviour as well as their own and society's attitudes to anti-social behaviour. Frequently they report that this type of play spills over into other areas of the environment so that it becomes invasive for other children. Educators are also concerned about the effects this may have on other children who choose not to engage in superhero play and who may resent its noisy, disruptive nature. The prevailing responses seem to be to ban it altogether, allow it only in the playground, or allow it indoors but with ongoing exploration of the issues it raises. There are a variety of suggested strategies to deal with these issues:

- Set up discussions in which the children can state how they feel about superhero play and listen to each others' points of view.
- Establish what the problems are and where they are occurring – indoors and/or outdoors – and what behaviours are impacting on other children.
- Encourage the children to explore solutions to the problems.
- Encourage the children to share in the process of making decisions about what happens in the classroom and playground. This can be done as a part of circle time or, if the problem is more serious, dedicated time may need to be allocated.
- Implement the agreed solutions and monitor their effectiveness. Be prepared to support the children by teaching conflict resolution strategies, helping them to be aware of their behaviour, how it affects others, and developing sensitivity.

Ultimately the objective should be to create a stimulating play/learning environment with a democratic and caring ethos. Because schools are a microcosm of wider society, many educators may feel the need to explain the reality of weapons and interpersonal violence. Children are protected from this reality by the fantasy element of superhero play. A teacher on an in-service course expressed the influence of her own personal value system when she explained that all superhero play was banned in her school as the children were taught that all violence, whether real or pretend, was unacceptable and led to injury or death. Whilst she felt that children had a right to develop their own play themes, she felt that this was an exception as, in her view, children learnt to be aggressive through such play. Of course this is a debatable point, and educators have to make and be prepared to justify their decisions to the children and other adults.

Whatever standpoint is adopted on superhero play or making guns and swords, children will inevitably create their own loopholes. For example, six year old Sam was observed for an hour during free play. He knew that war play was not acceptable but pursued his own interest in 'cowboys and Indians' anyway. He used a variety of constructional equipment to make weapons and then recruited two boys to enter his role play:

Mark: What's this one then?
Sam: It was a sword, then it was a arrow. A bow and arrow.
Mark: Can I have it?
Sam: Yeah. You hold it like this and put the arrows in there. Then you shoot it and it goes in their tummy then they're dead.
Jamie: Cowboys and Indians do that. Indians have got bows and arrows.
Sam: Cowboys have guns. Indians don't have guns though.

The conversation reveals some stereotypical views which focus on the conflict but without any understanding of the underlying causes or the moral implications. Sam's acceptance of how arrows kill people is quite matter of fact and is accepted readily by his friends. The role play continued for some time out of sight of an adult with the boys quite obviously containing the levels of noise and exuberance so as not to be detected. The interesting thing was that at review time Sam showed his 'bow and arrow' but explained to the group that it was a machine for doing jobs in the garden. Evidently children are good at subverting rules and 'playing the game' of conforming to the teachers' expectations even where this involves a dual paradoxical shift.

Guidelines for developing the quality of play

In order to support learning and development through play, educators need to create a high quality curriculum for young children which:

- provides opportunities to play alone, in pairs, in small and large groups
- provides opportunities to play with supportive adults who make appropriate interventions which are carefully tuned to the child's interests, motivations and ongoing cognitive concerns
- is content rich, relevant and meaningful
- recognizes where connections between areas of learning and experience can be made
- provides materials and resources to support creativity, inventiveness and originality
- supports independence, interdependence, making choices and decisions
- values and extends children's ways of knowing, thinking, reasoning and understanding
- helps children to acquire the tools for thinking, learning and playing to enable them to become master players and successful learners
- is culturally diverse, inclusive and reflects the languages, customs, cultures and lifestyles of different ethnic groups
- is enabling and empowering for children and the educators who work with them
- involves parents in the processes of playing and learning.

Intentions into practice: making it work

In translating intentions into practice, educators also need some descriptions of what they can expect children to learn in different play experiences. Understanding the breadth and complexity of this learning can demonstrate the valuable underpinning which play can provide.

Socio-affective and communicative skills and processes

- communicates with peers and adults in small and large groups
- conversational skills
- conveys ideas, comments on actions, gives directions
- joins in a game or activity
- assigns roles, takes on roles, stays in role
- negotiates rules, abides by rules
- plays alone/in parallel/collaboratively in pairs/in groups
- uses props/assigns meaning to objects
- uses abstract thinking to convey meaning and pretence
- manages self and others in play
- distances self to direct, negotiate, develop and extend the play
- establishes friendships – same and opposite sex
- uses conflict resolution strategies
- listens to others/understands perspective of others.

Investigation, exploration and problem-solving skills and processes

- creates, recognizes and solves problems
- observes closely and carefully
- raises and answers questions
- uses sensory exploration in investigating the properties and behaviour of materials
- uses fine motor skills in investigating, controlling and manipulating materials
- uses a variety of tools to assist investigation
- notices and communicates causes and effects
- uses descriptive language to convey experience, feelings and ideas, to organize, persuade and report accurately
- represents these through different media
- uses specific terms to describe and analyse experience (e.g. mathematical, scientific, technological)
- perceives and describes relationships
- perceives and describes classifications
- makes connections between existing and new knowledge
- makes predictions, tests ideas/hypotheses
- describes activities and conveys information

- collaborates with others towards agreed ends
- seeks help from peers/adults.

Creative and imaginative skills and processes

- understands the what if/as if nature of fantasy play
- able to pretend, conveys pretence, develops the pretence
- distinguishes fantasy and reality
- combines fantasy and reality
- generates and communicates ideas and imagination through language and different media – drawing, painting, modelling, writing, collage, printing, constructions and layouts
- combines materials and resources
- transforms materials and resources
- enjoys and conveys sensory experiences
- takes risks, refines ideas, edits work/products
- conveys abstract ideas verbally and through different media
- responds emotionally to experiences and expresses emotions verbally and through different media.

Many of these skills and processes are common to a wide variety of play experiences. Educators need to be aware of the more distinctive skills, forms of thinking and reasoning which are embedded in different activities which might typically be offered in pre-school and school settings. For example, sand, water and dough may promote sensory, investigative and manipulative skills which lead to scientific and mathematical knowledge and understanding. Dramatic and socio-dramatic play will lead to the development of imagination, cooperative play, pretence and representational thinking. Block play promotes classification, patterning, ordering, sequencing, balancing and seriation as well as creativity, representation and cooperation.

As educators track the children's use of the environment, resources, materials and activities, they need to ensure that the children are engaged in hands-on as well as brains-on activity. Many children will need the support of a more knowledgeable other to draw attention to the significance of what they have created, been absorbed in or played with. For example, a young child will not learn about floating and sinking just through playing with different objects in the water tray unless the specific terms and their meanings are introduced to develop conceptual understanding. Many of the skills, concepts and cognitive processes outlined above do not just emerge spontaneously through activity and experience. Skilled educators who use well-timed and carefully tuned interactions can support children's learning through play by recognizing 'teachable moments'. This is desirable if the teaching takes place within a child's zone of proximal development and leads both learning and development. They can also validate children's efforts, the learning processes they have used, the outcomes or products and their attitudes. It also gives status and value to play and self-initiated activities which then give the children the confidence in their abilities to take risks, be creative, inventive and to appreciate the significance of their play in relation to their learning.

The following case studies show how some of these principles can be realized in practice. They also demonstrate the interdependence of the play/learning environment, resources and materials, the managerial and organizational structures and the educator's role.

Creativity in a nursery class

The teacher wanted to stimulate the children's creativity through a wide variety of media. Materials and resources were made accessible to the children including different kinds of paints, pencils, chalks and crayons, sizes of brushes, types of paper, equipment for printing, glues, tools and a wide range of collage materials. The teacher planned some experiences where the children were taught how to use the materials and resources as well as specific techniques which they then developed in their self-initiated activities. These included observational drawing, mixing paints, selecting tools, media and equipment to create different effects, combining techniques and learning specific skills such as sewing and weaving. The children also looked at other works of art and regular exhibitions were held in the school which combined children's, teachers' and parents' contributions. The children's work was displayed well but it was not 'edited' by the adults. They were also responsible for taking care of the tools and resources and tidying up after themselves.

Through these processes the children were encouraged to explore the materials, play with ideas, make novel combinations, represent their ideas and experiences, learn to use and apply techniques and skills, and value their own and each other's creativity. They had opportunities to work at easels, on flat surfaces and on the floor for larger projects. They worked individually, in pairs, in groups and occasionally produced pieces that were contributed to by the whole class. The adults did not draw outlines for them to fill in, the children's work was valued and displayed sensitively and there were no adults' representations in the room. The children were inspired by the quality of the materials available, their freedom to choose, their ability to play with materials and ideas, the support provided through sensitive interactions with the educators and the fact that the processes and outcomes were valued. They combined workfulness and playfulness in these experiences and learnt that creativity is not the preserve of the gifted few.

Developing socio-dramatic play

A reception teacher was concerned about the repetitive and stereotypical nature of this type of play. She decided to use stories as a stimulus to developing the imaginative qualities of the children's play and encouraged the children to make their own props and suggest other resources. She found that the children initially responded to the stories as a stimulus but with experience they combined different stories, added their own interpretations and became involved in planning different themes. The adults noticed that they became more skilled at cooperation, negotiation, identifying needs, making props, managing and directing the play. The imaginative and creative qualities of their play were also stimulated as the children acted out a wider range of roles with greater complexities of actions and interactions. Adults were used in different ways by the children as co-players, or as a source of support for acquiring materials and resources to develop the play themes. As a result, more space was allocated to the role play area and more time was given to telling stories and listening to the children's stories. This contributed significantly to children's story comprehension. The educators in this team all noted that the children needed longer periods of time for play so that they could develop the chosen theme and organize their roles. As an extension, the older children were encouraged to draw their story themes and use emergent writing. Gradually these revealed a wealth of shared knowledge and experience and provided a record to demonstrate to parents the value of this approach to socio-dramatic play and its relationship to other areas of learning.

Linking play and work in an infants' school

The need for more space in an infants' school gave the teachers the opportunity to create a learning environment which supported their approach to play and learning in the curriculum. A large open space was created where sand, water, creativity and large block play were located. These areas were used by all the classes on different days, alongside other types of play provision in individual classrooms. The children were encouraged to make connections between teacher-directed and self-initiated activities. In a project on bridges, the children used a variety of constructional equipment to build and test different designs and reported back on their findings. Here they were playing with ideas and materials and one group role played being designers and builders, combining the 'what if' and 'as if' qualities of play.

In another example, the children visited the beach and did an environmental studies project. In school the children had access to sand and a collection of things found on the beach. They created their own miniature representations of their visit using these materials and some small world play resources. This was combined with a role play area, which became a travel agents and holiday shop so that the children extended their knowledge of their local area and more distant places. Their role play was supported by a wide variety of resources which were collected by the children and the teachers including brochures, booking forms, receipts, cheque books, maps and travel guides, postcards, posters, a globe and atlas and a large map of the world to show places that children had visited or where they had friends and relatives.

A whole school approach

A primary school appointed a curriculum coordinator for play across both key stages. She gave advice and support for developing a whole school approach and identified each teacher's requirements. She drew up a rolling programme of resource acquisitions over a three year period and was allocated time to play alongside the children to model her role and support the children with some of the more demanding technical and constructive equipment. The older children were encouraged to play with the younger ones on a regular weekly basis to extend the concept of peer tutoring. A further spin-off from this whole school approach was the re-design of the outdoor play environment, again with additional resources, delineated areas for ball games, chasing games and for sitting. The teachers, meal time assistants and children learnt traditional games and within a short space of time these approaches eradicated behaviour problems. The daily lunch time line up outside the headteacher's office became a thing of the past.

In each of these examples, it is evident that the educators involved all conceptualized play as an integral part of the curriculum. They were aware of the relationships between play and learning and were able to provide the enabling conditions to improve the quality of play in the different settings. They were prepared to change or adapt the learning environment, provide appropriate resources and support and to make time available for different kinds of play tutoring. The approaches adopted indicated their values and beliefs about the role of play and they had the confidence and expertise to implement these and, to a certain extent, to take risks in their practice. They were all prepared to adapt their practice in different ways to accommodate play and to enhance the quality of children's learning and experience.

Future directions

Improving the quality of play in both pre-school and school settings is a continuing concern. The expansion of pre-school provision has brought an unprecedented focus on the curriculum for children under five. As we have shown, the value of play to early learning and development has been recognized consistently in government reports. The OFSTED guidelines for inspecting maintained pre-school provision make frequent reference to the provision of a wide range of play activities as an indicator of the quality of the curriculum offered. However, the danger of a 'back to basics' curriculum which focuses on narrowly defined outcomes is very real (Wood, 1995). Therefore educators in all pre-school settings need to demonstrate how play can provide high quality learning experiences in a broad, balanced curriculum.

There are ongoing debates about implementing the National Curriculum requirements at Key Stage 1. Following a period of considerable upheaval teachers appear to be in a position to regain some control over how they choose to interpret the statutory requirements. In the revised curriculum (DfE,

1995) content in all the subject areas has been reduced and teachers have a little more flexibility in how time is allocated. In our view, incorporating play throughout Key Stage 1 is essential to supporting the quality of learning that children deserve to experience in their formative years. Close examination of this document indicates that rather than using it as an excuse to marginalize play, many of the attainment targets are difficult to achieve without utilizing a wide range of play activities and experiences. These can be seen as meaningful contexts in which children can

- reveal their existing knowledge, skills and competences
- use and apply these in different contexts
- understand the relevance and meaning of what they are learning
- combine areas of learning and experience
- make connections and relationships between these areas
- develop metacognitive skills and strategies
- develop positive attitudes towards learning.

Within these broad aims, educators can focus on more detailed intentions which underpin play in their individual settings and which allow for reciprocity between children and all those who have responsibility for supporting their learning and development. The extent of this responsibility should not be underestimated as we know that the quality of children's early experiences can determine their success in later life. In order to move forward the debates about play, early childhood educators need to articulate the nature of excellence in their practice and to communicate this through enabling children to become successful learners and master players.

Bibliography

Alexander, R. (1992) *Policy and Practice in Primary Education*, Routledge, London.

Alexander, R., Rose, J. and Woodhead, C. (1992) *Curriculum Organisation and Classroom Practice in Primary Schools*, DES, London.

Anning, A. (1991) *The First Years at School*, OUP, London.

Anning, A. (1994) Play and the legislated curriculum, in Moyles, J. (ed) *The Excellence of Play*, OUP, London.

Athey, C. (1990) *Extending Thought in Young Children*, Paul Chapman, London.

Attfield, J. (1992) The Possibilities and Value of Assessing Children's Learning Through Play at Key Stage 1, Unpublished M. Ed. thesis, University of Exeter.

Bateson, G. (1972) *Steps to an Ecology of Mind*, Ballantine Books, London.

Bennett, N. and Kell, J. (1989) *A Good Start? Four Year Olds in Infant Schools*, Blackwell, London.

Bennett, N., Wood, L. and Rogers, S. (1996) *Teaching through Play: Teachers' Theories and Classroom Practice*, OUP, Bucks.

Blenkin, G. and Kelly, A.V. (1993) Never mind the quality: feel the breadth and balance, in Campbell, R.J. (ed), *Breadth and Balance in the Primary Curriculum*, Falmer, London.

Blenkin, G. and Kelly, A.V. (1994) (eds) *The National Curriculum and Early Learning. An Evaluation*, Paul Chapman, London.

Booth, D. (1994) *Story Drama: Reading Writing and Roleplaying Across the Curriculum*, Pembroke Publishers, London.

Brostrom, S. (1995) Frame play amongst six year old children: possibilities and limitations. Paper presented to the European Conference on Educational Research, Bath, September, 1995.

Brown, A.L. and DeLoache, J.S. (1983) Metacognitive skills, in Donaldson, M., Grieve, R. and Pratt, C. (eds) *Early Childhood Development and Education*, Fontana, London.

Brown, M. (1990) *The High/Scope Approach to the National Curriculum*, High/Scope UK, London.

Brown, S. and McIntyre, D. (1993) *Making Sense of Teaching*, OUP, Bucks.

Bruce, T. (1987) *Early Childhood Education*, Hodder and Stoughton, London.

Bruce, T. (1991) *Time to Play in Early Childhood Education*, Hodder and Stoughton, London.

Bruner, J. (1966) *Towards a Theory of Instruction*, Harvard University Press, London.

Bruner, J. (1991) The nature and uses of immaturity, in Woodhead, M., Carr, R. and Light, P. *Becoming a Person*, Routledge/OUP, London.

Bruner, J.S., Jolly, A. and Sylva, K. (1976) (eds) *Play: Its Role in Development and Evolution*, Penguin, London.

Case, R. (1985) *Intellectual Development: Birth to Adulthood*, Academic Press, Routledge/OUP.

Chazan, M., Laing, A. and Harper, G. (1987) *Teaching Five to Eight Year Olds*, Basil Blackwell, Oxford.

Cleave, S. and Brown, S. (1991) *Early to School: Four Year Olds in Infant Classes*, Slough, NFER/Nelson, Slough.

Cohen, D. (1993) *The Development of Play* (2nd edition), Croom Helm, London.

Cohen D. and Mackeith, S.A. (1991) *The Development of Imagination: The Private Worlds of Childhood*, Routledge, London.

David, T, (1990) *Under Five – Under Educated?*, OUP, Bucks.

David, T., Curtis, A. and Siraj-Blatchford, I. (1993) *Effective Teaching in the Early Years: Fostering Children's Learning in Nurseries and in Infant Classes*, an OMEP (UK) Report, University of Warwick.

Dempsey, J.D. and Frost, J.L. (1993) Play environments in early childhood education, in Spodek, B. (ed) *Handbook of Research on the Education of Young Children*, Macmillan, New York.

DES (1989) *Aspects of Primary Education: The Education of Children Under Five*, HMSO, London.

DES (1990) *Starting With Quality: Report of the Committee of Inquiry into the Quality of Educational Experiences Offered to 3– and 4– Year Olds* (Rumbold Report), HMSO, London.

Desforges, C., (1989) Understanding Learning for Teaching, *Westminster Studies in Education*, Vol. 12, pp. 17–29.

DeVries, R. and Kohlberg, L. (1987) *Programmes of Early Education – The Constructivist View*, Longman, New York.

DfE (1995) *Key Stages 1 and 2 of the National Curriculum*, HMSO, London.

Donaldson, M., Grieve, R. and Pratt, C. (1983) *Early Child Development and Education*, Blackwell, Oxford.

Dowling, M. (1992) *Education 3 to 5: A Teacher's Handbook* (2nd edn), Paul Chapman, London.

Drummond, M.J. (1989) Early years education: contemporary challenges, in Desforges, C. (ed) *Early Childhood Education* Monograph Series No. 4, Scottish Academic Press, Edinburgh.

Drummond, M.J. (1993) *Assessing Children's Learning*, David Fulton, London.

Dunn, J. (1989) The family as an educational environment in the preschool years, in Desforges, C. *Early Childhood Education*, Scottish Academic Press, Edinburgh.

Early Years Curriculum Group (1989) *Early Childhood Education The Early Years Curriculum and the National Curriculum*, Trentham Books, Stoke on Trent.

Egan, K. (1991) *Primary Understanding: Education in Early Childhood*, Routledge, London.

Elkind, D. (1990) Academic pressures. Too much; too soon: the demise of play, Klugman, E. and Smilansky, S. *Children's Play and Learning Perspectives and Policy Implications*, Teacher's College Press, New York.

Feinburg, S. and Mindess, M. (1994) *Eliciting Children's Full Potential*, Wadsworth, California.

Forman, E.A. and Cazden, C.B. (1985) Exploring Vygotskian perspectives in education:

the cognitive value of peer interaction, in Wertsch, J.V. (ed) *Culture, Communication and Cognition*, Cambridge University Press, Cambridge.

Fromberg, D. (1987) Play, in Monighan-Nourot, P., Scales, B., VanHoorn, J. and Almy, M. *Looking at Children's Play*, Teacher's College Press, New York.

Garvey, C, (1991) *Play* (2nd edn), Fontana, London.

Guha, M. (1988) Play in school, Blenkin, G. and Kelly, A.V. (eds) *Early Childhood Education: A Developmental Curriculum*, Paul Chapman, London.

Gura, P. (ed) (1992) *Exploring Learning: Young Children and Block Play*, Paul Chapman, London.

Hall, N. (1994) Play, literacy and the role of the teacher, in Moyles, J. (ed) *The Excellence of Play*, OUP, Bucks.

Hall, N. and Abbott, L. (1992) *Play in the Primary Curriculum*, Hodder and Stoughton, London.

Hannikainen, M. (1995) *Young children's role play in a day care context: a Vygotskian perspective*, Paper presented to the European Conference on Educational Research, Bath, September 1995.

Hennessy, E., Martin, S., Moss, P. and Melhuish, E. (1992) *Children and Day Care: Lessons From Research*, Paul Chapman, London.

High/Scope Educational Research Foundation (1991) *Supporting Young Learners*, High/Scope Press, Ypsilanti.

Hohmann, M., Banet, B. and Weikart, D. (1979) *Young Children in Action*, High/Scope Press, Ypsilanti.

Howe, M. (1992) *A Teacher's Guide to the Psychology of Learning*, Blackwell, Oxford.

Hughes, F.P. (1991) *Children, Play and Development*, Allyn and Bacon, Massachusetts.

Hurst, V. (1994) The implications of the National Curriculum for nursery education, Blenkin, G. and Kelly, A.V. (1994) (eds) *The National Curriculum and Early Learning. An Evaluation*, Paul Chapman, London.

Hutt, S. J., Tyler, C., Hutt, C. and Christopherson, H. (1989) *Play, Exploration and Learning*, Routledge, London.

Johnson, J.E. (1990) The role of play in cognitive development, in Klugman, E. and Smilansky, S. *Children's Play and Learning: Perspectives and Policy Implications*, Teacher's College Press, New York.

Jones, E. and Reynolds, G. (1992) *The Play's The Thing: Teachers' Roles in Children's Play*, Teacher's College Press, New York.

Kelly-Byrne D. (1989) *A Child's Play Life: An Ethnographic Study*, Teacher's College Press, New York.

Kessler, S. and Swadener, B. (1992) *Reconceptualising the Early Childhood Curriculum: Beginning the Dialogue*, Teacher's College Press, New York.

King, R. *All Things Bright and Beautiful? A Sociological Study of Infants' Classrooms*, John Wiley, Bath.

Lally, M. (1989) *An Integrated Approach to the National Curriculum in the Early Years*, NCB, London.

Manning, K. and Sharp, A. (1977) *Structuring Play in the Early Years at School*, Ward Lock, London.

McAuley, H. and Jackson, P. (1992) *Educating Young Children: A Structural Approach*, David Fulton, London.

Meadows, S. (1993) *The Child As Thinker*, Routledge, London.

Meadows, S. and Cashdan, A. (1988) *Helping Children Learn: Contributions to a Cognitive Curriculum*, David Fulton, London.

Meckley, A. (1994a) Play, communication and cognition, *Communication and Cognition*, Vol. 27. No. 3.

Meckley, A. (1994b) *Disappearing pegs in the road: discovering meaning in young children's social play*. Paper presented to the American Educational Research Association Conference 6. April.

Meckley, A. (1996) Studying children's play through a child cultural approach: roles, rules and shared knowledge, *Advances in Early Education and Day Care*, Vol. 7, Social Development, J.A.I. Press.

Moyles, J. (1989) *Just Playing? The Role and Status of Play in Early Childhood Education*, OUP, Bucks.

Moyles, J. (ed) (1994) *The Excellence of Play*, OUP, Bucks.

Newman, F. and Holzman, L. (1993) *Lev Vygotsky: Revolutionary Scientist*, Routledge, London.

Norman, D. (1978) Notes towards a complex theory of learning, in Lesgold, A.M. (ed) *Cognitive Psychology and Instructions*, Plenum, New York.

Nutbrown, C. (1994) *Threads of Thinking: Young Children Learning and the Role of Early Education*, Paul Chapman, London.

Office for Standards in Education (OFSTED) (1993a) *First Class: The Standards and Quality of Education in Reception Classes*, HMSO, London.

Office for Standards in Education (OFSTED) (1993b) *Handbook for the Inspection of Schools*, HMSO, London.

Paley, V.G. (1981) *Wally's Stories*, Harvard University Press, London.

Pellegrini, A.D. (1991) *Applied Child Study: A Developmental Approach*, Lawrence Erlbaum, New Jersey.

Pellegrini, A.D. and Boyd, B. (1993) The role of play in early childhood development and education: issues in definition and function, in Spodek, B. (1993) (ed) *Handbook of Research on the Education of Young Children*, Macmillan, New York.

Rodd, J. (1994) *Leadership in Early Childhood Education*, OUP, Bucks.

Rogoff, B. (1993) The joint socialisation of development, in Light, P., Sheldon, S. and Woodhead, M. (1993) *Learning to Think*, Routledge/OUP, London.

Rubin, K., Fein, G. and Vandenberg, B. (1983) Play, in Etherington, E.M. (ed) *Handbook of Child Psychology. Vol. IV Social Development*, Wiley, New York.

Saracho, O. (1991) The role of play in the early childhood curriculum, Spodek, B. and Saracho, O. *Issues in Early Childhood Curriculum*, Teacher's College Press, New York.

Seifert, K.L. (1993) Cognitive development and early childhood education, in Spodek, B. (ed) *Handbook of Research on the Education of Young Children*, MacMillan, New York.

Siraj-Blatchford, I. and J. (1995) (eds) *Educating the Whole Child: Cross-Curricular Skills, Themes and Dimensions*, OUP, Bucks.

Smilansky, S. (1990) Sociodramatic play: its relevance to behaviour and achievement in school, in Klugman, E. and Smilansky, S. *Children's Play and Learning Perspectives and Policy Implications*, Teacher's College Press, New York.

Smith, E.A. (1994) *Educating the Under-Five's*, Cassell, London.

Smith, L. (1989) *Changing perspectives in developmental psychology*, Desforges, C. (ed) *Early Childhood Education*, Monograph Series No. 4, Scottish Academic Press, Edinburgh.

Smith, P. and Cowie, H. (1991) *Understanding Children's Development*, Blackwell, Oxford.

Sutherland, P. (1992) *Cognitive Development Today: Piaget and His Critics*, Paul Chapman, London.

Tamburrini, J. (1982) Play and the role of the teacher, *Early Child Development and Care*, Vol. 8, 3/4.

Tharp, R. and Gallimore, R. (1991) A theory of teaching as assisted performance, in Light, P., Sheldon, S. and Woodhead, M. (1993) *Learning to Think*, Routledge/OUP, London.

Tizard, B., Blatchford, P., Burke, J., Farquhar, C. and Plewis, I. (1988) *Young Children at School in the Inner City*, Erlbaum Associates, London.

Tizard, B. and Hughes, M. (1984) *Young Children Learning: Talking and Thinking at Home and in School*, Fontana, London.

Vygotsky, L.S. (1978) *Mind in Society* (Translated and edited by Cole, M., John-Steiner, V., Scribner, S. and Souberman, E.), Harvard University Press, Cambridge, Mass.

Webb, L. (1974) *Purpose and Practice in Nursery Education*, Blackwell, Oxford.

Wertsch, J.V. (1985) *Vygotsky and the Social Formation of Mind*, Harvard University Press, Cambridge, Mass.

Wood, D. (1988) *How Children Think and Learn*, Blackwell, Oxford.

Wood, L. (1995) Incomes and Outcomes, Times Educational Supplement, 13 October.

Wood, L., Bennett, N. and Rogers, S. (1995) Reception teachers' theories of play: pedagogical and policy implications. Paper presented to the European Conference on Educational Research, University of Bath, September 1995.

Wood, L. and Holden, C. (1995) *Teaching History at Key Stage 1*, Chris Kington, Cambridge.

Woodhead, M., Carr, R. and Light, P. (1991) *Becoming a Person*, Routledge/OUP, London.

Author Index

Subject Index